T0335292

A Sarong for Clio

Essays on the Intellectual

and Cultural History of Thailand

Cornell University

Maurizio Peleggi, editor

A Sarong for Clio

Essays on the Intellectual and Cultural History of Thailand

Inspired by Craig J. Reynolds

SOUTHEAST ASIA PROGRAM PUBLICATIONS
Southeast Asia Program
Cornell University
Ithaca, New York
2015

Cornell Southeast Asia Program Publications
640 Stewart Avenue, Ithaca, NY 14850-3857

Studies on Southeast Asia Series No. 66

Printed in the United States of America

ISBN: hc 9780877277965
ISBN: pb 9780877277668

Cover: designed by Kat Dalton

TABLE OF CONTENTS

ACKNOWLEDGMENTS

Although I had been thinking about it for some time, the idea of this volume was fleshed out over a Thai meal with Thongchai Winichakul in Singapore. A sabbatical semester supported by the National University of Singapore made possible for me to return to Canberra in 2013, after an absence of one and a half decade, and to relive in situ the intellectual excitement that marked my first encounter with Craig Reynolds.

I am grateful to the contributors, who believed in the project and joined it enthusiastically, and to Deborah Homsher at SEAP Publications, who secured a publisher for it. Craig Reynolds compiled the list of his publications. The two anonymous readers for the press provided constructive comments that greatly helped to improve each of the essays. Finally, Sarah Grossman, who inherited the project at SEAP, worked along with Fred Conner to ensure that the volume reached fruition in the best possible shape thanks to meticulous copy-editing and insightful editorial suggestions.

Craig J. Reynolds, circa 1964

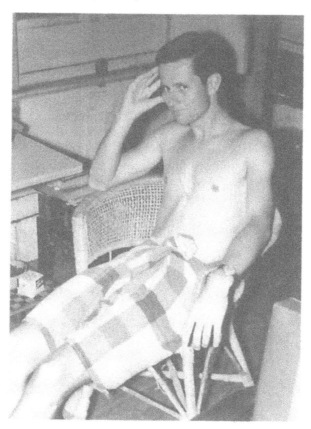

Conceived as a tribute to an innovative scholar, dedicated teacher, and generous colleague, it is also this volume's ambition to make a concerted intervention on Thai historiography, and Thai studies more generally, by pursuing in new directions themes and ideas that figure prominently in Craig J. Reynolds's scholarship.
Photograph by David Cadigan (courtesy of C. J. Reynolds).

ON HISTORY, THAILAND, AND THE SCHOLARSHIP OF CRAIG J. REYNOLDS

Maurizio Peleggi

The young man who looks at us from this black & white photograph with a disarming, perhaps vaguely wary smile, appears to be at exactly that early stage in life when "one closes behind one the little gate of mere boyishness—and enters an enchanted garden. Its very shades glow with promise. Every turn of the path has its seduction. And it isn't because it is an undiscovered country."[1] In this instance, it was an undiscovered and, in true Conradian spirit, also an exotic country—as testified by the loincloth wrapped around the young man's waist. A couple of years later, back in his home country and studying for a postgraduate degree, he received the visitation of Clio, the Muse of history. Did Clio show up in Homeric-named Ithaca, NY, draped in her customary tunic or, given the circumstances, in a Southeast Asian sarong?

I must beg for the reader's forgiveness, for this is admittedly mythological speech not befitting academic writing. Yet an exception might perhaps be permitted. Still frequently cited, "Buddhist Cosmography in Thai History" is an essay Craig Reynolds published at the beginning of his career, almost four decades ago.[2] This article examines the rejection in mid-nineteenth-century Siam of the traditional Indo-Buddhist cosmology—espoused in the "Sermon of the Three Worlds" (*Traiphumikatha*) originally composed in the fourteenth century and revised several times since—following the introduction of astronomic knowledge by the Christian

I thank Chris Baker, Patrick Jory, Tamara Loos, and Craig Reynolds, as well as Sarah Grossman, for comments and suggestions on an earlier version of this introductory essay, which stems from two decades of acquaintance with Craig and, most recently, a series of conversations that took place in Canberra in April–May 2013.

[1] Joseph Conrad, *The Shadow Line* (New York: Vintage Classics, 2007), 3.

[2] Craig J. Reynolds, "Buddhist Cosmography in Thai History, with Special Reference to Nineteenth-Century Cultural Change," *Journal of Asian Studies* 35, no. 2 (1976): 203–20, reprinted (with some changes) in Craig J. Reynolds, *Seditious Histories: Contesting Thai and Southeast Asian Pasts* (Seattle: University of Washington Press, 2006), chap. 8.

missionaries. In the *Traiphum* cosmology, the cosmos pivots around Mount Sumeru, the axis mundi, and comprises the world of desire, which encompasses the infernal regions and the four terrestrial continents; the world of form, which is the realm of the gods; and the formless world, or the realm of perfection.[3] This cosmology also furnished the spatiotemporal framework of traditional Lao and northern Thai chronicles (*tamnan*), which tell the story—partly factual, partly fictional, but no less real in its historical import—of local principalities, and even of major temples and Buddha images. In *tamnan*, "historical memory, the supernormal, the divine, and the miraculous are inextricably entangled."[4]

But what about Clio? To the historical-minded imagination of nineteenth-century Europeans, the mythological figure Clio conveyed the idea that "history offers maternal sustenance, as well as stern example."[5] Yet according to myth, Clio, along with her eight sisters, the Muses, who embody the various forms of artistic creation, was the daughter of Zeus and Mnemosyne, goddess of memory. It is Mnemosyne who leads Clio and her sisters in the chant that awakens the poet's memory, and fuels his narration. Like the Homer of tradition, the epic poet (*aoidos* in Greek) is blind, yet, thanks to Clio's inspiration, he can see that which is invisible to the eye: the past. "To remember, to know, and to see," writes classicist Jean Pierre Vernant, "are so many interchangeable terms."[6] Long before Herodotus and Thucydides, the past was for the ancient Greeks not a foreign country that confronts one with its otherness—"they do things differently there"—but a parallel dimension of existence accessible through the mediation of a divinely inspired seer. The poet's recitation, in fact, neither made the past come alive for his contemporaries nor transported them back in time. Rather, in a cosmological order where the realm of the living existed side by side with the subterranean realm of the dead (Hades) and the heavenly realm of the immortals (Olympus), the past formed an integral part of the cosmos:

> To explore it [i.e., the past] is to discover what is hidden in the depths of being. History as celebrated by Mnemosyne is a deciphering of the invisible, a geography of the supernatural.

Vernant's evocative definition of the archaic Greek idea of history as a geography of the supernatural strikes an uncanny analogy to the conception of the past espoused by *tamnan*. Like many other self-professed modernizers, the Thai "Victorian" aristocrats who reoriented their cultural coordinates to better deal with

---

[3] Frank E. Reynolds and Mani B. Reynolds, trans. and ed., *Three Worlds According to King Ruang: A Thai Buddhist Cosmology* (Berkeley: University of California Press, 1982). This is the translation of a text, *Traiphum phra ruang*, whose original composition is attributed to King Lithai of Sukhothai. The oldest extant version of the *Traiphum* is the recension composed by the order of King Taksin in 1776 to obviate for the loss of manuscripts in the sack of Ayutthaya. A beautifully illuminated manuscript, it is presently in the collection of the Museum of Asian Art, in Berlin.

[4] Peter Skilling, "Geographies of Intertextuality: Buddhist Literature in Pre-modern Siam," *Aséanie* 19 (2007), 105.

[5] Stephen Bann, *The Clothing of Clio: A Study of the Representation of History in Nineteenth-Century Britain and France* (Cambridge: Cambridge University Press, 1984), 1. See also by Bann, "Clio in Part: On Antiquarianism and the Historical Fragment," in his *The Inventions of History: Essays on the Representation of the Past* (Manchester: Manchester University Press, 1990), 100–121.

[6] Jean Pierre Vernant, *Myth and Thought among the Greeks* (London: Routledge & Kegan Paul: 1983 [Paris, 1965]), 77.

the challenge of Western imperialism sincerely believed that they had left mythical thinking behind, and entered an enlightened world ruled by instrumental rationality and technological progress. They accordingly developed not only constructive attitudes towards modern political, economic, social, and cultural realities, but also a novel vision of history, which was no longer regarded as a geography of the supernatural. In the second round of Thailand's engagement with modernity during the 1960s, a Thai technocratic elite was bred in the United States to engineer the kingdom's capitalist modernization, and thus counter communism, whose appeal was then at its peak in Southeast Asia, as well as in most of the so-called Third World. From the 1980s onwards, however, a widespread rejection of modernist paradigms in the social sciences has been matched by the recognition of the continuing force of myth—and not just "pop" myth a là Barthes, but religious myth, political myth, even historical myth. The latter, in particular, is an apparent oxymoron that troubles many historians, even though at least some are willing to acknowledge the spell that Clio exerts on them.

This volume testifies to an ongoing intellectual dialogue between its contributors and the individual who inspired these essays. Although he formally retired in 2007, Craig Reynolds continues to be extremely active academically; he has since published articles, commentaries, and three books of collected essays, and is now working on a new monograph. He continues to lecture, attend conferences, and conduct archival and fieldwork research on a regular basis. His scholarship remains a source of inspiration for students of Thailand of three generations—his peers, his former students and, increasingly, their students. Reynolds's record as a mentor is justifiably a major source of pride for him—a feeling that is reciprocated by those who studied under him. Even those who did not, including several Thai academics, have often resorted to his famously sharp criticism for improving articles and manuscripts. The range of nationalities and geographical locations of this volume's contributors, and the fact that historians are joined here by political scientists, testify to the influence of Reynolds's formal and informal mentoring within and outside the discipline of history.

Conceived as a tribute to an innovative scholar, dedicated teacher, and generous colleague, it is also this volume's ambition to make a concerted intervention on Thai historiography, and Thai studies more generally,[7] by pursuing in new directions themes and ideas that figure prominently in Reynolds's scholarship. The essays gathered here revolve around two themes in particular: the nexus of historiography and power, and Thai political and business cultures—often so intertwined as to be difficult to separate. The appendix, which contains Reynolds's complete bibliography to date, reveals the myriad ways these essays engage with his scholarship, as well as illuminating something about its nature. Reynolds belongs neither to the category of empiricist historians who fetishize archival documents as the repository of historical truth, be it macro- or micro-historical; nor to that of encyclopedic historians who seek to represent past human experience, or the zeitgeist of an age, by the narrative accumulation of data. Characteristic of

---

[7] This volume ideally follows in the footsteps of two earlier collections, Manas Chitrakasem and Andrew Turton, eds., *Thai Constructions of Knowledge* (London: School of Oriental and African Studies, 1991); and Andrew Turton, ed., *Civility and Savagery: Social Identity in Tai States* (Richmond, Surrey: Curzon Press, 2000). Reynolds was a contributor to the first volume, and discussed the latter in a review article, "Tai-Land and its Others," *South East Asia Research* 11, no. 1 (2003): 113–20.

Reynolds's historiographical style is what I like to call the "hermeneutical essay," the aim of which is to open up the possibility of alternative readings of the past by reframing historical facts and processes, either by examining sources that historians tend to neglect, or by extracting new meanings from the available sources. Taken as a whole, his books, articles, assorted essays, and book reviews form the movements of a historiographical score on Thailand's history, complete with recurring themes and occasional variations. Let us consider them more in detail.

• • •

Craig J. Reynolds's personal and professional involvement with Thailand over five decades parallels the experiences of several American students of Southeast Asia of his generation, who could not avoid confronting—whether in the tropical jungles or, more benignly, on college campuses—the Vietnam War. Military intervention was not, in fact, the only way the United States tried to counter the appeal of communism in Asia and Latin America. Possibly more effective, though far less discussed academically, was economic and social-development support delivered through the Peace Corps—an oxymoron revealing of the parallelism, if not complementarity, of this enterprise to army intervention. Still undecided about his future after graduating from Amherst College in Massachusetts with a BA in English literature, Reynolds joined the Peace Corps in 1963. As a result, for the first time in his life, he boarded an airplane. His assignment was to be a school teacher in Krabi, Thailand, a town on the western littoral of the southern peninsula; at the time, even the Thai Education Ministry officials looked down on it as an underdeveloped region. Today Krabi is a major tourist destination, boasting an international airport, luxury resorts, and a night market as varied as any in Thailand. At the time of Reynolds's posting, however, it was a sleepy fishing village, where the main excitement, he recounted, was the occasional escape from the local jail of small-time criminals.

On returning to the United States, Reynolds enrolled as a doctoral candidate in the recently established Southeast Asia Program (SEAP) at Cornell University, Ithaca, NY. As many have noted, nothing could be more different from the Southeast Asian climate and landscape than upstate New York, with its cold winters and deciduous forests. Yet the intellectual powerhouse gathered at SEAP, together with the Cornell Library's superb Southeast Asia collection in Olin Library (now known as the John M. Echols Collection on Southeast Asia), quickly established its reputation as the preeminent academic institution for the study of the region. Reynolds initially wanted to study linguistics,[8] partly because of his English degree, and partly because he believed that a doctorate in that discipline would give him a better chance at finding employment. For his redirection towards history he credits an enthusiastic cohort of fellow students—Akin Rabibhadana, Leonard Andaya, Noel Battye, Charnvit Kasetsiri, Richard Cooler, Reynaldo Ileto, Anthony Milner, Thak Chaloemtiarana, and Barbara Watson Andaya, all of whom have individually made significant contributions as the first US-trained generation of scholars of Southeast Asia—as well as inspiring teachers, including David K. Wyatt, A. Thomas Kirsch, Stanley J. O' Connor, and Oliver W. Wolters.

---

[8] Reynolds collaborated with Robert B. Jones and Ruchira C. Mendiones on an advanced language textbook, *Thai Cultural Reader* (Ithaca: Cornell University Southeast Asia Program Publications, 1970).

Wolters, a British émigré who entered academia in the 1960s after an earlier career in the colonial civil service, was the crucial figure in Reynolds's graduate education, instilling in him a taste for cross-disciplinary enquiry and conceptual sophistication. Although no abjuration apparently accompanied Wolters's professional transition from colonial administrator to academician (a transition I discuss below), the increasingly deadly American involvement in Indochina must have given him an uncanny sense of déjà vu, as he had served as an intelligence officer during the Malayan Emergency of the 1950s. To those who, like Reynolds, developed an academic interest for Thailand in the 1960s, the kingdom presented unique opportunities as a client state of the United States, and an enthusiastic ally in the Cold War fight against communism.

The political relationship between Thailand and the United States was behind the production of what to all intents and purposes represented a body of neocolonial scholarship. Such work was informed by modernist social-science paradigms (bureaucratic polity, loosely structured social system, modernization without development), and sought to prove there were deficiencies in Thai society that American-funded development programs were supposed to correct—*kanphatthana* (development) functioning as the antonym of *kommunit* (communism) in the Thai state's Cold-War rhetoric. This is not the place to examine how this neocolonial scholarship supported the US government's political objective to democratize Thailand as an anticommunist nation, perversely by supporting military dictatorship—a strategy pursued also in South Vietnam and throughout Latin America with much greater loss of human life. Even when not directly involved in devising anti-communist strategies,[9] American scholars of Thailand in the 1960s and 1970s tended to reinforce the hegemony of institutions such as the monarchy and the Buddhist monkhood (*sangha*) by conceptualizing them as fundamental elements of the Thai socio-cultural system.

Reynolds's own doctoral dissertation, which remains unpublished,[10] examines the reformation of the *sangha* in the same vein as other contemporaneous studies of Siam's institutional modernization—from the bureaucracy to the army and the school system.[11] The dissertation contains an especially valuable analysis of the schism between the mainstream Mahanikaya sect and the reformed Thammayutika, established in the 1830s by Prince (later King) Mongkut. But while completing his dissertation, Reynolds had already turned his attention to intellectual history. The first article he published foregrounded one of his abiding research interests—the politics of Thai historiography—by examining the challenge to the royal monopoly of knowledge by publicist and historian, K. S. R. Kulap.[12] This shift in research

---

[9] Eric Wakin, *Anthropology Goes to War: Professional Ethics and Counterinsurgency in Thailand* (Madison: University of Wisconsin Center for Southeast Asian Studies, Monograph no. 7, 1992).

[10] Craig J. Reynolds, "The Buddhist Monkhood in Nineteenth-Century Thailand" (PhD dissertation, Cornell University, 1973).

[11] See: Fred W. Riggs, *Thailand: The Modernization of a Bureaucratic Polity* (Honolulu: East-West Center Press, 1966); David K. Wyatt, *The Politics of Reform in Thailand: Education in the Reign of King Chulalongkorn* (New Haven: Yale University Press, 1969); and Noel Battye, "The Military, Government, and Society in Siam, 1868–1910: Politics and Military Reform during the Reign of King Chulalongkorn" (PhD dissertation, Cornell University, 1974).

[12] Craig J. Reynolds, "The Case of K. S. R. Kulap: A Challenged to Royal Historical Writing in Late Nineteenth-Century Siam," *Journal of the Siam Society* 61, no. 2 (1973): 63–90.

interests reflected also the elaboration of Reynolds's own historical method, in which the use of archival and non-archival Thai sources is married to a linguistic and conceptual sophistication that, back in the 1970s and 1980s, was still rather uncommon in Southeast Asian studies. This method, and the professional network on which it relies, has made Reynolds extremely popular among Thai academics in spite of being a *farang* (Westerner), for it is no secret, notwithstanding the polite welcome given to foreign researchers, that deep down many Thais doubt the ability of foreigners to understand Thailand.

Reynolds's profound interest in the literary aspect of Thai-language sources led him to translate in full the autobiography of Prince Wachirayan Warorot (one of King Chulalongkorn's many half-brothers, and the first supreme patriarch of the reformed Thai *sangha*),[13] and, subsequently, a foundational text of Marxist historiography that is discussed in the next paragraph. And yet, despite his own mastery of Thai and of the cultural code one must observe to effectively communicate in that language, Reynolds remains wary of the dangers inherent in employing a language that is not one's own for a scholarly purpose: "I am always worrying over the interface between Thai and English, and how and why the Thai-language world is so different."[14]

Reynolds's pioneering work on Thai intellectual history soon expanded to include the history of radical intellectuals—a line of enquiry that culminated, years later, in a sympathetic but not hagiographic study of Marxist militant intellectual Chit (Jit) Phumisak, which includes a full translation of his *Chomna khong sakdina thai nai patchuban* (The real face of Thai feudalism today, 1957).[15] Reynolds's new interests must be partly credited to the influence of Benedict Anderson. Although only a few years older than Reynolds, Anderson was already a lecturer in political science at Cornell University when Reynolds began his postgraduate studies there. Anderson himself turned his attention to Thailand in the 1970s after being banned from entering Indonesia by the Suharto government.[16] For his part, Reynolds has consistently exhibited an empathy with the maverick thinkers and intellectual outcasts—from Kulap and Chit to Nai Thim (author of a poem censored by King Chulalongkorn)[17]—who, regardless of social background, were bête noirs of the Thai establishment, and were as such arrested and prosecuted on charges of sedition, lese majesty, or communism.

Still, the label of politically engaged intellectual does not really suit Reynolds, who has, by his own admission, spent his entire life in classrooms, lecture halls, and

---

[13] Craig J. Reynolds, ed. and trans., *Autobiography: The Life of Prince-Patriarch Vajiranana of Siam, 1860–1921* (Athens: Ohio University Press, 1979).

[14] Craig J. Reynolds, written communication, September 2013.

[15] Craig Reynolds, *Thai Radical Discourse: The Real Face of Thai Feudalism Today* (Ithaca: Cornell Southeast Asia Program Publications, 1987).

[16] See Benedict R. O'G. Anderson, Ruth McVey, and Frederick P. Bunnell, *A Preliminary Analysis of the October 1, 1965, Coup in Indonesia* (Ithaca: Cornell Modern Indonesia Project, 1971). Attention garnered by that report led to Anderson being blacklisted from Indonesia. For a partial history of the botched attempt to keep this document confidential, see Benedict R. O'G. Anderson, "Scholarship on Indonesia and Raison d'État: Personal Experience," *Indonesia* 62 (1996): 1–18.

[17] Craig. J. Reynolds, "Sedition in Thai History: A Nineteenth-Century Poem and its Critics," in Manas and Turton, *Thai Constructions of Knowledge*; reprinted with changes in Reynolds, *Seditious Histories*, chap. 4.

libraries. In this regard his experience differs also from that of his British mentor, Wolters, who went through "two professional lives"—colonial civil servant first, academic later. Like Wolters, though, Reynolds, too, became an academic émigré when he moved to Australia in 1972 to take up a lectureship at the University of Sydney. There, and then at the Australian National University in Canberra, Reynolds has conducted his entire career, except for teaching semesters spent at Cornell University and the University of California, Berkeley.

The early to mid-1970s marked a critical transition in Australian political and social life with the beginning of its postcolonial transformation from white settlement to multicultural nation. The government, led by Labor party leader Gough Whitlam from 1972 to 1975, initiated a program of domestic reforms as well as a redirection of foreign policy, including the withdrawal of the Australian contingent from Vietnam. Moreover, there was increased engagement with Asian nations, which saw the first visit of an Australian prime minister to China, and talks with President Suharto over the Indonesian occupation of East Timor. At the same time, a postcolonial Australian identity, distinct from Britain, was being advanced: Australian history was included as a subject in the school curriculum, and the local arts were promoted (the iconic Sydney Opera House was unveiled in 1973, and later in the 1970s the Australian cinematic New Wave gained international appreciation). Most controversially, the territorial rights and cultural heritage of Aboriginal people received wide attention and partial recognition. The momentum in social and cultural change continued regardless of whether the Liberal or Labor party was at the helm of government. From 1983 to 1996, Australia came to be included, at least by the official government rhetoric, as part of the Asia-Pacific region (the Asia-Pacific Economic Cooperation, APEC, was established in 1989), while its population grew increasingly multiethnic.

Mirroring the socio-political and cultural transformation of Australia, the academic discipline of Asian Studies, which had been in decline from the end of the Vietnam War, achieved an unprecedented degree of importance and government funding in Australia during the first half of the 1990s. At the University of Sydney, where he worked for twenty years, Reynolds supervised his first doctoral students in Thai and Southeast Asian history, including Hong Lysa, Dhida Saraya, Greg Lockhart, Thongchai Winichakul, and Suwadee Tanaprasitpana. With Hong, Reynolds co-authored a seminal article, "Marxism in Thai Historical Studies,"[18] which traces the intellectual genealogy of the radical movement that a decade earlier had challenged the Thai military dictatorship, and whose publication preceded the study on Chit Phumisak mentioned above. Still, Asian history remained marginal to the curriculum of the history department at the University of Sydney in the 1980s. Because of this, Reynolds had to teach subjects outside of his own area of expertise, and so developed a familiarity with disciplines like anthropology and semiotics that most historians then deemed alien to their profession. Yet it was precisely his somewhat liminal position that gave Reynolds a preview of the shattering impact "theory" would make on the historical discipline in the following decade. "Are we in a position," asked Reynolds tongue-in-cheek in a piece for his department's centennial volume, "to follow the trajectory of the incoming poststructuralist missile

---

[18] Craig J. Reynolds and Hong Lysa, "Marxism in Thai Historical Studies," *Journal of Asian Studies* 43, no. 1 (1983): 77–104.

as it is about to implode within the Department of History? When and where should we station ourselves to observe the event?"[19]

The paradigm shift within history that started at the turn of the 1990s is known in the United States as "the history wars"—a hyperbolic label which nonetheless denotes how even in conflicts that are merely ideological, everybody is forced to take a position. Suddenly—and rather naively—many outside the historical profession discovered that, first, history is written by the victors, who control the archival record and erase from it the experience of the subjugated and the marginalized; second, historians' claim of holding a neutral, objective viewpoint on the past is illusory when not intentionally deceptive; and, third, the purported coherence, and explanatory power, of historical narratives is the product of literary rather than analytic techniques. The critique of the discipline of history and its practitioners was the salvo fired by the postmodern vanguard of cultural theorists who were striving for institutional recognition,[20] but it had a notable antecedent in Hayden White's often misunderstood study of the literary emplotment of history in the work of major nineteenth-century historians and historiographers.[21]

The other major blow to the epistemological credentials of the discipline of history was the result of Edward Said's criticism of Western students of the Islamic world (and, by extension, of Asianists and Africanists as a whole) as representing the intellectual arm of imperialist and neo-imperialist projects. An examination of the controversy ignited by Said's *Orientalism* lies outside the scope of this discussion,[22] but it is worth pointing out that his critique impacted mostly Anglophone academia, where the penetration of Marxism—in its historicist, structuralist, and neo-Marxist or Gramscian variants—had been far more superficial than on the continent. Reynolds's receptiveness to this debate is testified to by his essay "The Plot of Thai History,"[23] in which he deployed Hayden White's analytical framework to critique the emplotment of Thailand's past by royalist and nationalist historiography. Despite its publication in a somewhat obscure volume, this essay has exerted a major influence even on Thai

---

[19] Craig J. Reynolds, "Poststructuralism and History," in *History at Sydney: Centenary Reflections*, ed. Barbara Caine et. al. (Sydney: University of Sydney History Department, 1992), 106.

[20] See, as representative of the debate at the turn of the 1990s: F. R. Ankersmit, *The Reality Effect in the Writing of History: The Dynamics of Historiographical Topology* (Amsterdam: Noord-Hollandsche, 1989); and Dominick La Capra, *History and Criticism* (Ithaca: Cornell University Press, 1985).

[21] Hayden White, *Metahistory: The Historical Imagination in Nineteenth-Century Europe* (Baltimore: Johns Hopkins University Press, 1973). See also his *The Content of the Form: Narrative Discourse and Historical Representation* (Baltimore: Johns Hopkins University Press, 1987). The critical literature on White's oeuvre is considerable; for a sympathetic assessment see, for example, Herman Paul, *Hayden White: The Historical Imagination* (London: Polity Press, 2011).

[22] Edward Said, *Orientalism: Western Conceptions of the Orient* (New York: Pantheon Books, 1978). Among the many volumes that discuss the book's legacy, see: A. L. Macfie, *Orientalism: A Reader* (New York: New York University Press, 2000); and Daniel M. Varisco, *Reading Orientalism: Said and the Unsaid* (Seattle: University of Washington Press, 2007).

[23] Craig Reynolds, "The Plot of Thai History: Theory and Practice," in *Patterns and Illusions: Thai History and Thought in Memory of Richard B. Davis*, ed. Gehan Wijeyewardene and E. C. Chapman (Canberra: Australian National University, 1992), pp. 313–32. Thai translation by Ratchaniphon Janthara-ari et al., in *Thai khadi suksa ruam botkhwam thang wichakan phua sadaeng muthitajit* [Thai studies: Collected academic essays in honour of Dr. Neon Snidvongse], ed. Sunthari Atsawai et al. (Bangkok: n.a., 1992).

scholars thanks to a Thai-language version, and furnished the analytical lens for the thorough scrutiny of Thailand's nationalist narrative, and of the means by which it achieved hegemonic status. A number of studies written over the past two decades—some by Reynolds's own graduate students—have documented the parallels and points of contact in the projects of knowledge pursued by the Thai modernizing elite and by the French and British colonial regimes, and thus disproved the nationalist rhetoric of Thailand's exceptionality.

At the start of 1991, Craig relocated with his wife, Sue, and their two sons, Simon and Oliver, from Sydney to Canberra, where he took up a research position at the Australian National University. There he soon acquired some notoriety as a postmodernist—a label he seemed to enjoy despite (or perhaps because of) the fact that it often carried a derisory undertone in the intellectually conservative environment of the history division in what was then known as ANU's Research School of Pacific and Asian Studies. In practice, however, being a postmodernist meant for him little more than acquiring some familiarity with the poststructuralist and deconstructionist jargon, and voicing skepticism of wide-scope, Braudelian histories of Southeast Asia's *longue durée*. It was, rather, Reynolds's mix of intellectual inquisitiveness, sardonic humor, and occasional irascibility, which made his colleagues and students somewhat apprehensive. The syllabus of the graduate seminar on early Southeast Asian history Reynolds offered in my first semester at ANU, where I arrived at the start of the (Austral) fall semester of 1992, only weeks before the incidents of "Black May" in Bangkok, steered towards scholarly orthodoxy, its focal point being Wolters's work.

The main theme of Reynolds's scholarship in the early to mid-1990s was national identity, another ideological construct he proceeded to dissect with his customary dedication. Although he now doubts its conceptual usefulness, back then national identity must have seemed the ideal conceptual tool to demount the ideological mechanism by which the Thai state had achieved and reproduced its hegemony since the late-nineteenth century. Characteristically, Reynolds did not write at length on this topic, but the volume he edited, *Thai Identity and Its Defenders*,[24] oriented the debate on this subject for the next decade. By shifting his attention to globalization in the later 1990s, he was really looking at the other side of the coin of national identity, for widespread concern had started to be voiced by some Thai intellectuals about the negative consequences of the spread of "Western" sociocultural values that followed in the wake of the penetration of multinational capitalism. In fact, the same years saw a resurgence in Thailand of "Chineseness" as a prominent ethnic and cultural aspect of the identity of many of the kingdom's inhabitants. Reynolds reflected on these developments in a string of essays on the culture of Sino-Thai entrepreneurs, rooted in Chinese literary classics such as *The Art of War* and *Romance of the Three Kingdoms*, and on the genre of "how to" (*hao thu*) manuals, which enjoyed great popularity during the boom of the mid-1980s to mid-1990s.

But just when everybody—from academics to journalists and diplomats—was marveling at Thailand's "Newly Industrialized Country" status, the economy's bubble burst. Thailand's 1997 financial meltdown set in motion the chain of events that precipitated the country in an undeclared civil conflict, as most dramatically

---

[24] Craig Reynolds, ed., *Thai Identity and Its Defenders: Thailand, 1939–1989* (Clayton: Monash University Center for Southeast Asian Studies, 1991; reprint ed. Chiang Mai: Silkworm Books, 1993).

demonstrated by the Bangkok incidents of April–May 2010. In between renewed political violence, Thailand saw the enactment and abrogation of its most advanced constitution ever; the rise of the Thai Rak Thai party's brand of "capitalist populism"; and the return of sectarian violence and of the military's invention in the political process. Unlike in neighboring countries, where a steady process of economic and social change began with the end of the Cold War at the turn of the 1990s, Thailand seemed incapable of achieving social and political stability despite having suffered neither colonial domination nor communist dictatorship. The objective of national reconciliation premised on the erasure from social memory of the state's perpetration of political violence in the 1970s showed all its impracticability; at the same time, other long-standing sources of tension, such as the relations between Muslims and Buddhists in the south and the economic gap between the northeastern region and the rest of the country, were reignited.

For some in Thai Studies the kingdom's deepening political turmoil has been the cause of much excitement, intellectual militancy, and even some (regrettable) ideological posturing. Reynolds has contributed one or two commentaries on the vagaries of Thai politics, but most of his publications from the late 1990s to the present contribute to a long-term analysis of Thai intellectuals as the *trait d'union* between civil society and the body politic. Even though it was never coherently articulated, such a project forms a recognizable line of enquiry in Reynolds's scholarship. The latest installment is the intellectual biography of his longtime friend, economic historian Chatthip Nartsupha, one of the animators of the Political Economy Group at Chulalongkorn University in the 1970s.[25]

Around the time of Reynolds's official retirement in 2007, he completed three major projects. The first, *Seditious Histories*, a collection of new and revised essays, can be regarded as the compendium of thirty years of historical scholarship.[26] The essay on "Manual Knowledge" in this volume is almost a programmatic manifesto of the line of enquiry he has pursued over the last decade. Another collection of essays, *Tycoons, Warlords, Feudalists, Intellectuals, and Commoners*, was published in Thai the following year.[27] The third project is a posthumous tribute to O. W. Wolters, who passed away in 2000. In it Reynolds curates a selection of Wolters's essays on early Southeast Asian history, which are prefaced by a detailed biographical essay.[28] This essay provided an opportunity to pay tribute to Wolters's long-lasting contribution in conceptualizing early Southeast Asia as a cosmopolitan region where material goods, cultural practices, and faiths were imported from abroad and localized. At the same time, the essay addressed Wolters's role as an imperial agent. Reynolds wrestled with this question, arguably torn between gratitude towards his teacher and the demands of critical scholarship. As a result, his treatment of Wolters's "two

---

[25] Craig Reynolds, "Chatthip Nartsupha, His Critics, and More Criticism," in *Essays on Thailand's Economy and Society for Professor Chatthip Nartsupha at 72*, ed. Pasuk Phongpaichit and Chris Baker (Bangkok: Sangsan, 2013), 1–22.

[26] Craig Reynolds, *Seditious Histories: Contesting Thai and Southeast Asian Pasts* (Seattle: University of Washington Press, 2006).

[27] Craig Reynolds, *Chaosua khunsuak sakdina phanyachon lae khonsamaya* [Tycoons, warlords, feudalists, intellectuals, and common people] (Bangkok: Thammasat University, 2007; reprint ed. 2013).

[28] O. W. Wolters, *Early Southeast Asia: Selected Essays*, ed. Craig J. Reynolds (Ithaca: Cornell Southeast Asia Program Publications, 2008).

professional lives" may appear somewhat reticent on the nexus of knowledge and power that Wolters so obviously, if complexly, embodied.[29]

Reynolds's own lifelong contribution to the historiography of Thailand was celebrated by a panel at the 10th International Thai Studies Conference, held at Thammasat University in January 2008. On that occasion, I suggested that we could understand his craft as a historian in terms of the cultural practice Lévi-Strauss famously termed *bricolage*.[30] Marxism, feminism, semiotics, and deconstruction have all been among the many analytical tools Reynolds has used to approach the intellectual, social, and cultural history of Thailand from novel perspectives that led to the formulation of novel questions. Yet Reynolds has always handled these analytical tools in a functional, non-doctrinaire manner; when deemed no longer useful, he returned them to his professional toolbox without the need for misgivings or apologies. After the heart-warming Bangkok tribute, Reynolds took a further step to come full circle in his professional, and, indeed, existential, trajectory by going back to the South, a troubled region for more than a decade now, where his love affair with Thailand had started. The reason was to research the figure of Khun Phan, a somewhat notorious local policeman—part *nakhleng* (tough guy), part *khru* (guru)—who is representative of several strands of Reynolds's scholarship: Buddhism, magic, local knowledge, and power. First sketched in a 2011 article,[31] this larger-than-life figure of Buddhist law enforcer in Thailand's Muslim South—the latest addition to Reynolds's scholarly catalogue of mavericks, misfits, and outsiders—is now receiving book-length treatment.

Of late, Reynolds has also devoted much time to the fine art of writing book reviews. Reviews of academic monographs are odd cultural objects: uninspiringly written and dull to read in most (if by no means all) cases, often appearing long after the publication of the monographs they review, and disregarded by university administrators who compute publications for tenure decisions, they are nonetheless essential for keeping track of new scholarship and animating the intellectual debate. Taking advantage of the immediacy afforded by electronic media, especially when compared to the excruciatingly slow production time of academic journals, Reynolds has been posting his reviews on websites such as *New Mandala* and *Prachatai*. While written as discrete pieces, his reviews can be characterized as miniature sketches of portraits and landscapes of Thai public life.

Fortunately for those who count him as a friend and not just a colleague, Craig Reynolds is not one of those obsessive (and self-obsessed) academics whose sole topic of conversation is their "latest project." He enjoys literature and music, and is a

---

[29] Craig J. Reynolds, "The Professional Lives of O. W. Wolters," in Wolters, *Early Southeast Asia*, 1–38. On page sixteen Reynolds notes that, in the acknowledgment speech Wolters gave to the Association of Asian Studies upon receiving its Distinguished Scholar Award in 1990—a speech published in Cornell's *Southeast Asia Program Bulletin*, 1989–90 (p. 6)—he candidly (or self-deprecatingly?) admitted to having been, in his own words, "a member of the Malayan Civil Service. Yes, indeed, I was a 'colonial imperialist' and, perhaps in that respect, an unusual recipient of the award." The background research took Reynolds to Singapore to visit Changi Prison (or, to be more precise, the simulacrum of it erected on a new location), where Wolters had been interned by the Japanese in 1942, after the fall of Singapore.

[30] Claude Lévi-Strauss, *The Savage Mind*, trans. J. and D. Weightman (Chicago: University of Chicago Press, 1966 [Paris, 1962]).

[31] Craig Reynolds, "Rural Male Leadership, Religion, and the Environment in Thailand's Mid-south, 1930s–1960s," *Journal of Southeast Asian Studies* 42, no. 1 (2011): 39–57.

keen cook. Though he is most dependable when preparing Thai food (the discovery of which must have been, for someone raised on a typical 1950s American diet, a real eye-opener), he likes to experiment with other culinary traditions. In the end, though, the real pleasure of a meal, even more than from good food and good wine, comes from the spirit of conviviality: the conversation, gossips, and jokes that are exchanged at the table. Regarding the meals he and I have shared—at times in other people's company as well—in Canberra, Singapore, and various places in Thailand and the United States, the quality of the food has varied, but the conversation has been consistently good—food for thought, quite literally. It is in this convivial spirit that this volume is offered: as a source of intellectual delectation, but also as a more substantive source of nutrition to sustain an academic field, Thai studies. Despite the example set by scholars like Reynolds, Thai studies suffers from an overburdening parochialism, and badly needs to engage with conversations taking place within Southeast Asian studies as a whole as well as specific disciplines, least the near-obsessive attention to Thailand's unquestionably disturbing politics ends up reinforcing, however unintentionally, the myth of the kingdom's uniqueness, its standing apart from the historical experiences and sociopolitical realities of other countries in the region and elsewhere.[32]

• • •

The essays in this volume are arranged into two parts that expound on prominent themes in Reynolds's scholarship. Part I, "Historiography, Knowledge, and Power," contains four essays that examine different types of historical texts, including the dynamics of their production, circulation, reception, and assimilation into, or rejection from, the established canon; and, in two cases, the vicissitudes in the lives of their authors. Part II, "Political and Business Culture," features five essays that deal variously with Thai political discourse and political culture, as well as the media production of consumer culture.

Part I opens with Chris Baker and Pasuk Phongpaichit's study of the social life of *Khun Chang Khun Phaen*, a seventeenth-century oral epic committed to the page in the nineteenth, of which the authors recently produced a superb translation. The poem—a rare case of a literary work composed outside of the court and with an outlaw as protagonist—is approached in this essay just as Reynolds studied *hao thu* manuals—that is, as a sourcebook that offers its readers lessons on how to acquire and deal with power in the very pragmatic sense of the power to gain or bestow protection. By juxtaposing the figure of the king of Ayutthaya, the embodiment of formal authority as validated by Indo-Buddhist statecraft, to the figure of Khun Phaen, who represents individual power acquired through martial and exoteric training, the authors show how these two seemingly antithetical concepts of power are harmonized in the poem: institutional power requires the protection of powerful individuals like Khun Phaen to face threats to its authority, while individuals need formal authority to extract from it social validation and personal benefits. This

---

[32] This parochialism was stigmatized nearly four decades ago by Benedict Anderson in his "Studies of the Thai State: The State of Thai Studies," in *The Study of Thailand: Analyses of Knowledge, Approaches, and Prospects in Anthropology, Art History, Economics, History, and Political Science*, ed. Eliezer B. Ayal (Athens: Ohio University Center for International Studies, 1978), 193–247; reprinted in Benedict R. O'G. Anderson, *Exploration and Irony in Studies of Siam Over Forty Years* (Ithaca: Cornell Southeast Asia Program Publications, 2014), 15–45.

dialectic conception of power was eminently suited to the historical context of the late Ayutthaya period, marked by a series of dynastic upheavals and popular revolts; and where, therefore, preserving the safety of oneself and others was paramount. This utilitarian reading of *Khun Chang Khun Phaen* as a self-help manual was, however, forsaken in the nineteenth century as a result of the poem's assimilation into the courtly literary canon, which caused its sanitization along with the devaluation of Khun Phaen's potentially seditious powers.

Thongchai Winichakul's essay returns to the pioneering figure of the public intellectual K. S. R. Kulap, first studied by Reynolds and other Thai scholars. Popular historian, publicist, and publisher all in one, Kulap attracted in his lifetime the censorship of the authorities, who sent him to the asylum for a week to "cure" his alleged madness (the politically motivated accusation of madness is tackled also by James Ockey in chapter six of this volume). But whereas Reynolds argued that Kulap antagonized the authorities because his activity as a popular historian challenged the royal monopoly over the production of historical knowledge, Thongchai reframes the confrontation by seeing the charges of misappropriation and falsification of historical documents brought against Kulap in the context of the epistemic transition from history as the chronicling of events *believed* to have taken place, to history as the factual, verifiable account of (in Ranke's famous phrase) "what really happened." From this perspective, the disciplining actions to which Kulap was subjected are not only instances of class struggle centered on the production and circulation of knowledge,[33] but also of the epistemic conflict regarding how history must be written that was fought in the name of cultural progress. In this confrontation between two diverging historiographical modes, the burgher Kulap ironically stood for the old guard—the folk history tradition that was disowned at the turn of the twentieth century by the royal elite's advocacy of the empirical historical method, part and parcel of their embrace of modernity.

The disavowal of an individual rather than a cultural practice is the subject of Tamara Loos's essay, which further explores the localization in early twentieth-century Siam of modern genres of historical narration. Loos examines the autobiographical self-representation of Prince Prisdang, a half-brother of King Chulalongkorn, too, and also one of the signatories of the petition for the establishment of a constitutional monarchy in 1885 (further discussed by an essay in chapter five). The personal misfortune that befell Prince Prisdang, but not other petitioners, led him to a temporary self-imposed exile that, after his return to Siam in 1911, turned into virtual confinement. Prisdang died in Bangkok, impoverished and anonymous, in 1935. Yet his royally decreed disavowal also pushed him forcefully to seek self-exoneration, and avenge his tainted reputation as a traitor through writings. Loos considers in particular Prisdang's self-published autobiography (1930). This was not the first such work to appear in Siam—Prince Wachirayan's autobiography and Prince Damrong's memoirs came before it—but was the first to narrate a life from birth to old age in a non-didactic, self-centered (and self-interested) fashion, in an attempt to set the historical record straight, and claim moral compensation for having been deprived of the honors and wealth befitting his rank. Alas, Prince Prisdang's endeavor proved futile; designed to counter his elision from history,

---

[33] An apt parallel is the Inquisition trial of the miller Menocchio, famously reconstructed by Carlo Ginzburg in *The Cheese and the Worms: The Cosmos of a Sixteenth-Century Miller*, trans. John and Anne Tedeschi (Baltimore: Johns Hopkins University Press, 1980 [Turin, 1976]).

Prisdang's autobiography has itself been excluded from the Thai canon of this literary genre, despite this canon being (unsurprisingly) dominated by the life-stories of aristocrats and courtiers.

The final essay in Part I implicitly takes its lead from Reynolds's critique of the plot of Thai history by examining the art-historical narrative that links intimately the forging of a "Thai" style in art, sculpture in particular, to the unfolding of the Thai nation. The essay focuses on the discursive canonization of the Buddhist sculpture of the Sukhothai period as the greatest artistic accomplishment of the Thais—an appraisal first formulated by Prince Damrong, then validated by George Cœdès, and further elaborated by other students of Thai art. (Indeed, the predominance of Western scholars in this field until recently calls attention to the extra-domestic dynamics that made this master narrative hegemonic.) This appraisal rested, moreover, on a theory of cultural borrowing, for Prince Damrong argued that the distinctiveness of the Sukhothai images was due to the artful appropriation and combination by the Thais of the best features of foreign artistic traditions. The elaboration of a recognizably Thai–Buddhist imagery is a crucial element of the founding myth of Sukhothai as Thailand's golden age when "national" institutions and cultural expressions supposedly took shape and achieved maturity. Canonization of the Buddha images of Sukhothai as "classic" also affected the appraisal of the earlier and later styles in the art historical classification that since the 1920s is the ordering principle of the collection of the Bangkok National Museum.

Part II opens with Patrick Jory's essay, which traces the genealogy of republicanism in Thailand from the late-nineteenth throughout the early twenty-first century. Not unlike communism, republicanism has been cast off as alien, as—according to official political discourse—"un-Thai," because of its allegedly "foreign" origins. Jory shows that republican ideas have a longer history in Thailand than in most other Southeast Asian countries, starting with the petition of 1885 that caused Prince Prisdang's disgrace. While the history of the growing opposition to monarchic absolutism, culminating in the coup of June 1932, is well known, Jory pays special attention to the articulation of political ideas. In the coup promoters' incendiary proclamation composed by Pridi Panomyong, the term *prachatipathai* arguably defines the form of government to be instituted as "republic," rather than as "democracy," as is commonly translated. Of course, a constitutional monarchy was instituted instead, and although this came close to extinction between 1935 and 1951, it did so because of circumstance rather than by political design. Leftist intellectuals and Communist activists from the 1940s throughout the 1970s sought to abolish the monarchy as a vestige of feudalism, although one may argue that the republic they sought was perforce a Chinese-style "popular" one. In the current situation of a Yellow vs. Red color-coded political divide, in which both opposing factions rhetorically invoke "democracy," republican ideals are being re-appropriated by a newer generation of radicals, considerably different from the older ones. Yet whether republicanism has any chance to succeed in Thailand remains open to question.

Jim Ockey presents a deeply researched study of Cham Jamratnet (Chamratnet), affectionately known as "Teacher Cham," a long-time Member of Parliament for Nakhon Sithammarat who was twice jailed, and even subjected to psychiatric examination. Cham's political career began in the wake of the 1932 coup as an associate of Pridi, but he was also keen on stressing his faith in creative ways. After being elected to parliament in 1937, Cham developed an original rhetorical and campaigning style that, after the disruption of war, returned him to parliament in

1948. At this time, Cham expressed vocal criticism of his colleagues' corruption, and also started exhibiting eccentric behavior—both inside and outside parliament—that eventually led to accusations of insanity. Cham was declared sane by a parliamentary committee, but because of a delaying tactic, he lost his seat. Re-elected in 1957 and 1961, his outspoken criticism of Sarit earned him a five-year prison sentence while his mental sanity continued to be called into question. After his release, he successfully ran one last by-election in the capital, following which he became paralyzed under mysterious circumstances. In trying to make sense of Cham's unconventional personal and political life, and especially his presumed madness, Ockey draws an intriguing connection between the role of performance in Southeast Asia's political culture, dance as a medium of spirit possession in the Thai south, and the emergence in the 1940s of the authoritarian state and its double, the "medicalizing state,"[34] whose synergy eventually caused Cham to bend, though not to break.

The next chapter, too, is concerned with a controversial MP figure. It is not a biographical study, however. Rather, Yoshinori Nishizaki surveys with an ethnographer's eye the political landscape of provincial Thailand—a phrase which is to be understood literally here, as the essay's main analytical focus is the majestic Banharn-Jaemsai Observatory Tower built in Suphanburi by Banharn Silpa-archa, a MP for almost four decades who was also briefly prime minister in the mid-1990s, and which is named after him and his wife. Nishizaki adds to recent revisionist scholarship on Thai rural politics by arguing that Banharn has entrenched his personal power by fostering a "positive" identity in his native province. And what better for achieving such positivity than erecting, at the extravagant cost of 100 million baht, a soaring observation tower, which has since come to symbolize Suphanburi's pride of place within Thailand? What is more, even poor locals who cannot pay the entry fee to enjoy the panoramic view from the tower's observation deck seem to rejoice in the civic pride generated by it.[35] At the chapter's core is a Geertzian "thick description" of the ceremony that marked the laying of the tower's foundation stone, staged in December 1994. As for Banharn, the author urges us to look at him not as a corrupted godfather (*chaopho*) of provincial politics, but as a public figure who, to put it hyperbolically, is to Suphanburi what Pericles was to Athens—a visionary politician who has fulfilled his townsmen's immaterial desire for respect and admiration by the rest of the country.

Villa Vilaithong's essay traces the production and circulation of new knowledge on business practices that paved the way for Thailand's economic and consumer boom between the mid-1980s and mid-1990s by focusing on the monthly magazine *Khoo Khaeng*. Through the detail examination of articles, editorials, and advertisements published in *Khoo Khaeng* through the 1980s, before its success led the launch of the homonymous weekly magazine and daily newspaper during the first half of the 1990s, this chapter contributes a history of Thai economic journalism within the broader sociological narrative of the rise of corporate capitalism in Thailand, and the emergence of a class of conspicuous consumers that animated the

---

[34] See Davisakd Puaksom, "Of Germs, Public Hygiene, and the Healthy Body: The Making of the Medicalizing State in Thailand," *Journal of Asian Studies* 66, no. 2 (2007): 311–44.

[35] I visited the Banharn-Jaemsai Observatory Tower with Craig Reynolds in July 2008, and I must confess to having been far from impressed by it. Craig explained my blasé attitude as that of an Italian spoiled by exposure to great art and monuments.

boom years. By publishing news of the economic and business activities of every Thai province, instigating new approaches to retailing and marketing, producing research data on the changing habits of consumers, and organizing seminars and competitions for both business professionals and students, *Khoo Khaeng* performed the function of a manual—in the sense of a repository of esoteric knowledge that can be manipulated to achieve success, as also espoused in Chapter 1.

Finally, Kasian Tejapira contributes a commentary on the localization in the Thai political landscape of the neoliberal concept "good governance" in the wake of the Asian financial crisis of the late 1990s. The instrument for this localization was translation, as has often been the case in the course of Thailand's cultural interaction with the West. "Good governance" was lexically reconstituted in the Thai language as *thammarat*, a term etymologically related to the Buddhist "moral law" or dharma. Kasian argues that the coiner of this neologism, Chaiwat Satha-anand, and its chief advocate, Thirayut Boonmi (an ex-leftist of the generation that came of age in 1973), explicitly sought to create a space for the interpretation of "good governance" in Thai political discourse that was relatively autonomous from the International Monetary Fund's lexicon, and the policy imperatives associated with it. Eventually, however, *thammarat* has been reinterpreted and appropriated by different political groups—the military establishment, the corporate elite, communitarian activists, and royalist intellectuals—each having distinctive agendas, yet united by the objective of ousting media-tycoon-turned-populist-politician Thaksin Shinawatra.

And so the past blends into the present. The chain of events set in motion by the defenestration of Thaksin have led not only to outbursts of street violence but also to the return of the Thai military to the center stage of politics, the coup of September 2006 having been followed by a political stalemate and, dismayingly, by a second coup in May 2014. As students, friends, and—those among us who are—citizens of Thailand, we remain fully aware that moral rights and wrongs are not equally distributed in the country's recent history, and that political and social reconciliation can be achieved only through the public acknowledgement of the wrongdoings committed, the assumption of responsibility, and the redressing of the culture of impunity that has beset Thailand's public life since the 1960s. In honoring Craig Reynolds's scholarship, this book emphasizes the seditious elements in Thai history. But let us not forget that, as prominent public intellectual Sulak Sivaraksa put it, even loyalty demands dissent.[36]

---

[36] Sulak Siravaksa, *Loyalty Demands Dissent: Autobiography of a Socially Engaged Buddhist* (Berkeley: Parallax, 1998).

PART I

HISTORIOGRAPHY, KNOWLEDGE, AND POWER

CHAPTER ONE

THE REVOLT OF KHUN PHAEN: CONTESTING POWER IN EARLY MODERN SIAM

Chris Baker and Pasuk Phongpaichit

Craig Reynolds has drawn attention to the role of manuals (*tamra, khu mue, khamphi*) as a genre in Thailand's oral and written literature, and hence as a formative part of the Thai culture of knowledge.[1] Manuals, he notes, may be deliberate attempts to impose discipline—telling people how to fight a battle, behave as a monk, or conduct oneself in everyday life—but may also empower individuals by giving them access to knowledge that leads to success or survival. One consequence of the prominence of this genre is a tendency to read other literary works as if they were a manual, scanning these "virtual manuals" for lessons. Reynolds gives as an example *The Romance of the Three Kingdoms*, where the lessons in political maneuvering and battlefield strategy from a turbulent period of Chinese history are mined today for guidance in the warfare of business.

The folk epic *Khun Chang Khun Phaen* (*KCKP;* Khun Chang and Khun Phaen are the male protagonists' names) is another text that has often served as a manual because of several features. It is an original story, not adapted from an Indian, Chinese, or Javanese source. It was initially developed, not by court literati, but in an oral tradition of storytellers reciting tales for local audiences. Its central characters are not kings and gods engaged in heroic and fantastic exploits, but relatively

---

With thanks to Craig Reynolds, Charles Keyes, Thongchai Winichakul, Justin McDaniel, Trasvin Jittidecharak, Rachel Harrison, and two anonymous reviewers. In our translation of the poem *The Tale of Khun Chang Khun Phaen* (Chiang Mai: Silkworm Books, 2010), the Thai character *cho chan* is transliterated as the letter "j," and we retain that convention in the proper names here.

[1] Craig J. Reynolds, "Thai Manual Knowledge: Theory and Practice," in his *Seditious Histories: Contesting Thai and Southeast Asian Pasts* (Seattle: University of Washington Press, 2006), chap. 10.

ordinary people depicted with some realism. The text evolved from the interplay between performers and audiences over a long period, possibly centuries. Storytellers incorporated tales, true and imaginary, whose meanings resonated with the audience, and fine-tuned the episodes, characters, and language to satisfy the tastes of different audiences. By this process, the work became a depository of values, ways to understand the world, and lessons for living in it. The tale remained popular because it could be "read" to extract these meanings and lessons from generation to generation.

At a simple level, the text contains lessons for a boy about how to court a girl, and lessons for a girl about how to deal with his attention. At a deeper level, the whole story can be read as a cautionary tale for women in a society where social power rests with men.[2] Several lessons about proper behavior, similar to those found in nineteenth-century manuals, are embedded as speeches in the text. Passages from the tale on the practice of supernaturalism are today reproduced almost verbatim in manuals of *saiyasat* (the science of dark or supernatural power; lore).

One set of lessons embedded in the tale concerns power and politics. Today, this aspect is rarely if ever mentioned or commented upon. Indeed, when we have drawn attention to this aspect of the work before Thai audiences, the reaction has been surprise and disbelief. Yet, the plot in outline is about a young man who is accused of revolt, becomes an outlaw, and in the finale is hauled before the king. This plot resembles those found in popular literature all over the world about an ordinary man confronting wealth and power. The legend of Robin Hood is an example, and the comparison between the two will be pursued below.

In this essay, we discuss the lessons about power and politics in *KCKP*. First, we examine two concepts of power as represented by the two key characters, Khun Phaen and King Phanwasa of Ayutthaya. Second, we trace the interplay between these two concepts of power throughout the plot. Third, we discuss what the "writing" of these lessons into a literary work tells us about the era when the work was at its height of popularity. Finally, we examine how such literary manuals are read and revised across different eras, and speculate why this prominent aspect of a major literary work is now largely ignored. But first, some background on the work itself.

The Tale

KCKP is a long folk epic that developed in an oral tradition of storytelling for local audiences. The plot, set in the provincial urban society of central Siam, is a love triangle ending in tragedy. Khun Phaen is handsome and dashing, but his family is ruined after his father is executed by the king for an error on royal service. Khun Chang is the richest man in the local town, but is fat, ugly, and crass. The two compete for the lovely Wanthong. Khun Phaen woos and weds her, but Khun Chang uses his wealth and court connections to take her away. Khun Phaen abducts Wanthong from Khun Chang's house, flees with her into the forest, and kills two senior nobles sent in pursuit; he is accused of revolt and becomes an outlaw. The rivalry continues through pitched battles, court cases, trial by ordeal, imprisonment,

---

[2] See Chris Baker and Pasuk Phongpaichit, "Gender, Sexuality, and Family in Old Siam: Women and Men in *Khun Chang Khun Phaen*," in *Disturbing Conventions: Decentering Thai Literary Cultures*, ed. Rachel Harrison (London, UK: Rowan and Littlefield, 2014), 193–215.

treachery, and other mayhem. Tiring of this disorder, the king summons the three and commands that Wanthong be executed for failing to choose between the two men.

Nobody knows for sure when the tale began. Working from clues in the text, we suggest that it originated around 1600 CE, possibly based on true events that were taken up by storytellers. The tale became very popular as entertainment, and hence was lengthened and embellished to meet popular demand. Probably from the eighteenth century onward, the story was adopted by the court, converted to written form, extended with new episodes and sequels, and embellished with fancier poetry. The first printed edition appeared in 1872, but the work is known today through an edition published in 1917–18 by Prince Damrong Rajanubhab, half-brother of King Chulalongkorn.[3]

As a result of this long and varied history, the tale is complex. At some point during its history, probably in the late Ayutthaya era, a sequel was added about Khun Phaen's first son, Phlai Ngam. The plot of this sequel closely tracks Khun Phaen's own story and may have been adapted from an alternative version of the tale. This sequel was not placed at the end but inserted into the body of the tale, probably to preserve Wanthong's death as the dramatic ending. The insertion is easily seen because the scars of the surgery are visible in the text. For some of the analysis below, we have to imagine the tale prior to the addition of this "inquel."

PROTECTION: THE POLITICS OF EVERYDAY LIFE

Power in *KCKP* is the ability to protect.[4] Throughout the tale, characters seek protection against risks, dangers, and threats in order to ward off sorrowful hardship and achieve peaceful contentment. They look for someone on whom they can depend, and who will feed or support them. When the father of a main character dies, his servants lament that "we have lost our protector," and fear harassment by local officials (p. 47).[5] When news arrives that Khun Phaen has died during a military campaign, his mother-in-law's first thought is, "who'll protect us?" (p. 228). When a father announces he will give his daughter away to a husband, she protests, "my lord and master, do you no longer protect your child?" (p. 207).

The three main sources of danger are defined in the second chapter by recounting the deaths of the three main characters' fathers. The first source is nature, especially the wild forest. The father of the heroine, Wanthong, dies from a forest fever contracted on a trading expedition. The second is human wickedness—Khun

---

[3] Samuel Smith published the first printed edition in 1872. We have seen only a partial copy, but this is virtually identical to the edition published by the Wat Ko press in 1889 (*Khun chang khun phaen*, forty vols. [Rattanakosin: Wat Ko, 1889]), an original copy of which is in the William Gedney Collection at the University of Michigan library, from which we have published *Khun chang khun phaen chabap wat ko* [The Wat Ko edition of KCKP] (Chiang Mai: Silkworm Books, 2013). Prince Damrong's edition is reprinted in several forms, including a three-volume edition (Bangkok: Khurusapha, third printing, 2003).

[4] For a fuller treatment of this theme, see Chris Baker and Pasuk Phongpaichit, "Protection and Power in Siam: From *Khun Chang Khun Phaen* to the Buddha Amulet," *Southeast Asian Studies* 2, no. 2 (2013): 215–42.

[5] All page references to *KCKP* refer to Chris Baker and Pasuk Phongpaichit, *The Tale of Khun Chang Khun Phaen* (Chiang Mai: Silkworm Books, 2010).

Chang's father is killed by a professional bandit gang. The third is authority—Khun Phaen's father is executed by the king.

Finding protection from the third source of danger, authority, is the organizing principle of the social structure known as *sakdina*, at least when seen from below—the main characters' perspective in *KCKP*. Men donate some or all of their labor to a patron in return for protection from various forms of authority. In the classic form of *sakdina*, men become dependents (*phrai* or *that*) in the service of a *khun nang* noble. Khun Phaen's father is an effective patron in the provincial town of Suphanburi because he has an official post as a soldier and recognition from the king. As a result, local officials "shook their heads [and] knew never to cross him" (p. 8). After the father is killed, his servants lament that "nobody dared bully us, because everyone feared Khun Krai. But now they'll all come and push us around" (p. 35). But this classic form of patronage is not the only one. The same principles apply in many other circumstances. After being branded as an outlaw, Khun Phaen places himself under the patronage of a provincial governor who plans to employ him as a guard. The chief of a bandit lair gives shelter to fugitives who in turn must work as robbers. An abbot urges Khun Phaen to stay in the monkhood because the robe is protection against the dangers of conscription.

The model for the role of protector is a parent's custodianship of children, and especially the male in the combined role of father, husband, and householder. Good parents protect their children from all dangers, even the menace of sun, wind, and insects. Husbands shelter their wives like the spreading branches of a bo tree ("Oh, little bo tree shelter of your darling wife …," p. 748).

THE KING: FORMAL AUTHORITY

King Phanwasa of Ayutthaya and Khun Phaen are both presented as figures of power, but with power resting on very different bases. The king's power is legitimated by the political theory, infused by Buddhism, prevailing in late Ayutthaya. We shall call this "formal power" or "authority." Khun Phaen's power is based on education in the use of techniques and devices and we will call it "mastery."

The "Beautiful Apparition": Power Based on Supreme Merit

The king is generally introduced with a formal invocation similar to those in other literary works of the time:

Now to tell of the king emperor, ruler of Ayutthaya, the great heaven, who resided in a glittering crystal palace where throngs of palace ladies, / all just of age, radiant, fair, and beautiful, with figures like those in a painting, serviced the royal footsoles. The king slumbered in the golden palace / until dawn streaked the sky, when he woke from sleep and came to bathe in cool rosewater and was arrayed in splendid raiment. / Grasping a diamond sword in his left hand, he went out to the main audience hall to sit on a glittering crystal throne, surrounded by senior officials and royal poets. (p. 777)

These invocations present the king surrounded by abundance and beauty. This "beautiful apparition" is proof that he has accumulated the supreme stock of merit as a result of good deeds in previous lives and thus qualifies to be king.[6] In this kingly role, he has use of the formal machinery of state power—the wealth accumulated in the treasuries, the services of the nobles to carry out his wishes, and the labor of ordinary people to fight wars and perform various services.

This formal power makes the king supremely effective as a provider of protection. Two of the main items of royal regalia, the sword and multi-tiered umbrellas, are symbols of protection. In the invocations that preface his appearances, the king "protects the mass of the populace and soldiery so they are joyful" (p. 506) and "offers protection to the great and small throughout the world" (p. 402) so well that other territories eagerly seek the same shelter. In court formalities, the king is addressed as "lord protector," "divine protector," and "paramount protector." The young Khun Chang is taken to be presented as a royal page so that he will enjoy royal protection.

Concern over Revolt

To deliver protection, the king must preserve public order, which means defending the realm against enemies and quelling conflicts among the citizens. These duties depend in turn on the maintenance of his own authority. Threats to the king's authority and his ability to deliver protection are called "revolt" (*kabot*) and are a constant cause of concern.

In the court sources of mid and late Ayutthaya, "revolt" means a challenge to the authority of the king. It is applied to breakaways by subordinate cities or tributary rulers; dynastic challenges, especially during or after disputed successions to the throne; attempted military coups; and uprisings that may have millenarian aims. The word first appears in the later chronicles to describe a challenge for the throne by an alternative dynastic line around 1540, and appears regularly in the chronicles from the Naresuan era (1590–1605) onward, as such incidents become common, especially in the wake of frequent succession disputes.

In *KCKP*, when a city on the boundary between the spheres of influence of Chiang Mai and Ayutthaya is forced to submit to Chiang Mai, the king of Ayutthaya claims this forced defection amounts to a revolt. After Khun Phaen's army regains the city, its ruler is brought to Ayutthaya for trial. He pleads in his defense,

> My liege, please have mercy! I face a charge with a penalty of death. / I'm not dissembling or concealing matters. I did not revolt against the royal footsoles but acted in fear of danger. If I had not submitted to the Lao, I would be dead. (p. 263)

---

[6] Nidhi Eoseewong has argued that the theory of kingship of late Ayutthaya drew in part on the unquestionable, god-given power of the *devaraja,* but more on the idea derived from the Aggana (Akanya) Sutta that kingship came into existence because man needed protection from dangers and evils—especially those visited by man on man—and thus elevated a person "who was the handsomest, the best favored, the most attractive, the most capable" to become ruler. Later texts rationalized that "the person who is king is believed to have accumulated the most merit. This is indicated by his superior status in life, above all others in the same incarnation. He possesses the royal insignia, the palace, and a lifestyle of conspicuous wealth. The fact that he has the most accumulated merit is proven by his ascent of the throne." Nidhi Eoseewong, *Pen and Sail: Literature and History in Early Bangkok* (Chiang Mai: Silkworm Books, 2005), 323–24.

In the parallel military campaign later in the tale, the king of Chiang Mai is captured and brought to Ayutthaya for trial. Again, although the military circumstances are very different, the matter is judged within the framework of "revolt." Later in the tale, Khun Phaen becomes involved in a mock revolt led by his son pretending to be a Mon adventurer who has come to punish Ayutthaya for immoral rule. The king disdains such an attempt:

> I'm the pillar of the land. Though someone may have powers, he can't compete with me. It's known throughout the city that the guardian deities protect the royal lineage. / How can those who are mere servants of the royal dust crave the world? (p. 1053)

When a religious adept transforms himself into a giant crocodile and creates chaos along the Chao Phraya river, a senior noble assumes the adept was sent as part of a planned revolt: "Who entrusted you to come here? ... You have bold ideas of treachery and revolt." In his defense, the adept pleads: "As for the king, I had no thought of revolt" (p. 1112). Even a Chiang Mai princess caught using a love philter is accused by the king: "Truly you seem to be in revolt" (p. 1078).

Terrible Power

While the tale presents the standard theory of the king as protector through invocations and royal titles, the tale also seems intent on showing that the king's supreme power is also a supreme threat.

In several scenes at royal audience, the king is informed of some problem or misfortune, to which he reacts by directing some form of violence. When Khun Phaen's father misinterprets the king's order during a buffalo hunt, the king orders a summary execution:

> The king was inflamed with rage, as if a black vapor had blown across his heart. He bellowed like a thunderclap ... / Heigh! Heigh! Bring the executioners here immediately. I cannot keep him. Off with his head! Stick it up on a pole and raise it high! Seize his property and his servants at once! (p. 32)

When the king finds that Khun Phaen has evaded his duty as a trainee in the palace, the king reacts in a similar way (though quickly recants):

> ... he arrogantly dared to climb out over the walls. He is condemned to execution. Skewer his head on a pole as an example to others! (p. 310)

When Khun Chang fails in a trial by ordeal, the king exclaims:

> Don't leave him to pollute the earth. Cleave open his breast as an example to deter others. / He took Wai off to kill in a forest. Go and impale him in that same forest. (p. 769)

When the Chiang Mai ruler offends the king, his reaction is similar:

Why allow this king to remain a burden on the earth? Heigh! Phraya Jakri, raise an army immediately … / Don't spare this Chiang Mai rabble. Wherever they're found, slash them to dust. Lay waste their city and leave it deserted. Raze its walls and fortifications! (p. 543)

When a Chiang Mai princess is found guilty of using a love philter, the sentence is delivered immediately.

Ha! Heigh! Phraya Yommarat, take her away and slash her dead. Open her chest with an axe for public shame. Make an example of her to caution others. (p. 1078)

The king is also shown launching wars or other military actions, and the tale dwells on the human consequences. The recruitment of soldiers is portrayed several times in the tale, always as a brutal process, suggesting how much it was hated and feared: "They beat, bribed, and badgered people into the army. If a man could not be found, they impounded his wife and children" (p. 168). The tale also lingers on the aftermath of war, especially the sorrow visited on the families of slaughtered soldiers, and the human devastation when a city is defeated, its population is swept away into slavery, and its wealth dissipated by looting.

Royalist litterateur Prince Phitthayalongkon (Bidyalankarana)[7] noted that in *KCKP*, "The King is a queer and thoughtless autocrat."[8] Boonlua Debyasuvarn, the prominent mid-twentieth century literary critic from the royal Kunchon lineage, said at a debate in August 1974: "As for the ruling class as portrayed in *Khun Chang Khun Phaen*, can anyone who reads it say that it shows *good* rule? I say, we're awfully lucky not to have such a king ourselves!"[9]

In sum, the king is presented according to the prevailing political theory of late Ayutthaya as the possessor of supreme merit and thus also of supreme power, which enables him to protect the populace. But two other aspects of the way the king is presented in the tale bring this theory into question. First, the king is constantly concerned about "revolt," meaning any internal or external challenge to his authority. Second, seen from below, the king's absolute power is shown to be a terrible threat to life and property. Although he is also a giver of gifts and favors, particularly to those who bring him victory in war, this aspect receives much less emphasis than his capacity to deprive. All the major characters, and many of the minor ones, lose life, liberty, property, rank, spouse, or kin at the hands of the king.

KHUN PHAEN: MASTERY

Khun Phaen is also a figure of power, but the origins of this power stand in sharp contrast to that of the king. First, his power derives in part from resources found in the periphery, in the wild spaces of forests and hills. Second, his power

---

[7] Prince Phitthayalongkon (1876–1945) was as an author, editor, and translator, often writing under the pseudonym "No.Mo.So." He was a son of Prince Wichaichan, the last Front-Palace King (*upparat*) behind the Front Palace Crisis of 1875.

[8] Prince Bidyalankarana, "*Sebha* Recitation and the Story of *Khun Chang Khun Phaen*," *Journal of the Thailand Research Society* 33 (1941), 13.

[9] Quoted in Susan Fulop Kepner, *A Civilized Woman: M. L. Boonlua Debyasuvarn and the Thai Twentieth Century* (Chiang Mai: Silkworm Books, 2013), 297.

does not come from the formal hierarchy, but is something that can be learned and acquired by an ordinary man. Third, his power is not legitimated by the Buddhist idea of merit, but is underpinned by another aspect of Buddhism combined with other concepts of ancient and exotic origin.

Khun Phaen is born in the provincial town of Suphanburi, and retreats further into the periphery of forest and hill over the early course of the story. His family is minor nobility, but is ruined and impoverished because of his father's mistake on royal service. Khun Phaen is later elevated back to the minor nobility, but again reduced to penury and jail on royal command. Even after he is ennobled again by the king, Phaen refers to himself as a *phrai*, and his own mother mocks him: "You may be gentlefolk, but what level? Even now, they still call you 'Ai-Khun'" (p. 1024; *ai* is a prefix used for a subordinate).

Yet Phaen becomes a figure of power from skills that he learns. He enters the monkhood and studies with three abbots,[10] two of whom had been friends and teachers of his father. He passes on this learning to his own son, mostly indirectly through the texts he has collected in his library, and partly through direct instruction. Teachers, texts, temple, and family are the transmission lines for these skills.

Lore

This education primarily consists of military skills, but their application is not narrowly confined to war. Phaen famously uses these devices in his career as a lover, as well as to combat natural forces such as disease and the weather.

His skills include the ability to predict events and manipulate natural forces. Prediction is made through astrological reckoning and the interpretation of omens found in nature. Natural forces are manipulated through the command of spirits, and through the use of verbal formulas, natural substances, and constructed devices (especially yantra—geometrical diagrams filled with powerful symbols, words, and numbers). This manipulation operates through two pairs of forces: *repulsion* (warding off danger, or, in its most complete form, providing invulnerability) and *attraction* (inducing love, sympathy, or good fortune); and *constraint* (preventing an event or action, such as immobilizing an enemy) and *release* (removing constraints, such as undoing locks and chains, or ensuring a smooth delivery at birth).[11]

These skills have roots in three traditions. The first is a belief in spirits of the place and of ancestors, which is found throughout Southeast Asia and, indeed, in much of the world.

Second is a belief found in Indic tradition that mastery over oneself conveys mastery over natural processes. Through mental control and ascetic practices, a rishi or yogi attains supernatural abilities. In life stories of the Buddha, he was schooled in ascetic practice and acquired extraordinary powers—such as flying through the air,

---

[10] For a fuller account of this education, see Chris Baker and Pasuk Phongpaichit, "Protection and Power in Siam: From *Khun Chang Khun Phaen* to the Buddha Amulet," *Southeast Asian Studies* 2, no. 2 (2013): 215–42.

[11] See: Thep Sarikabut, *Phra khamphi phrawet* [Manuals of lore], six vols. (Bangkok: Utsahakam kan phim, n.d.); and Achan Hon Yanchot (Chayamongkhon Udomsap), *Saiyasat chabap sombun* [The complete *saiyasat*] (Bangkok: Sinlapa bannakan, 1995).

multiplying his body, and recalling previous lives.[12] In his studies of current-day forest saints and spirit mediums, Stanley Tambiah identified the idea of *itthi-rit*, meaning the mastery over oneself that delivers exceptional mastery over other natural forces.[13]

The third root also has Indic origins, but is more obscure. *Athan* (sometimes *athap* or *athanpawet*) is a Thai transliteration of Atharva Veda, the fourth of the great ancient texts of Hindu tradition.[14] This text contains a catalog of verbal formulas and devices for overcoming threats and difficulties that probably derives from north Indian folk practice some three thousand years ago. The difficulties and devices are similar to practices described in *KCKP*, identified in more recent anthropological studies of Thailand,[15] and found in Thai manuals of supernaturalism. *Athan* can mean protection, especially rites for protection of a palace or city, but is also used to refer to the whole range of verbal formulas, natural substances, and powerful devices. Verbal formulas are variously described as *mon* (mantra), *wet* (Veda), *akhom*, or *khatha*, all words that derive from the Hindu–Buddhist tradition of scriptures. Compound versions of these same terms (such as *khatha-akhom*) are used to describe the practice as a whole. Alternatively, the practice is described as *wicha* or *withaya*, the Pali–Sanskrit term for learning or knowledge—lore.

In Thai tradition, these three elements—spirits, mastery, and the formulas and devices of *athan*—are closely intertwined. For example, in his manufacture of a powerful sword, Khun Phaen first collects various metals that are invested with special qualities (such as having decorated the roof of a palace or served as the fastening on a coffin). These are then cast and forged following the procedures in a manual, including rites to transfer the mastery of the craftsmen into the weapon; and, finally, the spirits are convoked to instill extra power into the weapon.

In *KCKP*, an adept such as Khun Phaen is *khon di*, a "good person," and the practice as a whole is *thang nai*, the "inner ways," a phrase that nicely captures the depth of the knowledge, its arcane origins, and its reliance on the innate talent of the practitioner.

In sum, Khun Phaen's power derives from mastery over himself and mastery of textual knowledge, which lend him mastery over the spirits and obscure forces in the

---

[12] Victor Fic, *The Tantra: Its Origin, Theories, Art and Diffusion to Nepal, Tibet, Mongolia, China, Japan, and Indonesia* (New Delhi: Abhinav, 2003), 42–44.

[13] See: Stanley J. Tambiah, *Buddhism and the Spirit Cults in North-east Thailand* (Cambridge: Cambridge University Press, 1970), 49–51; and Stanley J. Tambiah, *The Buddhist Saints of the Forest and the Cult of Amulets: A Study in Charisma* (Cambridge: Cambridge University Press, 1984), 45, 315.

[14] Two main recensions of the Atharva Veda have survived. This inventory forms the first of four parts in the Shaunakiya, or northern recension. Dating is difficult and controversial, but may be around the eleventh- or twelfth-century BCE. Some scholars have speculated that this inventory is a record of local belief and practice in north India at the time the Vedas were composed. Others argue that the inventory may have earlier origins, perhaps in Central Asia. See: William Dwight Witney, *Atharva-Veda Samhita*, two vols. (Cambridge: Harvard University Press, 1905); Jarrod L. Whitaker, "Ritual Power, Social Prestige, and Amulets (mani) in the Atharvaveda," in *The Vedas: Texts, Language, and Ritual*, ed. Arlo Griffiths and Jan E. M. Houlson (Groningen: Egbert Forsten, 2004); and Axel Michaels, *Hinduism: Past and Present* (Princeton: Princeton University Press, 2004).

[15] About verbal formulas and devices for overcoming threats and difficulties, see, especially, Robert B. Textor, "An Inventory of Non-Buddhist Supernatural Objects in a Central Thai Village" (doctoral dissertation, Cornell University, 1960).

natural world. With these abilities, Khun Phaen is not only an accomplished soldier, but is able to extend protection to others. He provides protection to his wife when they are in danger, to his troops in battle, and to his horse. Beyond the battlefield, he offers protection in other ways. He protects the kingdom of Ayutthaya from the threat of Chiang Mai. He protects the people of Chomthong from the threat of being pillaged and swept from their homes as war prisoners. He provides money for one wife to buy herself out of slavery, and uses his skill with mantra to rescue another from illness. He spares people from the hated loss of freedom under corvée by declining the king's offer to raise a massive army, and even protects his rival Khun Chang from execution. Within the bottom-up theory of the politics of everyday life, in which protection is the key concept, Khun Phaen is thus portrayed as a figure of considerable power.

MASTERY AND AUTHORITY

How do these two forms of power co-exist, and how do they relate to one another in the political landscape? This question is developed through the tale.

Authority Undermined

In the prelude to the tale (the first two chapters), the authority of the king is plainly shown when he has Khun Phaen's father summarily executed. But in two military expeditions to the north, the ability of the king to impose his authority over vassals is shown as being utterly dependent on the mastery of Khun Phaen and people like him.

When Chiang Mai defies Ayutthaya, the king resolves to send an army north and asks for a volunteer to lead it. Not a single noble in the court volunteers. The nobles are portrayed as flaccid, and the king is powerless to command them. He is obliged to turn to the lineage of Khun Phaen's father, because of their known mastery. Khun Phaen, who at the time is aged around fifteen, is sent north at the head of the army.

In the replay[16] of this scene later in the tale, the limitation of formal authority is more clearly portrayed. When the king asks for a volunteer and none steps forward, he rants at his own nobles:

> You're good only at cheating your own men out of money by using your clever tongues. I don't have to support you with allowances. Your property and rank are a burden on the realm ... / ... Perhaps some slaves from some department or other will volunteer, and I can get rid of the lot of you at once to make room for appointing them in your stead. (pp. 544, 547)

Again the king is obliged to turn to the lineage of Khun Phaen. His son, Phlai Ngam, also aged around fourteen or fifteen, volunteers and asks the king to free his father Khun Phaen to accompany him. The scene continues to mock formal power. The king proposes to conscript a massive army, but Khun Phaen declines on the grounds that conscription will be "troublesome" for the people. Instead he asks for the release of thirty-five fellow prisoners who are skilled in lore, thus asserting the

---

[16] Because the "inquel" about Khun Phaen's son is similar in plot to his father's story, several scenes are replayed.

superiority of mastery over authority and its system of mobilizing manpower. At a roll call, the thirty-five relate their crimes, presenting themselves as threats to Buddhism, tax collection, merchant wealth, and the administrative frame—in short the underpinnings of the social order:

Next!

Ai-Thong from Chong Khwak, husband of I-Mak. I killed a Lao called Thao Sen, crept in to steal an alms bowl and shoulder cloth from a novice, thumped an old monk, and had a wrestle with the abbot.

Next!

Ai-Chang Dam, from Ban Tham. I burgled a tax collector and took all his money and property—good stuff and no small amount, including jewels.

Ai-Phao, husband of I-Phan from Ban Na-kluea. I poisoned Luang Choduek[17] and cleaned out his house.

Ai-Koet Kradukdam, husband of I-Khamdang, convicted of burgling the Department of Elephants with mahout Man, and robbing a forest Lawa. I'm invulnerable with a single testicle and twisted scrotum. (p. 552)

The text stresses the liminality of this army in other ways. Phaen is destitute. His hair is so long he can sit on it, and passersby mistake him for a madman. The ex-convict volunteers have nothing but sacking as clothes. On the march, they smash themselves with alcohol, *kanja*, opium, and *krathom* (a leaf chewed as an intoxicant). In an older text of this passage, they start looting even before they have left the confines of the capital, and continue to seize food, property, and women on the northward journey and return.

In both military expeditions, Khun Phaen triumphs, the king is overcome with relief, and both Khun Phaen and his troops are richly rewarded. The protection of the kingdom is shown to be dependent on the skills of Khun Phaen and his liminal-criminal colleagues.

The king attempts to limit the consequences of this dependence. After both victories, the king sends Khun Phaen away from the capital to guard a remote border. An old Thai saying runs, "After harvest, kill the bull; after war, kill the army chief."[18]

Confronting Wealth and Authority

In the main thread of the story, Khun Phaen and Khun Chang vie for the love of Wanthong. Khun Chang uses his wealth to suborn Wanthong's mother, and manipulates his court connections to get assistance from the king. He serves the king

---

[17] "Luang Choduek " is the official title of the head of the Chinese community in the capital, usually a very rich and influential person.

[18] The origin of the saying is probably *Rachathirat*; see Nithi Eoseewong, "Set suek kha khun phon" [After war, kill the army chief), *Matichon Sutsapda* 33, no. 1721 (August 9–15, 2013): 30.

as both a collector of taxes and keeper of the royal elephants in the strategic town of Suphanburi, and was presented at court in childhood. He first uses his access to the royal audience to have Khun Phaen sent north at the head of the army, then spreads a rumor that Phaen has been killed, and marries Wanthong before Khun Phaen returns. Later he appears at court and tries to frame Khun Phaen for revolt, as follows:

> Then he shouted at me provocatively, saying it was not a good idea to kill me; if he released me, I would go to Ayutthaya and tell everything; / then, were the king to come out, he would engage the king in an elephant duel, win a famous victory, and seize the city as ruler. These were his vile words. / He has built a royal lodge in the forest and a camp fortified with spikes. Very mischievously, he has constructed a toilet.[19] Before long, he will become a threat to the city. (pp. 393–94)

The king doubts the charge, but sends a force to bring Khun Phaen for trial. On finding Khun Phaen in the forest, one of the leaders of this force provokes Phaen with accusations of revolt: "Your lineage is nothing. Defying royal orders is a grave matter. You're full of ambition for kingship" (p. 405).

Equipping with Lore

In face of Khun Chang's deployment of his wealth and royal connections, Khun Phaen feels at a disadvantage. He asks, "How can I protect myself?" (p. 316), and resolves to equip himself to fight the powerful forces arrayed against him. This task takes him into the wild periphery.

> He left at dawn for the upland forests. / In search of what he needed, he delved into every nook and cranny, passing through / villages of Karen, Kha, Lawa, and Mon, and sleeping along passes through the mountains. (p. 317)

He forges a sword "according to the great manual on weaponry" (p. 317), instilled with supernatural power; acquires a personal spirit made from the fetus of a child who died with his mother in childbirth; and buys a horse sired on a "water horse."

Up to this point, Khun Phaen's mastery of lore has played only a small role in the story, but now that role dramatically increases. Moreover, his lore implicitly challenges aspects of royalty. The ingredients for forging his sword include metals from the summit of a royal palace, and ore from two mines used for making royal regalia weaponry. He names the sword *Fa fuen*, thunder before rain (translated as Skystorm), the name of a weapon among the regalia presented at the coronation of Khun Borom, the great hero king of Thai-Lao legend.[20] Later, Khun Phaen tells his son:

---

[19] At this time, a constructed toilet was one of the privileges of royalty. See "Phra aiyakan aya luang" [Criminal law code], section 115, in *Kotmai tra sam duang* [Three seals Law] (Bangkok: Khurusapha, 1955), vol. 4, 85.

[20] Souneth Phothisane, "The Nidān Khun Borom: Annotated Translation and Analysis" (doctoral dissertation, University of Queensland, 1966), 126. Sujit Wongthes argues that *Fa fuen*, literally "restored by the god," indicates a sacred weapon presented by Thaen, the creator

This Skystorm is superb. Tens and hundreds of thousands of other swords are not as good. Even the king's regal sword is not equal to mine. (p. 575)

With this equipment, he becomes more openly defiant. When his own personal spirit cautions him, "Hold off! Cool down. Don't kill him, Father. Don't you fear the power of the Lord of Life?" Khun Phaen snaps back, "No! I don't fear his power" (pp. 345–46). Starting in this stage of the tale, the text often introduces Khun Phaen with a mini-invocation similar though less elaborate than those that regularly introduce the king. These invocations celebrate Khun Phaen "whose mastery was unmatched," or "whose powers were famous everywhere."

The stage is set for a clash between mastery and authority. Khun Phaen abducts Wanthong from Khun Chang's house, and defeats the royal army sent after him, killing two noble officers. Now a wanted outlaw, he and Wanthong flee further into the wild periphery of forests and mountains where they live off lotus roots. When Wanthong becomes pregnant, they place themselves under the care of the governor of Phichit, who has a reputation for harboring those in trouble.

Play within a Play

There are two scenes outside the main thread of the plot in which Khun Phaen confronts a king other than King Phanwasa of Ayutthaya, and triumphs both times. These scenes seem to function like the "play within a play" in Shakespearean drama, predicting or mirroring events in the main plot.

In the first of the scenes, during his search for protective equipment, Khun Phaen visits a bandit lair in the western hills. Although the chief is not a "king," he appears very similar to one. Khun Phaen notes that he seems like "the lord of some country." A guard tells him that the chief "has put many passersby to death already." His residence is "furnished as well as any princely palace" with "throngs of young Lao and Thai girl servants, all just of age and good-looking. The sitting halls were spread with soft mats, pillows, and carpets, and strewn with items of gold, silver, nak, and nielloware" (p. 1176). Khun Phaen enters the chief's service, but they come into conflict ending in a physical struggle, and Khun Phaen's superior lore triumphs.

In the second of these scenes, during the campaign against Chiang Mai, Khun Phaen and his son use lore to enter the Chiang Mai palace with the aim of capturing the king, but first take a tour, violating the sacred space of the palace interior, and inspecting the various "forbidden" women—from queen to consorts to lady attendants. Finally, they approach the sleeping king and use superior lore to drive away the king's protective spirits. Waking up and discovering himself defenseless, the king surrenders himself, his realm, and his family into Khun Phaen's hands.

Mastery and Authority

In the texts of *KCKP* assembled in the palace in the mid-nineteenth century and used in the earliest printed editions,[21] there are four places that raise the question of whether mastery can defy authority.

---

god of Tai tradition. See "Dap 'Fa fuen' khong Khun Phaen chuea dieo kap phi banpachon kasat mueang Nan nai tamnan" (Khun Phaen's *Fa fuen* Sword, Same Name as the Ancestral Spirits of the Nan King in Legend), *Matichon Sutsapda* 33, no. 1724 (August 30, 2013), 77.

[21] See above, note 3.

The monks who teach lore to members of Khun Phaen's lineage are convinced that their pupils can defy the monarch. The teacher of Khun Phaen's father asks Khun Phaen in bewilderment why his father let himself be executed by the king: "I'm still disappointed that he died without putting up a fight. He must have lost his knowledge" (p. 122). Phaen explains that his father had taken the oath of allegiance and would not go back on his word, and hence renounced his mastery and allowed himself to be killed.

Similarly, after release from jail, Khun Phaen visits his old teacher, who is bewildered as to why his pupil languished in jail for a dozen years. "What was up? Didn't you have faith in your knowledge? Or was it fun lying in the jail?" (p. 558). Khun Phaen replies, "I was not lacking in power," but again explains he had taken an oath that he would not escape and refused to break his word.

When Khun Phaen and Wanthong are outlaws in the forest, and Wanthong becomes pregnant, Khun Phaen decides to turn himself in. He reasons, "If I give myself up, rather than being captured in the forest, the punishment should be light. Besides, I can create obstruction with the power of my knowledge" (p. 426). When brought before the king, "Khun Phaen intoned a mantra he had decided on in advance, and blew it with faith in its lore. The king's mood relaxed, and he turned his face towards them" (p. 436). The king promptly absolves Phaen of the serious charge of murdering two senior nobles.

Similarly, when Phaen's son Wai goes to seek pardon for his mother, he equips himself with many devices and "recited prayers to his powerful teachers for the king's anger to recede." The king feels "love and concern for him on account of the power of the lore" (pp. 812–13), and promptly issues a pardon (though it turns out to be too late).[22]

In the two instances when Khun Phaen uses lore on the king, it is effective. In the two instances when he or his father refrain from using lore to defend themselves, Phaen can rationalize the decision by reference to personal loyalties.

DENOUEMENT: REVOLT AND SACRIFICE

Khun Phaen and Wanthong leave Phichit and return to Ayutthaya to surrender to the king. In the old version of the tale, their return was quickly followed by the climactic scene of confrontation.

The rivalry between Khun Phaen and Khun Chang has caused two pitched battles, the death of two senior nobles, a court case, ordeal by water, and other mayhem. In short, it has disrupted the social peace that it is the king's duty to preserve, and thus represents a challenge to his authority, a revolt. He summons all the parties to the audience hall, where the king sits in judgment over the whole dispute. The charges that the king brings do not concern the wrongs that Khun Chang, Khun Phaen, and Wanthong may have done to one another, but the ways their actions are undermining or impugning royal authority.

---

[22] The message arrives too late to forestall the execution and Khun Phaen makes only a half-hearted attempt to thwart it. Phra Wai angrily accuses his father, "You have stunning mantras, powerful enough to immobilize people in droves. Why didn't you blow one to stun this executioner and stop him? She died because you didn't help her. Or have you lost your powers?" (p. 826). Khun Phaen explains to his son that her death was predestined in astrology and thus impossible to prevent.

On hearing of Khun Chang's efforts to prise Wanthong away from Khun Phaen, the king calls Khun Chang a robber (*chon*), alluding to the Law on Theft, which reserves its highest punishments for acts that disturb public order. He continues, "It turns out I'm not the Lord of Life. You think I'm just a lord in a mask play with no authority." He adds that Khun Chang "deserves to be knocked unconscious right here, thrashed countless times, and have a ripe coconut stuffed in his mouth" (p. 798). This punishment comes from clause 1 of the Code of Crimes against Government, about infringing on the prerogatives of the monarch.[23]

The king turns to Khun Phaen's son (now called Phra Wai) and again explodes against both the disruption of public order and the impugning of royal authority:

> Phra Wai has acted arrogantly. It seems the country has no master. / People don't pay attention to the law but do whatever they like. If they slash and kill one another, it'll be a danger to the populace. That angers me. / ... There are courts and codes of law. Or perhaps you think I can't make a judgment. (p. 798)

With the phrase "a danger to the populace," the king alludes to the Law on Conflict,[24] which deals extensively with threats to public order, and he proposes that Wai be punished appropriately with both fines and the lash.

By logic, the king would now confront Khun Phaen in the same way, and the issue of their competing power would rise to the surface. Instead, the king turns to Wanthong, accuses her of being the root cause of the conflict, and insists she choose between the two men. Wanthong is terrified. She mumbles that the two men have different meaning for her life, and she tacitly refuses to make a decision. The king's anger comes down on her head:

> You cannot say which one you love! Your heart wants both of them, so you can switch back and forth, having a reserve deeper than the deepest sea ... / Heigh! Phraya Yommarat, go and execute her immediately! Cleave open her chest with an axe without mercy. Don't let her blood touch my land. / Collect it on banana leaves for feeding to dogs. If it touches the ground, the evil will linger. Execute her for all men and women to see! (p. 801)

This condemnation and sentencing have nothing to do with the laws on marriage. The penalties prescribed for adultery and bigamy were fines, caning, and public shaming (being paraded around town with hibiscus flowers), not capital punishment.[25] Throughout the tale, neither Khun Phaen, Khun Chang, or other characters criticize Wanthong for bigamy. Only Wanthong chastises herself for being "two-minded," and then in fear of social reprobation, not criminal retribution. The telling flourish in the king's speech is the order "Don't let her blood touch my land." In the Ayutthaya laws, the only place where this instruction appears is Clause 1 of

---

[23] *Kotmai tra sam duang*, vol. 4, 5–6.

[24] Ibid., "Phra aiyakan laksana wiwat ti da kan" [Law on conflict], vol. 3, 184 (especially the preamble).

[25] Under the law, the cuckolded husband had the right to execute his errant wife, but only after first exercising his right to execute the adulterer. See "Phra ayakan laksana phua mia" [Law on marriage], clauses 8 and 9, *Kotmai tra sam duang*, vol. 2, 210–11.

the Law on Revolt.[26] This is a sentence for revolt, not for a woman's failing to choose between two men.

Although the judgment appears to be about Wanthong's behavior, the issue at stake is the king's authority. In simple terms, Wanthong is in revolt because she has defied his order to make a decision between the two men. More broadly, as the build-up to this climax has shown, the king is concerned about royal authority confronted by a family equipped with mastery. Wanthong becomes a sacrificial victim whose death evades any resolution of the issue of authority against mastery. This finale can be evaluated in many different ways. Viewed from the king's perspective, it can be rationalized as a practical solution: he needs the services of Khun Phaen and his son as soldiers, and the services of Khun Chang as a collector of taxes and keeper of elephants, while Wanthong is expendable. In terms of the plot, the sacrifice of Wanthong provides a dramatic and enigmatic ending that has probably been a key factor in the story's lasting popularity. In terms of the tale as a manual, a repository of lessons about power, the sacrifice leaves the issue unresolved because, of course, it cannot be resolved. As David Chandler concluded about some nineteenth-century Cambodian tales, "In a sense, the texts 'answer' questions that no one dared to ask, but in the end, what do they *explain*? No more, and of course no less, than songs at the edge of the forest, as night comes on, the time *entre chien et loup*."[27] As a depository of meanings, values, and lessons, the tale maps the territory and lays out the issues but does not provide answers to unanswerable questions.

Besides, in truth, the mastery represented by Khun Phaen and the authority of the king are not irredeemably opposed but delicately balanced.[28] The king relies upon the likes of Khun Phaen and his ancestors to fight his wars. At the same time, Khun Phaen and others who share his lineage accept honors and titles from the king because of their obvious social benefits.

WRITING THE MANUAL

The discourse on power in *Khun Chang Khun Phaen* is embedded in the plot of the story and hence is probably an old part of the tale rather than a later addition. The story presents King Phanwasa according to the political theory of the era—he is king by virtue of his supreme stock of merit and provides protection to the populace through the machinery of the *sakdina* state. But, the tale also questions this theory in

---

[26] To paraphrase, the law reads: anyone who attempts to dethrone the monarch, or who attempts to do damage to the monarch with weapons or poison, or who refuses to submit tribute as a governor, or who encourages enemies to attack, or who gives information to enemies, is liable to punishment of death and seizure of property for a. the entire clan; b. seven generations of the clan; or c. the whole clan, ensuring no successors; with the executions to linger over seven days "without letting the blood or corpse fall on the realm but be put on a raft and floated with the current 240,000 *yochana* to the next country" [Law on revolt, clause 1], *Kotmai tra sam duang*, vol. 4, 124.

[27] David Chandler, "Songs at the Edge of the Forest: Perceptions of Order in Three Cambodian Texts," in *At the Edge of the Forest: Essays on Cambodia, History, and Narrative in Honor of David Chandler*, ed. Anne Ruth Hansen and Judy Ledgerwood (Ithaca: Cornell Southeast Asia Program Publications, 2008), 45, emphasis in original.

[28] Especially in the eighteenth century, kings were attributed with supernatural powers deriving from mastery, and this belief survives in folk tradition down to the present. In *KCKP*, however, the king is never portrayed exercising such powers, only Khun Phaen and other warriors or adepts.

several ways. First, viewed from below, the exercise of kingly authority can have terrible results. Second, in practice, the king is dependent on other powerful figures, such as Khun Phaen, and regularly faces challenges to his authority ("revolt"). Third, others also have the mastery to offer protection and thus can rival the king's power.

We have no way of knowing how this discourse was "read" in the past by those who heard the story. As with any manual or "virtual manual," many readings are possible. For example, the take-away might be that the execution of Khun Phaen's father at the start of the tale and his wife at the end proves the supremacy of royal authority and shows that claims of mastery are relatively impotent. But equally, the message could be that royal authority is terrible, hollow, and fragile. A third reading might be that formal authority is no more or less powerful than other authority, but, because it is embedded in institutions, is dangerous to defy.

The key point is not how it was interpreted, but the very fact that it was "written." This discourse on power is found in a work derived from oral tradition and believed to have been popular entertainment for commoners in late Ayutthaya. By contrast, almost all other surviving Thai sources prior to the mid-nineteenth century, including chronicles, laws, oral histories, and heroic and romantic literature, originated from the court and reflect its views. Accounts by visiting foreigners also largely present information and views gleaned from the court circle. *KCKP* is an important exception.

Revolt and Defiance

The era of late Ayutthaya was peppered with revolts. Many erupted at the time of royal succession. From 1610 onward, all but one of the twelve successions involved battles that varied in degrees of severity. The dynasty was ejected and replaced in 1629, 1688, 1767, and 1782. With the exception of the Burmese sack in 1767, the pretender came from senior nobility, but these events were far from simple palace revolutions. Nobles and their armed retainers divided into rival camps. In 1688 and 1782 (and possibly on other occasions for which historical information is scant), the monkhood became involved, and armed bands and mobs came in from the provinces. The initial putsch was often followed by aftershocks and counter-attempts for several years. Provinces broke away—particularly strategic centers such as Khorat and Nakhon. The purges that restored order could be massive and brutal. Besides events related to the succession, there were other revolts. Mobs marched on the city, led by figures that might be dynastic pretenders or local men-of-prowess (a description popularized by O. W. Wolters, meaning men who exude universally recognized leadership qualities). And foreign forces interfered, too: Japanese in the 1610s, Patani forces in the 1660s, Macassars in the 1680s, and Chinese merchants in the 1730s all attempted to stage a coup in the capital. Thus, it is not surprising that the most prominent work of popular literature of this era should contain a discussion of power in the plot and be able to be read as a guide, a manual.

As many modern anthropologists have discussed, claims of invulnerability are a form of defiance. As Andrew Turton notes, at an individual level, belief in invulnerability involves a "lessening of fear and deference ... Even more fundamentally assertive and challenging to notions of fixed social hierarchies is the underlying assumption of the perfectibility, or at least the potential for self development, of any who would learn or practice."[29] Turton and Shigeharu Tanabe note that invulnerability is linked to "distinctly peasant ideas of legitimacy" and to a "theme of boldness, of overcoming fear and disparagement—crucial if fear is seen as an ideological mediation between coercion and consent."[30] Turton also argues that a reputation for invulnerability is "virtually a requirement of leadership" at the local level, and suggests that beliefs in invulnerability count among the local "traditions of hope," ideas about the past that can serve as the basis for "hopeful and courageous social mobilization against all odds."[31] Cohen, Turton, and Reynolds have all noted the subversive, "counter-hegemonic" way that *kshatriya*, the Indic term for "warrior" and the origin of a Thai word for "king" (*kasat*), has been appropriated in an alternative transliteration to mean expertise in invulnerability itself (*chatri*).[32]

One well-known development of this theme of defiance, subversion, and hope is the tradition of "men of merit," *phumibun* or *phu wiset*, who led several millenarian revolts, particularly in the late-nineteenth century, but also before and since.[33] There are several similarities between the *phumibun* and Khun Phaen. Both claim the power of invulnerability and the ability to transfer it to others. Both draw on the tradition of self-mastery. Both use *athan* devices, such as yantra and enchanted water or oil. But there are also at least two important differences.

First, *phumibun* observed the Buddhist precepts and practiced Buddhist forms of meditation to acquire exceptional merit (*bun*) that was their qualification to lead. Though Khun Phaen is educated by abbots inside Buddhist *wat*, there is virtually no reference in his life story to Buddhist precepts, texts, or symbols in his education. In rites to summon his powers, he convokes a long list of spirits and Indic deities in which the Buddha may appear as just one among many. While the term *bun* appears in *KCKP* in many conventional phrases, Khun Phaen is never described as possessing exceptional *bun*. In the invocation-like phrases that announce his appearance in the text, he is famed for his powers (*sakda*, *rit*), not his merit (*bun*). Second, the *phumibun* is essentially a messenger who brings news that the millennium is nigh, that the Future Buddha is about to appear and usher in a just social order. The *phumibun* promises no less than a shift from one era to another, and thus demands an extraordinary leap of belief among his followers. But the promise represented by Khun Phaen is less dramatic, more accessible. He is merely an alternative agent of protection, the service that everyone wants.

The tale of *KCKP* goes beyond the technical manuals of invulnerability and supernaturalism by creating the figure of Khun Phaen, an embodiment of these skills, and a potential model for a historical actor.

---

[29] Andrew Turton, "Invulnerability and Local Knowledge," in *Thai Constructions of Knowledge,* ed. Manas Chitkasem and Andrew Turton (London, UK: School of Oriental and African Studies, 1991), 172 (with some editing of the original punctuation).

[30] Andrew Turton and Shigeharu Tanabe, "Introduction," in *History and Peasant Consciousness in South East Asia,* ed. Turton and Tanabe (Osaka: National Museum of Ethnology, 1984), 4, 7.

[31] Turton, "Invulnerability and Local Knowledge," 170, 176.

[32] See: Andrew Turton, "Invulnerability and Local Knowledge," in ibid., 158–59; Paul T. Cohen, "From Moral Regeneration to Confrontation: Two Paths to Equality in the Political Rhetoric of a Northern Peasant Leader," *Mankind* 17, no. 2 (1987); and Craig J. Reynolds, "Thai Manual Knowledge: Theory and Practice," in Reynolds, *Seditious Histories,* 234.

[33] Charles F. Keyes, "Millennialism, Theravada Buddhism, and Thai Society," *Journal of Asian Studies,* 36, no. 2 (1977): 283–302.

REVISING THE MANUAL

Today this political aspect of the tale seems to be ignored. Sombat Chanthornwong's subtle and thoughtful discussions of the political aspects of classical Thai literature conspicuously omitted *KCKP*.[34] Cholthira Satyawadhna analyzed *KCKP* from the viewpoint of masculinity and violence[35] and Boonlua Debyasuvarn concluded that *KCKP* demonstrates that "Thai society is a society without principle,"[36] but neither examined the issue of power.

The political aspect of the tale has been obscured in part by the way that *KCKP* has changed over time. Big tales that loom large in popular culture do not remain constant, but are themselves subject to political forces. This can be clearly seen from the history of Robin Hood, a medieval English tale that shares many affinities with *KCKP*, and that has sources for reconstructing its history over several centuries.

The Changing Meanings of Robin Hood

In Stephen Knight's historical analysis of the Robin Hood legend,[37] there is no clear identification of an actual man named Robin Hood. In the earliest sources, mostly law-court records from the thirteenth and fourteenth centuries, the name is used as an epithet for criminals and outlaws. By the fifteenth century, ballads appeared all over England in which Robin Hood is a rebel against the church and the nobility. He robs and he refuses to serve the king. He lives in the forest and wears a green costume that recalls a wild, anti-civilization spirit-figure from Anglo-Saxon legends. From the late-fifteenth century, playlets about Robin Hood were performed at local festivals, especially the May festival. In some of these events, the Robin Hood character was identified with the May King or Summer Lord, a lord of misrule with deep roots in antiestablishment popular culture. In this era, Robin Hood was "the hero who stands for an alternative and natural force of lordship, one who has the will and the power not only to elude but also to resist and if necessary destroy the agents of the world of legalism, of finance, and of regulation."[38] In the sixteenth century, authorities suppressed these performances, and a total ban was enacted in 1592.

In the seventeenth century, there was a deliberate attempt to bring this rebellious tradition under control by rewriting the script. Dramas began to appear in which Robin Hood was given a noble background, and his exploits became less threatening to the social order. He becomes an earl fallen on hard times. He no longer fights against the church and the power structure, but against individual corrupt officials. He no longer defies the king, but appeals to the king to help suppress his corrupt

---

[34] *Bot wichan wa duai wannakam kan mueang lae prawatisat* [Essays on literature, politics, and history] (Bangkok: Kopfai, 1997).

[35] Cholthira Satyawadhna, "Kan nam wannakhadiwichan phaen mai baep tawan tok ma chai kap wannakhadi thai" [Application of western methods of modern literary criticism to Thai literature] (MA thesis, Chulalongkorn University, 1970).

[36] Boonlua Debyasuvarn, *Wikhro wannakhadi thai* [Analyzing Thai literature] (Bangkok: Social Science Association of Thailand, 1974).

[37] See: Stephen T. Knight, *Robin Hood: A Complete Study of the English Outlaw* (Oxford, UK: Basil Blackwell, 1994); and Stephen T. Knight, *Robin Hood: A Mythic Biography* (Ithaca: Cornell University Press, 2003).

[38] Knight, *Robin Hood: A Complete Study*, 81.

enemy and restore his rightful position. By the eighteenth century, Robin Hood had also become a nationalistic figure, representing values of charity, bravery, and moral uprightness that were supposed to form the national character. By the twentieth century, this version had evolved largely into a tale for children.

Revising KCKP

This summary shows how the political meanings of a popular literary work can change radically over time. Precisely because the story is popular, its meanings are contested and manipulated. In the case of *KCKP*'s evolution, the paper trail is more fragmentary and less historically deep than that for Robin Hood's transformation, yet there is enough evidence from the later phases of its history to suggest it underwent similar modification.

A collection of *KCKP* manuscripts telling the whole story was assembled in the Bangkok palace in the mid-nineteenth century.[39] Between then and the publication of Prince Damrong's standard edition in 1917–18, *KCKP* underwent several changes. For example, of the four instances cited above that show that Khun Phaen or his teachers believe his powers exceeded those of the king, three were changed so that such an assertion is unclear.[40] Other editing was similarly subtle. For example, in the early text, Khun Phaen's father is introduced as *khon di*, a good person, a term for someone with expertise in lore. In the standard version, this was changed to *phu phakdi*, a loyal fellow, which is a substantial change of meaning achieved by adding one syllable.

In the mid-nineteenth century texts, Khun Phaen kills only as a soldier on the battlefield. By the time of the 1917–18 standard edition, he brutally murders a wife, threatens to kill another, kills two innocent peasants, and tries to kill his own son. His heroic character is substantially diminished by these changes.

Similar changes can be detected in revisions made by the court in the Second Reign, though the sources are meager. In versions preserved in popular drama and believed to represent the old story, Khun Phaen is clearly the hero and Khun Chang the villain in the rivalry over Wanthong. But in the version that emerged from the Second Reign salon, Khun Phaen has become a cruder and clumsier character who is partly responsible for his own difficulties.[41]

Earlier revisions can be detected, though dimly. The "inquel" about Khun Phaen's son, which was probably added in the late Ayutthaya era, obscures the political meanings of the plot by inserting fifteen years in the story and fifteen chapters between Khun Phaen's "revolt" and Wanthong's execution. Looking further

---

[39] Chris Baker and Pasuk Phongpaichit, *The Tale of Khun Chang Khun Phaen* (Chiang Mai: Silkworm Books, 2010), 902–3.

[40] In the first instance, Khun Phaen's explanation that his father did not use his lore because he had taken an oath was omitted. In the third, Khun Phaen's assertion "I can create obstruction with the power of my knowledge" was changed to "I think there'll be ways to ask for a pardon." In the fourth, the line stating the king was "feeling love and concern for Phra Wai on account of the power of lore" was changed to say that the king "felt merciful." See Baker and Phongpaichit, ibid., 122, 426, 436, 812–13, where the changes are detailed in the footnotes.

[41] Sukanya Pathrachai, "'Khun Chang plaeng san' ton thi hai pai chak sepha Khun Chang Khun Phaen chabap ho samut" ['Khun Chang changes the letter': A passage missing from the library edition of Khun Chang Khun Phaen), *Phasa lae wannakhadi thai* [Thai language and literature] 8, no. 1 (1991): 29–37.

back for revisions is impossible because there are no sources,[42] but the momentum and direction of change is clear.

Overlooking the political aspect of *KCKP* is also a function of changes in the way the tale is consumed and taught. Since the early nineteenth century, the emphasis has shifted away from the plot to the performance, from content to style. Recitation became more stylized, increasingly emphasizing sound rather than meaning, reaching an extreme in the "beggar" style, in which a single line is drawn out for several minutes of ululation, obscuring all meaning. At court, music was added to the performance, and gradually became more important than the text. In the preface to his edition in 1917, Prince Damrong explained that the editorial committee "has the aim of preserving poetic works that are good examples of Thai language, rather than trying to preserve the story of *Khun Chang Khun Phaen*."[43] In keeping with this aim, today's schoolchildren are taught extracts, mostly from the Second Reign revision, as examples of fine poetry and moral values. University literature courses also concentrate on the versification. In academic studies and university theses on the poem, only that of Cholthira examines the plot while others focus on characterization, social background, and ethical values.[44]

Today, Kukrit Pramoj's summary and exposition of the tale, originally serialized in his newspaper *Siam Rath* in 1988, and still in print as a book, is probably read by more people than the original text, not least because it is a highly readable work by an accomplished writer.[45] Kukrit sums up the meaning of the work as follows.

> The loyalty of the characters in *KCKP* can be used as a model for officials and people in general. It is an ultimate form of loyalty without question. Even severe royal punishment does not make the loyalty of any of the characters diminish. They continue to remain loyal. Moreover, several of the characters have command of lore and supernatural powers, including keeping protective spirits. But when they must face royal punishment, their skills—whether from mantra or

---

[42] Sujit Wongthes suggests that the story goes right back to a hero legend of great antiquity. See "Khap sepha lae Khun Chang Khun Phaen mi ton tao thi Suphannaphumi" [Reciting *sepha* and KCKP originate from Suwannaphum], *Matichon Sutsapda* 33, no. 1721 (August 9-15, 2013), 77.

[43] Baker and Pasuk, *The Tale of Khun Chang Khun Phaen*, 1362; translated from Prince Damrong Rajanubhab, "Tamnan sepha" [History of *sepha*], preface to *Khun Chang Khun Phaen* (Bangkok: Khurusapha, 2003 [1917]), 28.

[44] Cholthira Satyawadhna, "Kan nam wannakhadiwichan phaen mai baep tawan tok ma chai kap wannakhadi thai." On characterization, two examples are: Saowalak Anantasan, *Wannakam ek khong thai (Khun Chang Khun Phaen)* [Major Thai literature: *KCKP*] (Bangkok: Ramkhamhaeng University, 1980), and Suvanna Kriengkraipetch, "Characters in Thai Literary Works: 'Us' and 'the Others,'" in *Thai Literary Traditions*, ed. Manas Chitakasem (Bangkok: Chulalongkorn University Press, 1995). Studies of social background include Arada Kiranant, "Kan chai saiyasat nai sepha rueang Khun Chang Khun Phaen" [Use of Supernaturalism in *KCKP*], *Warasan phasa wannakhadi thai* 2, no. 2 (1985), and Woranan Aksonphong, "Kan sueksa sangkhom lae watthanatham thai nai samai rattanakosin ton ton chak rueang Khun Chang Khun Phaen" [Study of society and culture of early Bangkok from *KCKP*] (MA dissertation, Chulalongkorn University, 1972). Studies of ethical values include Phramaha Suradech Surasakko (Intarasak), "Itthiphon khong phra-phuttha-sasana tor wannakhadi Thai: sueksa chapo korani sepha rueang Khun Chang Khun Phaen" [Influence of Buddhism on Thai literature: A case study of *KCKP*] (MA thesis, Mahachulalongkorn University, 1965).

[45] Kukrit Pramoj, *Khun Chang Khun Phaen: chabap an mai* [*KCKP*, a new reading] (Bangkok: Dokya, 2000 [1989]).

various amulets or spirits—totally lose their force, and provide no protection against the royal will.[46]

Kukrit instructs readers to find a lesson in *KCKP* that is starkly different from our discussion of mastery and authority. As Saichon Satyanurak has recently shown,[47] Kukrit feared that the monarchy had lost much of its formal political power, and was intent on remaking Thai kingship as a focus of moral and cultural power. It is fascinating that Kukrit and Prince Damrong, two key figures in shaping the modern Thai monarchy, should also have had key roles in the modern evolution of *KCKP*. As Reynolds concluded on the role of manuals in general,

> Manuals in themselves are not orthodox or authoritarian. They are polysemic, amoral, apolitical. If a teacher, or institution, or powerful or socially influential individual insists on using manual knowledge in a particular way, then the knowledge in the manual is bent for certain purposes.[48]

---

[46] Ibid., 21.

[47] Saichon Satyanurak, *Kukrit kap praditkam "khwampenthai"* [Kukrit and the crafting of "Thainess"], two vols. (Bangkok: Sinlapa Watthanatham, 2007).

[48] Craig J. Reynolds, "Thai Manual Knowledge," in *Seditious Histories*, 241.

CHAPTER TWO

FABRICATION, STEALTH, AND COPYING OF HISTORICAL WRITINGS: THE HISTORIOGRAPHICAL MISCONDUCTS OF MR. KULAP OF SIAM

Thongchai Winichakul

Every historian of Siam must have heard of K. S. R. Kulap.[1] His reputation is the result of wrongdoings in the writing of history and the production of knowledge. His misconducts were considered so serious that he was committed to a mental asylum for at least seven days, after which he came to be regarded as insane. The imputations he was found guilty of in two court cases, in 1901 and 1906, concerned primarily the fabrication of history. But his notoriety had also to do with the tampering of historical documents he purloined from the royal archives. The charge of fabrication blemished his life and reputation to the extent that, in the Thai language, a syllable of his name, *ku*, has since become shorthand for "fabrication/to fabricate."[2]

---

[1] An earlier version of this article appeared in Thai. See: Thongchai Winichakul, "Ku lob lok taeng baep phrai phrai: khwamphit khong ko.so.ro. kulap thi tatsin doei nak prawattisat ammat" [Fabrication, stealth, copying like a plebeian: The wrong-doings of Mr. Kulap that was adjudged by the aristocratic historians], *Ahan* 3, no. 2 (2011): 12–28. This is not an English translation of that article, but a new version of it. I removed the Thai version's social commentaries, and this English-language version includes new sections, in particular, on the folk-temple tradition of historiography, which I added based on the comments I received after the Thai version was published. I am grateful to the Asia Research Institute, National University of Singapore, for support during the final stage of the research and writing of this article. Thanks to Thanapol Limapichat for comments and assistance in finding materials by and about Kulap, and to Bunphisit Srihong, whose research and works about Kulap have been very valuable for writing this essay.

[2] Nakharin Mektrairat, in his introduction to K. S. R. Kulap, *Ayatiwat* (Bangkok: Thailand-Japan Friendship Society, 1995 [1911]), 14, questions this explanation, for the word *ku* had long been present in the Thai language. Its earlier meaning, however, was not even close to "fabrication," "falsehood," or "lie."

Kulap's persistent notoriety in Thailand owes largely to a portrait of him that was sketched by Prince Damrong Rajanubhap, the "Father of Thai History."[3] Damrong portrays Kulap as an abnormal character, narcissistic and boastful, especially about his knowledge and his possession of old books and historical materials. The causes of his ill repute—the fabrication of history and the alteration of documents—are also reported by Damrong, who claims Kulap intentionally altered the published version of those materials in order to cover up the tracks he left in the royal archives.[4] Thanks to Damrong, generations of Thai intellectuals are familiar with Kulap's reputation for fabrication, stealth, and the tainting of historical records.

Craig J. Reynolds,[5] along with several Thai scholars,[6] has argued that Kulap got himself in trouble because, up until the early twentieth century, historical writing was the exclusive prerogative of aristocrats, and, indeed, was usually commissioned by the king. As a commoner of humble origins, Kulap trespassed into the exclusive realm of aristocratic authority regarding the production of historical knowledge. While by and large I concur with this view, with some reservations to be mentioned later, I have been bothered by the specific charges on which he was adjudged: stealth, illegal transcription, and fabrication of history. Those previous studies of Kulap take the charges for granted and never question them. While Kulap's actions may be regarded as a form of resistance to power, and even a path-breaking moment in the democratization of knowledge production, was he really guilty as charged? The royal elitist view about Kulap's wrongdoings has gone unquestioned.

Did Kulap really steal documents, make unauthorized copies, and fabricate history? What did he actually do that was considered a fabrication? How did he modify or alter texts in ways that were considered illicit, and why did he do so? Legally speaking, whenever a wrongdoing is perpetrated, there must be two components to constitute an offense: first, an action; and second, a rule or law or another normative measure stipulating what actions are wrong. For the case of Kulap, what were the rules or criteria for determining right or wrong transcription, and for the creation or fabrication of history? Were these rules and criteria the same over time, or did they change? What if there were other criteria than the ones distinguishing right and wrong in the practice of historical writing, since they were not the law? As a matter of fact, there were contemporaries of Kulap who performed similar creative acts but were not considered wrong. On the contrary, several of them were rewarded and praised, and became famous for what they did. Were there different sets of rules and criteria for different people? Or was this a case of Thai-style justice, in which the application of the law varies depending on the status, class, and connections of the defendant?

---

[3] Damrong Rajanubhap, "Nithan ruang thi 9 ruang nangsu ho luang" [The ninth story: On the documents in the royal archives], in *Nithan borankhadi* [Stories from the past] (Bangkok: Dokya Publication, 1994 [1939]), 146–72.

[4] An unpublished research paper by Bunphisit Srihong found Damrong's account of Kulap to be replete with major factual and interpretive mistakes; thus, Damrong's characterization of Kulap may be mistaken.

[5] Craig J. Reynolds, "The Case of K. S. R. Kulap: A Challenge to Royal Historical Writing in Late Nineteenth-Century Thailand," *Journal of the Siam Society* 61,2 (July 1973): 63–90; and Craig J. Reynolds, "Mr. Kulap and Purloined Documents" in *Seditious Histories: Contesting Thai and Southeast Asian Pasts* (Seattle: University of Washington Press, 2006), 55-79.

[6] Chai-anan Samudavanich, *Chiwit lae ngan khong thianwan lae k.s.r .kulap* [Life and works of Thianwan and Kulap], second printing (Bangkok: Bannakit, 1981).

This essay does not deny Kulap's actions, but it questions how those actions were understood, framed, and adjudged. The main argument is that Kulap's actions were misjudged by people who subscribed to the emerging ideas and practices of modern historiography, while Kulap and his and writings were products of an outgoing, obsolete mode of historiography, whose standard practices, ideas, values, and criteria were different from the modern one. Both Kulap and his chief adversary, Damrong, practiced historical writing at the time of a historiographical transition, at the moment when two types of episteme, one in decline and the other on the rise, overlapped. In the early years of modern historiography in Siam, the older tradition of historical writing continued alive and well. In this older mode, the criteria for credibility, truthfulness, fabrication, creation, transcription, alteration, and how to create historical writing were different from those of modern historiography. Kulap operated in the old fashion, but was (mis)understood, charged, and adjudged by the standards of modern historiography. Perhaps at this moment of transition between the two historiographical modes, the criteria used to distinguish correct from incorrect practice were still intermingled and inconsistent.

KULAP'S HISTORIOGRAPHICAL MISCONDUCT

Let us begin by looking more closely at Kulap's actions, the charges and accusations that were moved against him, and the deliberations and judgments that followed. K. S. R. Kulap (1835–1922)[7] was a commoner, but grew up under the tutelage of a princess; in his teens, he was educated in a royal temple, Wat Phra Chetuphon, as a Buddhist novice. He had the opportunity to study English, French, and Latin under the French Bishop of Bangkok, Jean-Baptiste Pallegoix. Afterward, he became a monk and studied Sanskrit, literature, and ancient jurisprudence with a famous court scholar, *Phraya* Si Sunthonwohan. After leaving the temple in 1860, he spent the next fifteen years working as a clerk in various foreign companies. During that time he traveled to Singapore, Penang, Sumatra, Manila, Batavia, Macao, Hong Kong, Calcutta, and also to Europe and China.[8] Between 1884 and 1891 he served in the government office of the marine police, although by the 1880s he was apparently already known to be among the literati. A more detailed biography of Kulap can be found in previous studies about him.

Here I will only summarize the cases in which Kulap was considered to be responsible for wrongdoings about historical writings. Kulap was not formally charged in a court. According to the procedures of absolute monarchy in Siam, he was initially criticized by the king. Then, his actions were twice formally investigated by special committees set up by the king, which found him guilty of fabricating history and lying both times, and once of lèse-majesté as well. Finally, in another case, Kulap was committed to a mental asylum without adjudication. Damrong's

---

[7] Records of Kulap's birth and death dates are inconsistent. According to Mananya Thanaphum, *K. S. R. Kulap* (Bangkok: Chulalongkorn University Press, 1982), 5, 71, he was born on March 23, 2377 BE, and died on March 24, 2464 BE. Because until 1941 the Thai (lunar) year ran from April to March, Kulap must have been born in March 1835 and died in March 1922, one day after turning eighty-seven. However, in Kulap's autograph will, it is stated that he was eighty-seven in 2462 BE (April 1919–March 1920). See Mananya, *K. S. R. Kulap*, 204. Reynolds, *Kulap and Purloined Documents*, 79 (note 25), also mentions this inconsistency.

[8] Chai-anan, [Life and works of Thianwan and Kulap], 194–95.

later account added to Kulap's notoriety by bringing up more charges, such as the stealth of documents.

The first case was in 1883, when Kulap published for sale *Khamhaikan khunluang hawat* ("The testimony of the king who fled to the temple," hereafter *The Testimony*). He claimed that this was a document of the late 1760s, from the end of Ayutthaya. The publication excited many people in the literati circles of Bangkok at the time, especially collectors and antiquarians, with the notable exception of King Chulalongkorn. The king had seen the original text, which was not yet widely known at that time, and realized that the version Kulap had published was altered. The king's discontent with the published text was obvious, as he subsequently wrote in his famous *Royal Ceremonies in Twelve Months*:

> The printed edition [of *The Testimony*] ... is so suspicious. It was undoubtedly altered by somebody ... [If it were authentic] it would have been as wonderful as pure [*borisut*] gold ... But whoever taints the authentic one by mixing it with the [im]pure elements, is robbing the treasure from us all. Anybody who claims to love books should not do this. Even though it is not clear when the book was altered, [the printed edition] is obviously tainted.[9]

Nevertheless, there was no investigation into this case, possibly because the king had not positively concluded that Kulap was responsible for the alteration. Probably his alleged misconduct was not yet widely known. On the contrary, Kulap's fame as an avid collector of old books and an expert in traditional lore had been on the rise since 1881. In 1884, he was invited to become a member of the Vajiranana Library, the exclusive club of elite intellectuals at that time. Commoners were not allowed to be members. Prince Phichitprichakorn, the president of the library, invited Kulap to be assistant treasurer. But the throne rejected the invitation on the grounds that "Kulap was not a royal or a noble, and the king was not familiar with him."[10] It is not clear whether King Chulalongkorn knew by then about Kulap's behavior, or just suspected him.

The second case took place early in 1901, when Kulap published an essay about the cremation of Crown Prince Wachirunnahit (1878–95) in *Sayampraphet*, the journal of which he was both editor and publisher. His description was based, or so he claimed, on ancient customs. But it was not correct. The king ordered an investigation. At first Kulap claimed that he consulted some seventy old books as well as several elders. But the royal investigation found out that the old books did

---

[9] King Chulalongkorn, *Phraratchaphithi sipsong duan* [The royal ceremonies in twelve months] (cremation volume for the royal funeral of Prince Chanthaburi Narunart, 1953), 216–17. This volume was first published in 1889 and reprinted many times since (including the edition consulted here). However, there is one very important discrepancy in this particular passage among the various editions—the word "impure" (*mai borisut*). In the 1953 edition, as in most other subsequent editions, the word in this passage is "pure," not "impure." The same passage was quoted *verbatim* by Damrong in his story about Kulap ([The ninth story]), citing the original edition of *The Royal Ceremonies* (*Phraratchaphithi sipsong duan*). The word in Damrong's citation is "impure." Judging from the context of the passage, I believe the correct word here must be "impure" for the sentence to make sense. The 1953 and subsequent editions must therefore be incorrect, missing the negative prefix *"mai"* (not) in front of the word for "pure." Here I follow Damrong, but put the word in brackets to mark the difference from the 1953 edition.

[10] Mananya, *K. S. R. Kulap*, 24.

not exist, and neither did the elders to whom Kulap claimed to have talked. In conclusion, his wrongdoing in this case was that "there was no truth in his essay. Kulap wrote the piece entirely from his own conjecture." The result of the investigation was published in the government's gazette as a way to censure his actions in public.[11] No further punishment was needed.

The third case took place at about the same time as the second. Kulap wrote a biography of the Supreme Patriarch Putsathewa (Sa). He even offered two thousand copies of the printed biography to the king to distribute for free as a cremation volume at the patriarch's funeral. The king believed that Kulap's bragging that he knew the patriarch pretty well was self-promotion on his part. In fact, Kulap's biography was full of mistakes, suspicious statements, and factual errors. So the king ordered another investigation. The committee found that Kulap was guilty on seven counts, all involving factual errors. In addition, the fact that he had offered an untrustworthy book to the king made his action a crime of lèse-majesté. Showing mercy, King Chulalongkorn, however, suspended the jail term and, instead, had Kulap placed on probation because of his old age.

The fourth case, in 1906, involved Kulap's story about Sukhothai published in *Sayampraphet*.[12] It recounts Sukhothai's defeat and territorial loss to Ayutthaya during the reign of King Chunlapinket, the son of King Pinket. Anybody with some knowledge of Thai history would recognize right away that the story is entirely fictional: there were no kings so named in the Sukhothai period. In fact, the two names are derived from the official names of King Mongkut (Chomklao) and Chulalongkorn (Chulachomklao). The king was furious at Kulap's mockery and, especially, at the association of his name with defeat and the loss of territories. Kulap was punished by confinement to a mental asylum for seven days.[13]

Kulap was a prolific writer for more than forty years—from his first piece of writing in 1879 until his death in 1922. It is fair to say that he was among the first professional and full-time writers, publishers, and public intellectuals in Siam. But throughout his career, there were other publications of his that suffered from similar problems as the cases cited here, although they were less known or unknown and not as controversial. For example, in 1908 he announced his discovery of an authentic legal text dated from 1744, in the late Ayutthaya period. As it turned out, it was an edition of the *Laws of the Three Seals* from the late 1780s with intentional tampering on its cover to make it look old and authentic.[14] There is another example from 1910,

---

[11] *Ratchakitchanubeksa* [The Royal Gazette], March 31, 1901 (Rattanakosin Era 119).

[12] I based the summary of this case primarily on the account by Damrong, [The ninth story], which is full of doubtful facts and errors (see above, footnote 3). However, the argument related to this case in this article can be made even if Damrong's account is taken for granted.

[13] The Thai word for mental asylum at the time, *rongliangba*, was very close to the word for stable, *rongliangma*. Reynolds (1973), in writing that Kulap was sent to a "stable," must have misread the word. Prince Damrong, in his introduction to *Chotmaihet ruang taisuan nai kulap* [Records on the investigation of Kulap] (cremation volume for the royal funeral of Princess Khaekhaiduang, November 12, 1929, Bangkok), and others, such as Anek Nawikkamun, *Ruang pralat nai muangthai* [Strange stories in Thailand] (Bangkok: Sangdaet, 1993), confirm that Kulap was sent to an "asylum." Reynolds later corrects his misreading in *Kulap and Purloined Document*, 66. Damrong wrote that the punishment was seven days of confinement, but Anek (ibid., 52) cites evidence suggesting that Kulap might have been in the asylum for more than a month.

[14] See Damrong's introduction to [Records on the investigation of Kulap], third and fourth pages (unnumbered).

which has never been mentioned before. It concerns an essay Kulap published in the newspaper *Chinno sayam warasap*, in which he cited a passage allegedly taken from one of King Mongkut's writings, although, in fact, the passage was his own. On that occasion, King Chulalongkorn ordered Kulap to "send his confession and publish it in five newspapers."[15]

The seven counts of guilt on which Kulap was adjudged in the third case mentioned above (the supreme patriarch's biography) are representative of how elite intellectuals at the time viewed his misconduct around historical writings, and also of the criteria they used to judge Kulap's actions. These counts of Kulap's "untrustworthiness" were detailed as follows:

1. He falsely promotes himself by boasting to have in his possession some books that do not exist.
2. He fabricates materials, facts and stories thereby deceiving people, such as writing something without basis, or citing from a particular text that does not exist. He also inserts his words into books written by other people.
3. He destroys the knowledge that is already known to be true ...and questions the truth that some have already said or written about.
4. He fails to preserve the original texts. All books in his possession are altered, unauthentic.
5. He guesses about matters that he doesn't know.
6. He exaggerates beyond evidence and facts.
7. He is careless about wording or idioms in his writings.[16]

The investigation concluded that Kulap was guilty on three separate charges:

1. Complete falsehood (fabrication)
2. Falsehood mixed with some truth/ facts
3. Facts/ truth mixed with some falsehood

Despite the fact that the investigative commission picked at him on every detail of misconduct and every other possible mistake, Kulap refused to admit his guilt. Although the commission gave him several opportunities to confess to obtain a reduced punishment, his "confessions" were not satisfactory. On one occasion he wrote: "I humbly never intended to lie; never."[17] The commission took more time than necessary because, as it reported to the king, Kulap's confession statements were "not honest," "insincere," "not genuine or earnest," and "still concealing his true mind."[18] Was Kulap just being stubborn, or did he not confess his guilt because he genuinely believed that he was not guilty? Is it possible that the same action was considered to be wrong by some and not by others, making the latter unable to confess but seemingly culpable in the former's eyes? Given that this was a

---

[15] I thank Thanapol Limapichat for this information. I have yet to investigate further into this case.

[16] These are not verbatim translations. On each count, the original adds one example case. For details and the original words, see [Records on the investigation of Kulap], 45–46. See another summary of these counts in Reynolds, *Kulap and Purloined Documents*, 70–71.

[17] Ibid., 10.

[18] Ibid., 4, 9, 11, 13.

contestation about historical writings, the question to ask is whether those involved were speaking the same language of historiographical practice.

KU FOR "FABRICATION"

According to the *Royal Institute Dictionary, ku* means inventing a fact.[19] According to the widely used Matichon Thai Dictionary,[20] *ku* was "slang among the royal elite at the time of King Chulalongkorn to mean acting or speaking with exaggeration; nowadays, it means saying or writing a story not based on facts, for example, a politician *ku* this story to draw attention away from the problem."

It is hard to deny that Kulap wrote some pieces without adequate evidence and some that were not even based on facts. The story of King Pinket and Chunlapinket of Sukhothai, for instance, is unquestionably untrue. But in some of the cases in which he was found guilty, his writings might be considered to be reasonable historical interpretations based on the knowledge and evidence that was available at the time, for example, his mistakes about details of the royal cremation of Prince Wachirunnahit. In the case of the patriarch's biography, it was rather a matter of carelessness for not checking the evidence. Those two acts of negligence were common to other historians of the time, including Prince Damrong—"the Father of Thai History"—and King Chulalongkorn, and some present-day historians as well.

An example of a false historical interpretation that misled Thai historians for half a century was Prince Damrong's distinction of two categories of *phrai*, or serf. He wrote that *phrai som* referred to all Thai males eighteen years of age. Once they turned twenty, they became *phrai luang*.[21] Assuming that Damrong belonged to the generations close to the time when serfdom and slavery were officially abolished in 1905, Thai historians took his interpretation for granted. As it turns out, he was completely wrong, not even close, for *phrai luang* was the term for serfs who belonged to the king, and *phrai som* for those who belonged to the nobles.[22] Even today, it is not clear how Damrong arrived at his interpretation. Needless to say, in this case no investigation was launched, no punishment meted, and no detention in a mental asylum suffered. No part of Damrong's name, say, "Dam," became a slang term for "fabrication." On the contrary, Damrong's essay remains a classic of historiography that every Thai history student is assigned to read, even though the prince's interpretation could be classified, according to the commission that investigated Kulap's case, as a lie devoid of any truth.

---

[19] *Royal Institute Dictionary* (Bangkok: Royal Institute of Thailand, 2011 [1950]).

[20] *Matichon Dictionary of the Thai Language* (Bangkok: Matichon Publishing Group, 2004).

[21] Damrong Rajanubhap, "Laksana kan pokkhrong prathet sayam tae boran" [The Siamese government in ancient times], repr. in *Prawattisat lae kan muang* [History and politics] (Bangkok: Thammasat University, 1975), 14.

[22] The misinterpretation was cleared up in the 1970s, first by Chai Ruangsilp, *Prawattisat thai samai ph.s. 2352–2453 dan sangkhom* [Thai social history, 1782–1910] (Bangkok: Ruangsilp Publication, 1974); and subsequently by Piyachat Pitawan, *Rabop phrai nai sangkhom thai, ph.s. 2411–2453* [The serfdom system in Thai society, 1868–1910] (Bangkok: Thammasat University Press, 1983) and Anchalee Susayan, *Khwam plianplaeng khong rabopphrai lae phonkrathop to sangkhom thai naisamai phrabatsomdet phrachunlachomklao chaoyuhua* [The change in the serfdom system and its impacts on Thai society in the reign of King Chulalongkorn] (Bangkok: The Toyota Foundation, 2003).

We may think of many other cases of historiographical mistakes and fabrications, both intentional and not. Some are better known or more important than others, such as the case of Lady Moe or Thao Suranari.[23] Past and present hagiographies of Thai monarchs are full of exaggerations, euphemisms, hyperboles, fabrications, dishonest glorification, and so many white and plain lies; but they have attracted neither investigation nor punishment. As a matter of fact, they are usually praised, if not rewarded. Professional historians sometimes create historical narratives without adequate evidence. We make a reasonable supposition of what might have happened and put forth a good-faith interpretation by connecting the dots between the missing elements. A sensible supposition sometimes is restated over and over again until its origins as a hypothesis is forgotten, and it becomes an accepted fact or truth. Two well-known examples in Thai historiography suffice to make the point: the long-held theory that ancestors of the Thai people originated from the Altai in Mongolia, and the belief that there was no slavery in Sukhothai.

The question, therefore, is what constituted *ku*? Once, in his review of a late-eighteenth-century historical document, King Chulalongkorn found that some words, and even sentences, had been added to the original document. Yet the king remarked that "the insertions are of a different kind from [those in] *Sayampraphet*; or, to put it in today's [i.e., the King's time] parlance, there was *ku* but not the same kind of *ku* as in *Sayampraphet*."[24] So, what constituted "genuine" *ku* as that allegedly perpetrated by Kulap in *Sayampraphet*?

WHEN FABRICATION WAS NOT *Ku*

Before the modern practice of historical writing became dominant, a story about the past did not need to be based on verifiable evidence or empirical facts. The basis for its credibility or truthfulness was not objective truth. What constituted truthfulness was not objective fact, and the verification of truth was not based on evidence. The modern historical sensibility is a particular mode of thinking, a belief system underlying a particular form of historiography, whose credibility and truthfulness rest upon empirical facts. In Siam, the older tradition of stories about the past survived well into the modern time. It is fair to say that by the early twentieth century, the premodern historiographical tradition and practice coexisted with modern historiography.

A piece of historical writing in the premodern historiographical mode, therefore, may be full of creative and imaginative stories, which is to say, fiction according to today's standard. The insertion or addition of elements that would enhance understanding of the meaning of the story was common. After all, a religious or court chronicle was considered a literary text, not an objective record of facts. Not only were embellishment, hyperbole, exaggeration, and fictive elements allowed, but

---

[23] See: Saiphin Kaewngamprasert, *Kanmuang nai aunusawari thao suranari* [Politics in the monument of Thao Suranari] (Bangkok: Matichon Publishing Group, 1995); and Charles Keyes, "National Heroine or Local Spirit? The Struggle over Memory in the Case of Thao Suranari," in *Cultural Crisis and Social Memory: Modernity and Memory in Thailand and Laos*, ed. Charles F. Keyes and Shigeharu Tanabe (London and New York: Routledge/Curzon, 2002), 113–36.

[24] King Chulalongkorn, *Phraratchawichan chotmai khwamsongcham khong phrachao paiyikathoe kromluang Narinthewi* [The royal critical study of the memoir by Princess Narinthewi], fourth reprint (Bangkok: Ton Chabab Publication, 2003 [1908]), 29.

they were integral to the genre. The successful creator of such a story would be rewarded, both in this world and possibly in the otherworld as well, not investigated, denigrated, and punished. Moreover, a royal chronicle or an old religious doctrine needed purification from time to time, especially after a political or societal disaster. A doctrinal purification did not mean the cleansing from the text of superstitious or implausible elements (by today's standard), or the verification of the stories by checking facts and evidence. Rather, it usually involved some modification of the text (including alteration, insertion, and addition of new elements that were not in the texts before), in order to restore the doctrine—the codification of social order—to its proper, "correct" condition.

These practices contravene the modern handling of historical documents, for the modern historical sensibility venerates authenticity and historicity. A history of the modern historical sensibility and modern historical practice in Siam must be a separate project. I have dealt with it to some extent elsewhere,[25] though far from adequately. Suffice it to say that the modern historical sensibility emerged in Siam around the mid-nineteenth century, and became prevalent among the intelligentsia of the late-nineteenth century. Among the fundamentals of the emerging modern practice of history was, first, the idea of linear historical time, as reflected in the growth of antiquarianism and of writings that contrast the past and present conditions of various things, such as King Chulalongkorn's *Royal Ceremonies* and Kulap's *Ayatiwat*.[26] As a matter of fact, this past–present contrast is the most common theme in Kulap's works. A second fundamental is the advocacy of historical authenticity and modern historical methods, as reflected in the rising concern for historical preservation and the increasing number of critical examinations of historical evidence, such as King Chulalongkorn's work on the memoir of the late-eighteenth-century Princess Narinthewi,[27] and several critical studies of the old royal chronicles. Third, the need for a new type of historical narrative, as reflected in Chulalongkorn's speech at the inauguration of the Antiquarian Society in December 1907;[28] the collection of chronicles and histories of various polities in the new territory of Siam; and the creation of a new master narrative of Siam's history that merged two historical ideologies: the notion of Siam's civilized antiquity, and the allegory of Siam's anti-colonial history.

Kulap and his approach to writing were accused and adjudged according to the criteria of modern historiographical practice, such as factuality, evidence, and authenticity. But what if Kulap still operated in the older historiographical mode? Was Kulap's practice the same as that of premodern chroniclers? Or did it more plausibly reflect the transition from the older historiographical mode to the modern one? Is it possible that at such a transitional moment, two different historiographical modes coexisted, coalesced, contested, and clashed? Did Kulap represent the legacy of the older practice, while the royal elite represented the emerging modern historical practice and sensibility?

---

[25] Thongchai Winichakul, "Siam's Colonial Conditions and the Birth of Thai History," in *Unraveling the Myths of Southeast Asian Historiography*, volume in honor of Bass Terwiel, ed. Volker Grabowski (Bangkok: River Books, 2011), 23–45.

[26] King Chulalongkorn, [The royal ceremonies]; and K. S. R. Kulap, *Ayatiwat* (1995 [1911])

[27] King Chulalongkorn, [The royal critical study].

[28] Chris Baker, trans., "The Antiquarian Society of Siam Speech of King Chulalongkorn," *Journal of the Siam Society* 89, nos. 1 and 2 (2001): 95–99.

STEALTH

Stealth (Thai *lob*), according to the *Royal Institute Thai Dictionary*, means "acting secretly, not wanting anybody to know about the act." According to the *Matichon Dictionary of the Thai Language*, *lob* means doing something secretly. Prince Damrong states matter-of-factly that Kulap stealthily took materials from the royal archives, and transcribed them before returning them to the archives. Fearing that his illegal acts might eventually be discovered, Damrong explains further, Kulap had to cover up his tracks by altering those texts, making them different from the authentic ones in the archives in order to claim that he got them from elsewhere.[29] According to Damrong, *The Testimony* was a prime example of the texts lifted from the archives and of which Kulap created a new copy, as a result of which he enjoyed fame among the Bangkok literati for his antiquarian expertise and possession of rare historical materials. But did Damrong report proven facts or merely express his understanding of what happened—that is to say, his opinion?

During his lifetime, Kulap gave dozens of books to the Vajiranana Library, founded in 1880 as an exclusive literati club of the elite, and lent and exchanged historical materials with the library's members. Some of those materials were the items identified as transcriptions from the royal archives.[30] If Kulap wanted to cover up his secret acts, why did he give to the library items he had allegedly taken from the archives and transcribed and altered, such as *Aphinihan banphaburut* [Our ancestors' miracles]?[31] As a matter of fact, Kulap often offered his new publications to the king and the aristocrats, both for free and for sale. These were the publications that landed him in trouble, including his conviction for lèse-majesté when he offered to the king publications that were adjudged as fabrications and lies. Would Kulap offer to the king a document that he intentionally and secretly fabricated, knowing that willful falsification was a transgression?

Furthermore, Kulap did not hide or try to deflect attention from himself and his publications. On the contrary, he was always bragging and boastful in his journal about the materials in his possession and his publications, including the allegedly altered documents. Kulap routinely resorted to self-promotion in his paper, partly to sell his other publications, partly because he was a narcissist (perhaps Damrong was right on this point). It should be noted that newspapers were the "new media" of the time, and that collecting old stuff was also in vogue. His desire for publicity seems illogical in light of the accusation that he altered the texts to cover up his alleged illegal actions. Is it possible that Kulap did not try to hide or cover up what he did? Is it possible that he did not consider tampering with historical documents a wrongdoing, which is also why he could not genuinely confess despite the undeniable conclusions of the investigation? Is it possible, finally, that the originals of several titles were not taken from the royal archives, and that, therefore, there was no track that needed to be covered up by altering the documents?

The notion that the historical materials in Kulap's possession included those he secretly took from the royal archives is questionable. At the exhibition for the Bangkok Centennial Celebration in 1881, Kulap took the elite literati by surprise by displaying 150 items from his personal collection of rare books and historical

---

[29] Damrong [The ninth story], 151.

[30] Mananya, *K. S. R. Kulap*, 28–30; Chai-anan, [Life and works of Thianwan and Kulap], 197.

[31] Sujit Wongthes, ed., *Aphinihan banphaburut lae pathomwong* [Miracles of our ancestors and the beginning of the dynasty] (Bangkok: Matichon Publication, 2002), 10–11.

materials.[32] Among them was *The Testimony*, which he later published, and for which he was admonished by King Chulalongkorn. The number and value of his exhibits were so impressive that he became renowned among the Bangkok elite literati and aristocrats as a collector of rare historical materials, and as a scholar of old customs and tales. He commanded their respect, and several even called him *achan*, "teacher." It was at this exhibition that Kulap was introduced to *Kromluang* [Prince] Bodin Phaisansophon, the officer in charge of the royal archives who later provided him with access to the archives. This indicates that even before gaining access to the archives, Kulap had assembled quite an impressive collection of historical materials. Unlike what Prince Damrong and others believed, he did not get *The Testimony* from the royal archives.

In fact, Kulap had his own networks for finding and acquiring historical materials. In his correspondence with G. E. Gerini dated March 1893, Kulap informed Gerini of how he was searching for the same rare materials as Gerini, through his (Kulap's) network of government servants, old people, and monks in various temples.[33] Although it is not clear how extensive or effective these networks were, or for how long Kulap relied on them, he clearly made use of them to acquire historical materials for his own collections. In any case, it appears that Kulap did not rely on the royal archives alone or as much as Damrong and later historians believed he did.

We may say that Kulap was among the first collectors of rare and historical materials in Siam, and probably the first Thai to do so outside the elite circles of the court and officialdom. Damrong, who had both authority and authoritativeness, especially at the time when he was minister of the interior between 1892 and 1910, ordered provincial governors and officials to look for historical materials and send them to Bangkok. Kulap did not have such power. He was, rather, a modern literary entrepreneur. Given that he eventually donated a number of old materials in his collections to the Vajiranana Library, we may say that he helped collect valuable historical materials that otherwise might be scattered around in temples and private collections. Thus, it would seem that, rather than stealthily removing materials from the archives to build up his own collection, he did the opposite. But if he did not need to cover up the sensitive origin of his materials, why did he tamper with them?

COPYING AS CREATION

The *Royal Institute Dictionary* defines *lok* (ลอก) as a verb meaning "to write, transcribe, copy from an original manuscript or model ... or thought." According to the *Matichon Dictionary of the Thai Language*, *lok* means "to transcribe or copy [something] from the original to make it one's own." In Siam, as in most world civilizations, composing a written work did not entail that it should be an original

---

[32] See: *Ngan sadaeng nithatsakan sinkha phunmuang thai nai phraratchaphithi somphot pharakon khrop roi pi ph.s. 2425* [The exhibition of Thai local products in the Bangkok centennial celebration, 1882] (Bangkok: Ton Chabab Publication, 2000); and Saran Thongpan, "Y E Yerini kap k. s. r. kulap lae wongwichakan khong sayam nai plai satawat thi 19" [G. E. Gerini and Kulap and the academia in Siam in the late nineteenth century], *Muang Boran* 31, no. 3 (2005): 74–86, citation p. 75. According to Reynolds, "The Case of K. S. R. Kulap," 70, Kulap's exhibit included more than a thousand items/books. Here I follow Saran, who gives us the titles of all books in that exhibit.

[33] Saran [G. E. Gerini and Kulap], 76–82.

creation. On the contrary, copying, compiling, and excerpting from previous texts was common practice. In Hindu-Buddhist doctrinal culture, the more sacred or authoritative a text was, the more it was supposed to be not created anew, but to be re-created. The Dhammasastra, the source of all laws in a Hindu-Buddhist society, is said to have been created by transcribing the inscription on the wall of the Universe. The codification of the social order was thus created by copying the immanent supreme law. The composition of a religious commentary, a royal chronicle, a treatise on knowledge, or a practical manual assumed the veneration of the prior texts, which were honored by incorporating parts of them into the new text. Indeed, lifting certain passages from the preexisting texts was a norm, which was even encouraged in cases in which the text was considered sacred. In Theravada doctrinal culture, the composition of a text by copying is regarded as a major form of merit-making, not only because of its orthodoxy, but because it contributes to extend the life of Buddhism. A monk or scribe who reproduces the texts would be rewarded.

Before the emergence of the modern idea of individual authorship, orthodoxy and convention were the basis of textual creation. Originality and creativity took place within, and under the guidance of, orthodoxy. The author was not the sole creator of the text. After all, truth and wisdom were assumed to derive from tradition, not from some future discovery. The method for the transcription–creation of a sacred or authoritative text did not entail reproducing the old text verbatim, however. In the Theravada tradition, after a calamity had befallen a society—for example, the fall of a kingdom or a serious sectarian conflict in the *sangha*—the restoration of the social order and the *sangha*'s unity usually involved religious reform based on doctrinal purification. The reexamination of the Tipitaka meant the reproduction of the sacred doctrine to ensure its accuracy, on the one hand, and, on the other, the explanation of the calamity or disorder that had occurred. This was the method to renew the relevance of the Buddhist Dharma to the changing reality. Apart from the correct transcription, therefore, the text must also be altered, usually by adding an exegesis dealing with the past, in order to make the doctrine relevant to the present time. Copying and inserting additional exegesis were common methods of producing a new edition of an authoritative text. Likewise, a royal chronicle was updated, revised, and re-created from time to time, especially after turmoil or for the celebration of a special era.

> [The] long tradition of writing "history" has rested on the continual practice of what is known as "recension of the chronicles" ... [In] fact, the recension of the chronicles involved everything from correcting the style and spellings, to extending the coverage, inserting new materials, and altering old materials ... Hence, recension of the chronicles was not simply a matter of adding materials to bring an old version up to date, but also involved a complete revision of the view of the past to accord with ideas prevalent at the time of recension.[34]

All royal chronicles in Siam were created in this way. As late as the second half of the nineteenth century, shortly before Kulap's time, *Chaophraya* Thiphakorawong (1813–70) was commissioned in 1869 to compose the royal chronicles of the Bangkok Reigns. He did so by copying and altering available materials as he saw fit. According to a study of his composition of the chronicle of the First Reign, he

---

[34] Nidhi Eoseewong, *Pen & Sail* (Chiang Mai: Silkworm Books, 2005), 290.

transcribed from the "… 'old account,' meaning the account from the royal chronicle composed by Phra Phanarat, though the style and wording were altered in some places. The 'new account' means the parts Thiphakorawong wrote anew. The 'old–new mixture' means the old account interspersed by the new one."[35] Kulap's method was not much different from Thiphakorawong's. A work by Kulap, *Anam sayam yut* (*The battle between Siam and Annam*, 1903), illustrates how he wrote history. His account of the battle followed closely that in the royal chronicle of the Third Reign. Then he added miscellaneous knowledge at various places in the text, some of which is relevant to the account, and some not. According to a study of this book by Kulap, he inserted miscellanea "… from many kinds of sources, written at different times for different purposes, compiled them [with the chronicle], and edited them to make a new piece of writing with its own character."[36] Some of the additions were taken verbatim from the original source, some were written by Kulap himself. This is how he composed most of his writings, including those that landed him in trouble.

We cannot talk about an "original" text, since every manuscript in this tradition was a copy of previous texts with additional insertions, which were in turn copies of previous texts, and so on. For example, the royal chronicle by Phra Phanarat—the "old account" on which Thiphakorawong relied—was a transcription from several previous royal chronicles, added and edited by him to justify the beginning of the new dynasty. The "authenticity" of a text was not particularly important, either, since the value of renewal and relevance was more important. As for the notion of plagiarism as we understand it today, it did not exist yet; rather, what would be considered plagiarism today was a legitimate method for composing texts in premodern times. Indeed, the creation of a new text by copying and altering an old text earned high merits and was usually rewarded.

In the older historiographical practice, it was not unusual to give a new title to a work, despite the fact that it was a based on copying the "old accounts" and adding passages. Since it was not understood as illegitimate appropriation, it was not intended to confuse or to mislead the reader. It was a new "edition" of the old text, and thus deserved a new title. One work can have more than one title, too. For example, Kulap composed for publication in *Sayampraphet* a series of writings entitled *Aphinihan kan prajak* (Renowned miracles). But when, later on, he collected the pieces into a book, he changed the title to *Aphinihan banphaburut* (Our ancestors' miracles). *The Testimony*, and its kindred *Khamhaikan chao krungkao* (The testimony of the old Ayutthayans), were primarily the same text, except that the latter contained several insertions, hence it represented a new work, and was given a new title.

It would appear that Kulap really made copies of old texts. He also altered them, and not in small ways; he sometimes added pages. The inserted passages he sometimes lifted from other sources, sometimes he wrote following his own interpretations. He did not hide his methodology; on the contrary, there was every

---

[35] Narumol Thirawat, Preface, in *Chaophraya* Thiphakorawong, *Phraratchaphongsawadan krung rattanakosin ratchakan thi 1 chabap chaophraya thiphakorawong chabap tuakhian* [The royal chronicle of the First Bangkok Reign by *Chaophraya* Thiphakorawong, the autograph manuscript], ed. Nidhi Eoseewong and Narumol Thirawat (Bangkok: Amarin Printing, 1996), fourth page (no page number).

[36] Witthawas Meesangnil, "Anam sayam yut: prawattisat niphon prachachon" [The Thai–Annam battle], in *Khlon tid low khon mai tid krob* [Mud on the wheel, man in the box], volume in honor of Dr. Dhida Saraya, ed. Suthachai Yimprasert (Bangkok: Faculty of Arts, Chulalongkorn University, 2002), 22–23.

reason to announce publicly one's possession of a valuable text and accomplishing the creation of a new text. Kulap always bragged about his works. Because the act of producing a "new" text was typically rewarded, Kulap was proud of his creations and might even think of offering them to the king as an appropriate form of tribute.

Kulap's misfortune was the consequence of the transition that was taking place from the older practice of history to the modern one—a moment when two different historiographical modes coexisted and occasionally clashed. Kulap represented the older practice of history while the royal elite represented the emerging, modern one. Indeed, all the cases involving Kulap's writings could be seen to be moments when the modern practice of history drew a boundary line to separate itself from the older one. Novel demarcations were being drawn between the historically true and the historically false, fabrication and creation, verifiable evidence and imaginative interpretation, virtuous copying and plagiarism, authenticity and continuing renewal, authorship and divine authority. Of course, power relations were also implicated in this confrontation.

THE FOLK OR "TEMPLE" PRACTICE OF HISTORY

So far, this essay has considered the different modes of historical practice according to the convenient temporal dichotomy premodern vs. modern. My argument refers mostly to the court and aristocratic textual culture for both modes, implying that the court's historiographical culture had already changed, while Kulap's stayed rooted in the past. The ensuing distinction and confrontation between the two modes suggest another dimension, that is, the social location of knowledge production. Kulap was not part of the court culture; his historiographical practice descended genealogically from the folk, or temple tradition, not the court.[37]

The temple tradition of historiography was suggested by historians of Siam decades ago. There are several historical documents and chronicles known for not being part of the court's literature—for example, *The Testimony* and its kindred, *The Testimony of the Old Ayutthayans*. Many local legends, and the local chronicles of cities that Damrong ordered provincial officers to search for, belong to folk literature, not to courtly literature (even provincial courts). The best known historiographical tradition outside the court, especially in the Lanna region (present-day northern Thailand), is that of Buddhist chronicles, which were written by monks and circulated within temples.[38] In Siam's case, the discovery of Van Vliet's *Chronicle of Ayutthaya*, a work by a seventeenth-century Dutch merchant, suggests the existence

---

[37] This distinction between methodologies implies the hierarchy or class difference between the folk/monks and the aristocrats. I do not suggest rigid or sharp breaks between the two in each dichotomy. As we will see later, more nuances and hybrids are always present, even for the case of Kulap. The cut-and-dry dichotomy is for the sake of a clear argument. Like any other analytical category, those dichotomies only suggest the different characteristics and parameters of the contestations as seen from different angles and perspectives. Needless to say, the dichotomies are not truth, they are tools.

[38] See: Winai Pongsripian, "Traditional Thai Historiography and Its Nineteenth-Century Decline" (PhD thesis, University of Bristol, 1983), part 1; and David Wyatt, "The Chronicle Traditions in Thai Historiography," in *Southeast Asian History and Historiography: Essays Presented to D. G. E. Hall*, ed. C. D. Cowan and O. W. Wolters (Ithaca: Cornell University Press, 1976), 107–22. Here I mean only those chronicles of temples and Buddhist relics. This does not include the Buddhist royal chronicles that were produced in various courts in Lanna. These latter were the court's literature, though not of the Siamese court.

of a parallel historiographical tradition outside the court. It is a chronicle of the kings and battles of Ayutthaya, but its substance is quite different from the one produced by the court.[39] The royal chronicle of Ayutthaya that Rama I commissioned a Buddhist monk to write in 1797 to mark the beginning of the new Chakri dynasty, and the new capital Rattanakosin, was similar in style and content to others in the same genre of court literature. However, a decade earlier, the same monk had composed another chronicle of Ayutthaya, *Samghitiyavamsa*, whose substance and style belong to the tradition of Buddhist temple literature.[40] Unfortunately, knowledge of the temple (or folk) historiographical traditions that flourished before modern historiography is still underdeveloped. Historians have mistaken this as a genre of historiography that preceded and led to the genre of royal chronicles, and failed to recognize its parallel existence and production with courtly literature.[41] Although some scholars have pointed to the temple or folk historiographical tradition as operating in parallel to the courtly one, so far we have not understood much about it.

Let us return to Kulap. As we have seen, among the historical materials in his possession before he gained access to the royal archives, the item that made him first famous, and then infamous, was *The Testimony*. Judging from his correspondence with Gerini in 1881, we can assume that the network of monks, former local government employees, and villagers on which Kulap relied to obtain old materials was not his only one. In fact, by that date he must have already collected at least 150 items, which he had likely obtained from temples and folks who were local intellectuals far from, the court. These historical texts were produced and circulated outside the court and parallel to it. Another corpus of historical texts that is associated closely with Kulap is that known as *Our Ancestors' Miracles* or *Pathomwong* [Our ancestors]. The two are variations of the same corpus of texts: the folk stories of miracles from the beginning of the Thonburi-Bangkok period. Nidhi Eoseewong tried to find out if Kulap had authored *Pathomwong*, or transcribed it from the prior text(s).[42] As it turns out, there are about twenty versions of the same text in the National Library today.[43] Kulap donated one of them to the library, and also published it in his journal. Many versions are different from Kulap's, and some seem older. It is not known which one, if any, was the "original" one. It is unlikely that Kulap was the author, or that his version served as the source of others. But it is likely that Kulap's version was his own transcription-creation, based on an older version (or more), which combined various parts he selected, with the addition of his own comments and remarks to make the text more interesting for contemporary

---

[39] Chris Baker, Dhiravat Na Pombejra, Alfons van der Kraan, and David K. Wyatt, *Van Vliet's Siam* (Chiang Mai: Silkworm Books, 2005), 179–244.

[40] Craig J. Reynolds, "Religious Historical Writing and the Legitimation of the First Bangkok Reign," in *Perceptions of the Past in Southeast Asia*, ed. Anthony Reid and David Marr (Singapore: Heinemann Education Books, 1979), 90–107.

[41] See: Wyatt, "The Chronicle Traditions"; Charnvit Kasetsiri, *The Rise of Ayudhya* (Kuala Lumpur: Oxford University Press, 1976), and "Thai Historiography from Ancient Times to the Modern Period," in *Perceptions of the Past*, ed. Reid and Marr, 156–70.

[42] See: Nidhi Eoseewong, *Kanmuang thai samai phrachao krung thonburi* [Thai politics in the reign of King Taksin], second printing (Bangkok: Matichon Publication, 1993), 217–21 (notes 1, 2 of chapter 2); and Sujit [Miracles of our ancestors], introduction.

[43] Sujit [Miracles of our ancestors], [19]–[30].

readers. Finally, Kulap gave his work a new title. Fortunately for him, there was no investigation into this case.

MIXED HISTORIOGRAPHICAL PRACTICES IN TRANSITION

Kulap, however, was not frozen in the old mode of historiography. His works reflect the transitional, or hybrid, practice of history writing that belonged to different episteme. This essay does not suggest that the two historiographical modes were exclusive, or isolated from one another. Rather, it indicates the parameters for the coexistence and contestation of different historiographic practices during the epistemic transition of the second half of the nineteenth and lasting into the early twentieth century. The leading Siamese elite intellectuals of the period, such as King Chulalongkorn and Prince Damrong, were apparently aware of the epistemic changes underway, engaged with them, and advocated and employed the modern historiographical practice. Kulap, too, engaged with the changes, even though he may seem to represent the legacy of the folk or premodern practices. Let us consider the three fundamentals of the emerging modern historiography as the cornerstones for assessing Kulap's engagement with the new method. One of the major threads running through Kulap's oeuvre, as well as his journal *Sayampraphet*, is the shape of things in the past, and the comparison drawn, more or less explicitly, with their present, different shape. *Ayatiwat* (1911), a collection of essays mostly about the changes in various customs, written over many years, is evidence of this line of enquiry. Similar to King Chulalongkorn's treatise on the royal ceremonies, Kulap in these writings casts the gaze of the present upon the past, revealing a new sensibility that saw the differences between the past and the present according to a linear temporal framework.

Kulap also engaged in modern historical methods. Toward the end of his life, in 1914, he published *Poet hu poet ta* [Eye opening], a study of the chronicles of Ayutthaya, "comparing facts and fictions" (or lies). This is a meticulous, critical study of many debatable issues in the history of Ayutthaya based on the consultation of, and comparison between, the accounts found in different sources about the same events. The book demonstrates Kulap's impressive knowledge of chronicles, both the royal chronicles produced by the court and those in the folk/ temple tradition, such as *The Testimony*. He also referred to records by the Burmese, Mon, old treatises, and manuscripts, including previously unknown materials he claimed were in his possession, namely, the "Thonburi manuscript from the Ho Sastrakhom,"[44] and the "Records of Dvaravati" (*Chotmaihet thawarawadi*), written in Pali using Khmer scripts by an Ayutthayan temple abbot, which was discovered by Bishop Pallegoix, and which Kulap inherited because he had been a disciple of the Pallegoix.[45] He said that this manuscript was among his exhibits in 1881 as well.[46] This study deals with many issues that remain controversial among Thai historians even today; for example, whether the Burmese vice-king (*uparacha*) was shot dead by an unknown soldier rather than killed by King Naresuan in the famous elephant duel of 1592;[47] the supposed erection of a stupa to commemorate that event; and the questionable

[44] K. S. R. Kulap, *Poet hu poet ta* [Eye opening] (Bangkok: n.p., 1914), 43–45.

[45] Ibid., 86–89.

[46] Ibid., 92–93.

[47] Ibid., 115–27.

account of the final eight reigns of the late Ayutthaya period leading to the end of the kingdom.[48]

This is definitely not a work based on the transcription-creation of a preexisting text. It is a historiographical commentary, or a "critical examination," in the mode King Chulalongkorn encouraged fellow elite intellectuals to engage.[49] It is worthy of note that around those same years a number of landmark works in the transition to modern historiography were published, namely, King Chulalongkorn's inaugural speech at the Antiquarian Society (1907);[50] his critical examination of the memoir of Princess Narinthewi (1908);[51] King Vajiravudh's *Thiao mueang phra ruang* (1908), which established one of the two master narratives of Thai history;[52] and Prince Damrong's lengthy introduction to the royal autograph edition of the chronicles of Ayutthaya (1914)[53] and his classic, *Thai rop phama* (1917),[54] which established another master narrative of Thai history.[55]

Yet Kulap's works were different from those by elite intellectuals on at least two counts. First, he relied more on folk historical literature, even in his most critical study, *Poet hu poet ta*. Moreover, as also shown in this study, he treated them as equivalent to the royal chronicles and other official documents. He still made use of *The Testimony* long after the king had discredited it. His accounts and interpretations, too, followed the mode of the folk history of Ayutthaya. For example, his stories about the late Ayutthaya period are to a large extent similar to those in *The Testimony*. Second, a study on Kulap notes that he carried on the old-fashion historiography in his writing style and formal conventions. On the contrary, the prose of elite historiography underwent change as its character became analytical and interpretive.[56] Nevertheless, in *Poet hu poet ta*, Kulap incorporated a novel convention that had not been adopted yet by his elite counterparts: endnotes. His 150 "calling for witnesses" (*ang phayan*)—that is, references—took up almost two hundred pages. Also noteworthy is that Kulap presented this book to the king, both as an offering and for sale, as he had always done before.

---

[48] The latter one is the subject of the now classic work by Nidhi Eoseewong, *Pen & Sail*, 287–341. This article was first published in 1979, sixty-five years after the publication of Kulap's book.

[49] Chulalongkorn, [Critical study of memoir by Princess Narinthewi], 46.

[50] Baker (trans.), "The Antiquarian Society of Siam."

[51] Chulalongkorn, [Critical study of memoir by Princess Narinthewi].

[52] King Vajiravudh, *Thiao mueang phra ruang* [Journey to the land of King Ruang] (Bangkok: Khurusapha, 1983).

[53] Damrong Rajanubhap, "Introduction," *Phraratcha-phongsawadan chabap phraratcha-hatthalekha* [The royal chronicles of Ayutthaya, the royal autograph edition], vol. 1, seventh printing (Bangkok: Khlangwitthaya, 1973).

[54] Damrong Rajanubhap, "Phongsawadan rüang thai rop phama" [A history of the Thai wars against the Burmese], in *Prachum phongsawadan* [Collected Chronicles], part 6, vols. 5–6 (Bangkok: Khrurusapha, 1963).

[55] On the significance of these texts in modern Thai historiography, see Thongchai, "The Birth of Thai History."

[56] Witthawas, [The Thai–Annam battle], 22–27. Nidhi [Thai politics in the reign of King Taksin], 221, makes a similar observation.

Mis-categorization in Transition

The categorization of a literary genre rests on particular criteria and expectations. But because such criteria and expectations change over time, a categorization may change, too. Today, a historical novel is not judged by the same standards as is academic history. Moreover, the latter belongs to a different category than does history as presented in popular magazines, made-for-television documentaries, Wikipedia entries, and weblogs. At the time of the epistemic transition in Siam, when different modes of historiography co-existed, contested, and clashed, confusion and discord also occurred in the evaluation of historical writings. Kulap's *Anam sayamyut* was originally published in his journal in 1899 as a series of episodes, each having an individual title. It is likely that Kulap wrote one episode at a time, similar to the work of a columnist in a modern magazine. Indeed, Kulap's was popular history for the new print culture. The essays were compiled and published as a single volume in 1903. Kulap advertised his book as "a story good for learning, containing useful lessons for government services, but more entertaining than *The Three Kingdoms* or the *Ramakian*."[57] May this phrasing be taken to suggest that Kulap did *not* consider his book to be history?

Another intriguing story written by Kulap is that of the kings Pinket and Chunlapinket of Sukhothai, who lost territories to Ayutthaya (1906), about which I propose here a hypothetical explanation. First of all, Kulap must have been very naïve if he thought that he could fool the elite intellectuals into thinking that this was a genuine story of Sukhothai. Second, this is not the transcription of a previous text, or the compilation of disparate sources. It is not difficult to recognize that it was entirely Kulap's own writing—his own original creation, so to speak. Is it possible that Kulap composed this piece without intending to fool anybody into thinking that it was a genuine story? It seems obvious, and undeniable, that the plot was a commentary on the loss of Siamese territories to the French in Indochina during King Chulalongkorn's reign. But it did not purport to be a true historical account. Kulap might well have been guilty of lèse-majesté, but anybody who thought that Kulap was tampering with history, and thus deserved punishment for fabrication, may likewise be considered unreasonable.

Kulap's story, as an allegory mocking the supreme ruler, should be considered as belonging to the literary genre of satire. In Siam, satire was not uncommon, as attested by *Raden landai* [Lord Landai],[58] a parody about a mendicant described as if he was a courtier living in the palace. In fact, this tradition was well known throughout the region, from the Lao story of Siang Miang to the Thai story of Sri Thanonchai, both of which are tales about a clever commoner who makes a fool of the king. There were other folk stories that served as commentaries on power, and as lessons to both rulers and subjects. The turn-of-the-century royal elite knew about, and even wrote in the mode of, satirical literature, such as King Chulalongkorn's *Wong thewarat* [Heavenly genealogy], which mocks his relatives in the court. A well-known work of courtly literature, *Nang Noppamat* [Lady Noppamat], written anonymously in the early nineteenth century, while not a satire, depicted its setting, Sukhothai, in so much detail that some misunderstood it for a genuine Sukhothai story. Most intellectuals, however, had no problem recognizing that it was a work of

---

[57] This advertisement appeared in *Bundittayaphasit* in 1907. I thank Thanapol Limapichat for this information.

[58] *Raden* is a Javanese title of nobility.

fiction. Nobody unreasonably asserted that *Nang Noppamat*, or any of the stories mentioned above, were fabricated history. I suggest that in the case of the King Pinket and King Chunlapinket story, the real reason why Kulap got into trouble was not because he fabricated history, as ruled by the court, but, rather, because his satire seemed too close to actual history. The setting was Sukhothai, the plot concerned the loss of territories, and the narrative style was suggestive of nonfiction. Had Kulap obviously written it as a fiction, he might still have been found guilty of lèse-majesté, but not of fabricating history.

Another pertinent question to ask is whether, by 1906, Sukhothai was already in the realm of historical knowledge. The story of Sukhothai, and of its founding hero, Phra Ruang, had been part of the folklore of the upper Chao Phraya valley region for a long time. It was similar to folk stories of the remote and legendary past found in other regions, such as Saenpom and Khotrabong. Moreover, Sukhothai was not yet considered the past of "Siam," that is to say, the Ayutthaya-Bangkok kingdom, whose chronicles made no mention of Sukhothai and Phra Ruang. In the early 1830s, a stone inscription, throne, and other artifacts were discovered in Sukhothai. Despite this discovery, and some attempts at deciphering the inscription, Sukhothai did not become part of Siam's history right away. It did so only when enough facts were established, and fragments of history constructed, to make a solid connection. Until then, Sukhothai remained in the realm of legend, in a vague and remote past one might call prehistory. The formulation of the narrative of Sukhothai occurred in the final two decades of the nineteenth century. As we can observe in some historical writings from that time, by the 1890s the upper Chao Phraya valley was considered "northern Siam."[59] The history of Sukhothai was integrated into the official narrative of Siam's history in the early 1900s.

Accordingly, it is likely that Kulap's knowledge of Sukhothai in 1906, just at the time when the fable was becoming reality in the public imagination, still came from the folk and temple tradition. It is also probable that Sukhothai and King Chunlapinket in Kulap's perception were not the same as those known to elite intellectuals. For Kulap, Suthothai was at best semi-legendary, prehistorical, and his story was not supposed to be taken as serious history. It was neither fiction nor nonfiction, according to modern historiographic criteria. It was an allegory, a story told to convey a moral lesson, and it should not be judged by the criteria and requirements of a historical study. To take Kulap's story as historical and adjudicate it accordingly were anachronism in action.

GUILT BY BIRTH

Kulap was not the only one to write about history during the historiographical episteme's transitional period. There were many others, including some elite intellectuals, who also transcribed and created new texts, made incorrect insertions and wrong interpretations, and wrote stories that, later, were interpreted differently

---

[59] See, for example, Prince Patriarch Wachirayan Warorot, *Pramuan phra niphon prawattisat-borankhadi* [Collected works: History and studies of the past] (Bangkok: Mahamakut Royal College, 1971), 5–20; and King Chulalongkorn, *Phraratchaniphon wichan ruang phraratchaphongsawadan kap ruang phraratchaprapheni kantang phramaha upparat* [The royal commentary on royal chronicles and on the customs of the appointment of the royal heir apparent] (Bangkok: cremation volume for the funeral of Mr. Phongcharoen Songsiri, February 11, 1973), 2.

in new contexts. For example, Thiphakorawong, who was from a generation earlier than Kulap, belonged like him to the older historiographical culture.[60] Even though, according to Henry Alabaster (an Englishman who, in the 1860s, was at the court of Siam), Thiphakorawong was among the "modern" minds of Siam,[61] by the end of the century his royal chronicles of Bangkok were seen by the elite as being full of problems, and needing a thorough "cleaning up." But Thiphakorawong was never accused of *ku* or *lok*, or found guilty of historical malpractice. His name did not take up any negative connotation. Kulap's persecution, therefore, may not be entirely attributable to his historiographical practice. There must be other factors beyond the intellectual ones.

The argument made by previous studies that Kulap was among the first commoners who trespassed into a territory that was the aristocracy's monopoly—the production of history—may provide the answer here. Until then, knowledge of royal customs and history, the subjects of Kulap's interest about which he claimed expertise, and for which he was punished, were in the hands of the royal elite. Thanks to the print media, which were the "new media" of that time, Kulap was able to make his way into the aristocrats' realm. Kulap's knowledge, his prolific production, his ability to acquire via his personal networks historical materials, and his possession of rare and valuable documents were comparable to those of elite intellectuals, even though Kulap could marshal neither personal nor governmental authority. Still, he was able to demonstrate his intellectual prowess by means of his own journal. He broke the monopoly of printing knowledge. He challenged and tested the limits of the elite intellectuals' power.[62] Moreover, he was boastful, commonly showing off his expertise and intellectual prowess. He frequently challenged those readers who did not believe him. To his credit, he often backed up his arrogance with facts or documents about which people had never heard. And, indeed, many among the aristocratic elite appreciated his talents and even invited him to join the elite's exclusive scholarly club, the Vajiranana Library, and to deliver lectures at two prestigious intellectual fora, the Chomrom Bantoeng Thatsanakan and the Witthayathan Sathan (in 1896 and 1897).[63]

It is not far-fetched to assume that there were also elite intellectuals who detested Kulap's repute. In *Nithan borankhadi*, Prince Damrong presented Kulap as an ostentatious character who, in reality, was a fake. In a hierarchical society like Siam's, a commoner who dared to challenge the status quo was despised twice—for his arrogance and for his disrespect of the social hierarchy. Kulap ultimately was judged guilty of being a commoner who did not know his proper place in society. The charge that he fabricated history was perhaps framed by the presupposition that he should not have known about royal customs or veracious history. The charge that he stole documents from the royal archives was perhaps deemed credible by the belief

---

[60] See: Chalong Suntharawanit, "Wiwatthanakan kan khian prawattisat thai cak caophraya thiphakòrawong thüng somdet kromphraya damrong rachanuphap" [The evolution of history writing from Chaophraya Thipakorawong to Prince Damrong Rajanubhab], *Sinlapakorn* 16, no. 4 (1976): 68–82; and *Chaophraya* Thiphakorawong, [The royal chronicle of the First Bangkok Reign], introduction.

[61] Henry Alabaster, *The Modern Buddhist; Being the Views of a Siamese Minister of State on His Own and Other Religions* (London, UK: Trubner & Co., 1870).

[62] Reynolds, "The Case of K. S. R. Kulap," p. 90.

[63] See: Mananya, *K. S. R. Kulap*, 25–27; and Chai-anan, [Life and works of Thianwan and Kulap], 196–97.

that he should neither have had access to those documents nor held rare items in his private possession. Thus, by virtue of his personal history, his knowledge of Siam's history could not possibly be correct. He was not supposed to write about history. He was expected to behave according to his place in the social hierarchy.

Strong social hierarchy still persists in Thai intellectual culture today. Intellectual criticism in this social milieu is a delicate, sometimes risky business, as illustrated by the case of Kulap, depending on who is under criticism and who the critic is.

THE HISTORIOGRAPHICAL MOMENTS

Previous studies on Kulap paid attention to the politics or power relations in the production of historical knowledge. In these readings, Kulap resisted, and even transgressed, the exclusive intellectual realm of the elite. This essay has considered the case of Kulap in terms of the epistemic transition in the practice of history: the coexistence, contestation, clash, and mixture of the concepts and practices underlying two different historiographical modes. Kulap represented the older tradition of folk-temple, or popular tradition, of historiography, whereas the elite intellectuals represented, and advocated for, the modern one. The punishment of Kulap was one of the moments when the contestation was decided in favor of modern historiography by establishing new standards, criteria, and expectations for history writing, while condemning the older, traditional practice of employing fabrication, lies, plagiarism, copying, fictions, and fruits of insanity.

Despite being punished and humiliated in 1901, and again in 1906, Kulap kept writing and publishing for another decade or so. Among other works, he composed and compiled *Anam sayamyut* (1903), a chronicle-like biography of the first four kings of Bangkok (1907); *Ayatiwat* (1911); and the already mentioned *Poet hu poet ta* (1914). His style of history writing remained the same. He continued to be boastful as before, and to offer his books to the king. In the introduction to *Ayatiwat*, which he published when he was seventy-eight years old, Kulap wrote about himself:

> At the age of seventy-eight, Kulap is still healthy, mentally and physically, and as active as before. He does not need glasses. He can pass a thread through the eye of a needle, can read the newspaper in the evening when it gets dark, and can hear clearly noise which is far away. His teeth are strong enough for hard food. He is still strong and energetic, can work hard like he used to do at a younger age. As long as he is physically healthy, his mind remains sound, not crazed, and not forgetful.[64]

This was not just an introduction to a book. It was a public announcement that Kulap was not, and had never been, crazy. Shortly before his death (he probably died on March 24, 1922), Kulap wrote his will, in which he bequeathed his possessions to the Vajiranana Library. If anything, one might take this last act by Kulap as evidence of his madness, for no Thai would bequeath their possessions to a library—not in the past, and not even today.

---

[64] Kulap, *Ayatiwat* (1995 [1911]), no page number; this quotation is from the second page of the introduction of the original manuscript, as opposed to the introduction of the reprint in 1995.

CHAPTER THREE

RENEGADE ROYALIST: AUTOBIOGRAPHY AND SIAM'S DISAVOWED PRINCE PRISDANG

Tamara Loos

The central place Professor Craig J. Reynolds gives to Thai language sources, and his dogged search for meaning in the deserted corners of the archive as well as on the streets of provincial Thailand, have inspired the following essay. Reynolds's method emphasizes texts, which he consistently anchors to their authors and their relevant contexts. His 1979 study and translation of a Thai autobiography constitutes one of the first of that genre, and even in his essays on Thai intellectuals and writers Reynolds excavates their biographical details, thereby grounding our understanding of Thai history in the lives and experiences of real people. This approach has motivated me to dig deeply into the political and emotional journey of one man, Prince Prisdang Chumsai (1852–1935), who led an extraordinary life that ended in bitter disappointment.[1] An examination of his singular life opens a window onto the larger constraints of Thai culture and history. Prince Prisdang's account reveals the sharp edges bordering Siam's culture of authority in the late nineteenth and early twentieth centuries.

Although he can hardly be regarded as a political radical, Prince Prisdang nonetheless antagonized King Chulalongkorn, and as a result paid a highly personal price involving exile, blacklisting, and social shunning. His efforts to avenge history's erasure of him are the subject of this chapter, which initiates a project about the history of Siam through social biography.[2] Although it follows the life story of a particular individual, the larger project places him within the cultures and societies in which he lived, particularly that of Siam during the most turbulent and exciting period of its recent history. Prince Prisdang was born in 1852, just as the challenges of imperialism threatened Siam's leadership, and he died shortly after a coup

---

[1] I am grateful to the following colleagues and friends for their assistance with this essay: Ida Aroonwong, Chairat Polmuk, Sherman Cochran, Maria Cristina Garcia, Apikanya McCarty, Lorraine Paterson, David Vernon, and Rachel Weil.

[2] The term "social biography" comes from Nick Salvatore, *Eugene V. Debs: Citizen and Socialist* (Urbana: University of Illinois Press, 1982), xi.

overthrew the absolute monarchy and established a constitutional form of government in 1932. Prisdang's life encapsulates more than the political, however. His dramatic personality and the relative abundance of personal and official documents written by him offer an unprecedented opportunity to weave the individualized, emotive dimension of human life into historical scholarship. Historical contingency and specificity confront readers of his letters, memoranda, and autobiography, bringing Siam's history vibrantly alive.

What follows considers three elements in the history and historiography of Prince Prisdang. First, it explains the moments leading up to his decision to live in exile in 1890, a cataclysmic event that occupies primacy of place in his life story. Second, it examines the primary sources for the causes of his exile. I privilege documents composed by Prisdang, and reveal how political aims and affective impulses motivate the story he tells, which changes depending on historical context and intended audience. The third section begins with a peculiar scene from 1930, when Prince Prisdang staged the distribution of his autobiography. It then broadens out to locate Prisdang's narrative in the context of other early forms of life writing in Thai history in an effort to reveal the uniqueness of his autobiography.

HISTORICAL CONTINGENCY: THE MOMENT OF EXILE

Prince Prisdang has nearly been expunged from the mainstream record of Thai history. When he is mentioned, he appears either as a traitor or a political reformer who overstepped the boundaries of his authority.[3] Scholars conclude that after years of service as the first and highest-ranking diplomat and representative of Siam to eleven countries in Europe and to the United States, Prince Prisdang offended King Chulalongkorn (r. 1868–1910) by recommending in 1885 that Siam become a constitutional monarchy, rather than an absolute monarchy, as the surest way to avoid colonization. The background to the 1885 petition bears telling.

The mid-1880s proved challenging for Siam's ruling elite, who witnessed British colonization of the rest of Burma, the permanent exile of Burma's monarch to British India, and French colonization of northern Vietnam. An understandably anxious King Chulalongkorn privately wrote to Prince Prisdang, then stationed in Paris, for advice about how Siam should best proceed to maintain its independence. The Burmese ambassador in Paris had previously consulted Prisdang as the British took over, so he knew exactly what the imperial stakes were, and how the fall of a kingdom was "negotiated" through lies disguised as diplomacy that justified colonization in the name of civilization. Prince Prisdang tested the limits of the advice he could candidly give by explaining his reluctance to provide the king with counsel because his opinion might be too strong and incur the king's displeasure. The king insisted that the prince be frank. Prince Prisdang's sixty-page response—a draft co-written in 1885 and signed by several key Siamese royal and noble elites

---

[3] For a subtle treatment of Prisdang based on his writings, see Nigel Brailey, ed., *Two Views of Siam on the Eve of the Chakri Reformation: Comments by Robert Laurie Morant and Prince Pritsdang* [*sic*] (Arran, Scotland: Kiscadale Publications, 1989); and Kullada Kesboonchoo Mead, *The Rise and Decline of Thai Absolutism* (London: Routledge Curzon, 2004), 93–125. For a view that hews closer to Thai official sources, see David Wyatt's description of the 1885 petition as a "*treasonable* challenge" to the king's authority in his *The Politics of Reform in Thailand: Education in the Reign of King Chulalongkorn* (New Haven: Yale University Press, 1969), 90 (emphasis added).

residing in Europe—called for the adoption of Western political principles that "had become the standard for measuring civilized nations."[4]

The recommended reforms extended beyond changing the absolute monarchy to a constitutional one—the document respectfully but clearly requested a cabinet system, legal equality for all Siamese subjects, freedom of speech, new laws regarding succession, changes in the appointment and salary system for government officials, and so on. The king, realizing the correspondence was no longer private, wrote a measured response several months later, politely agreeing with most of the suggestions, which were gradually implemented after 1888, except for a few including the one regarding the constitutional monarchy, free speech, and legal equality (royalty had a separate court for several more decades).

Most historians, to the extent they comment on Prince Prisdang's fall from grace, point to his catalyzing role in drafting the proposal as the cause. They base their conclusion on the fact that King Chulalongkorn recalled to Siam most of those who signed the petition, including Prisdang, in 1885.[5] However, this fails to explain why Prisdang began to live in exile in 1890, nearly five years after his recall to Siam. It also fails to elucidate why none of the others felt they had to leave Siam, but, on the contrary, were appointed to some of the highest posts in the administration.

When Prisdang returned to Siam from England in 1886, he witnessed his mother's agonizing death from cholera and had his home repossessed by the monarch, who briefly lent him a houseboat until the cremation ceremony for Prisdang's mother was over.[6] Unlike his princely peers similarly recalled from Europe, he failed to secure a posting in Siam adequate to his training. By 1888, petition co-signer Prince Naret had been named minister of the capital, Prince Sawatdi had become the minister of justice, and Prince Phitthayalap (Sonabanthit) served in many roles including the minister of public works and of the palace.[7] By contrast, the diplomatic skills of Prisdang were not fully utilized in his new position as director general of the Post and Telegraph Department.[8] Depressed at his sudden

---

[4] Eiji Murashima, "The Origin of Modern Official State Ideology in Thailand," *Journal of Southeast Asian Studies* 19, no. 1 (March 1988): 84. In the prince's autobiography, he credits Prince Sawatdi, then only nineteen years old, as a major influence on the content of the petition. Prisdang, *Prawat yo nai phan ek phiset phra worawongthoe phraongchao prisdang tae prasut pho. so. 2392 thung 2472* [Brief history of special colonel Prince Prisdang from birth in P.S. 2392 until 2472] (Bangkok: 2472/1930 [1970]), 60.

[5] Parties to the petition included Prisdang, Prince Bidyalabh (Phitthayalap, aka Sonabanthit), Prince Naret, Prince Svasti Sobhon (Sawatdi Sophon), and seven junior officials. All of the princes except for Prisdang were invited to sit on King Chulalongkorn's cabinet by 1892, when it was created and "staffed by men whom he [the king] could trust," according to Wyatt, *The Politics of Reform in Thailand*, 94.

[6] Prisdang, *Prawat yo*, 64–65. He actually borrowed a boat from Nai Sanphet before King Chulalongkorn's brother, Prince Chakkraphat, lent him a houseboat, but simplified this (or forgot the details) in his autobiography. See National Archives (Bangkok) [herafter NA], Krasuang Tang Prathet [Ministry of Foreign Affairs; hereafter K.T.], 6.26/2, Phraworawangthoe Phra-ongchao Prisdang, Prisdang to Phanurangsi, May-August R.S. 109 [1890], 13.

[7] Wyatt, *The Politics of Reform in Thailand*, 93 fn. 16, 100; *Ratchasakunwong* [The Royal House], Cremation volume for Nai Sanan Bunyasiriphan (Bangkok: Prajan Pub., 1969), 63.

[8] Bonnie Davis, *Royal Siamese Postal Service (The Early Years)* (Bangkok: Siam Stamp Trading Co., 1983), 16. Prince Phanurangsi was the director-general from the opening of Siam's first post office in 1883 until 1886, when Prisdang returned to Bangkok.

change in circumstances, Prisdang purchased a gun and contemplated suicide, marking his emotional nadir.[9] A different kind of death occurred instead: most histories fail to mention Prisdang again.

In 1890, he was finally allowed to travel abroad when he accompanied Prince Phanurangsi, by then the minister of war, to Japan on a diplomatic mission. When Prince Phanurangsi fell ill and required care on the return journey, they made an unplanned stop in Hong Kong so that Phanurangsi could recover. From Hong Kong, Prisdang wrote the telegrams excerpted below that led up to his decision to flee Siam. The illness, the stopover, and the telegrams that led to his drastic decision were unanticipated. Instead, they unfolded in the moment.

One can imagine Prince Prisdang anxiously dashing off a telegram to Siam's minister of foreign affairs, Prince Thewawong,[10] on October 10, 1890, from a Post and Telegraph Office in Hong Kong. Prisdang wrote:

> Unless I have a reply about middle of next week what H. M. the King's pleasure is, I will take it for granted you have abandoned me. I must go obtain best possible employment for living in disguise for I am not able to maintain my present position. Will you be [good] enough to inform me by telegraph immediately what has been decided.[11]

The subject of the decision was not explained. The telegram sent in response from Bangkok to Tokyo, which Prisdang may have shred in rage or used to wipe away tears of anguish, is not recorded. However, from that moment, Prisdang began living in exile and disguise. He did not return to his native country, Siam, for over twenty years, though this was not for lack of desire to return home. He feared for his life.

He expressed that fear in a letter, written in English, to Prince Thewawong on October 22, 1890:

> After having fully truthfully explained my reasons for keeping myself away from malicious intention of doing me harm and the circumstances ... and after having submitted my life which if of no value to anyone is yet the most valued by each to the pleasure of H. M. the King and doing all in my power under the circumstances to avoid anything which may be unpleasant and regrettable, I have now to take for granted that I must be left to my own resource [*sic*] and not wanted to return for none of my praying [*sic*] has been granted ... I forgive them all who did me wrong and harm and pray that they may be forgiven ... With profound regrets, your most humble, Prisdang.[12]

---

[9] Prisdang, *Prawat yo*, 65.

[10] Prince Thewawong was King Chulalongkorn's half-brother (both were sons of King Mongkut) and also the elder brother of three of the king's queens (who were also daughters of King Mongkut). Thewawong was Siam's minister of foreign affairs for thirty-eight years.

[11] NA, K.T. 6.26/2, Phraworawongthoe phraongchao Prisdang, Telegram from Prisdang to Thewawong, 10 Oct. 1890.

[12] NA, K.T. 6.26/2, Phraworawongthoe phraongchao Prisdang, Prisdang to Thewawong, 23 Oct. 1890.

His fear that he would be harmed with the tacit consent of the king persisted through his first years in exile. In a confidential memo written for Frank Swettenham, the British resident of Perak, nearly a year later, in October 1891, Prince Prisdang recorded that, after deciding that he should not return to Bangkok in 1890, he attempted to enrobe as a monk in French Cambodia. However, he was informed that the Siamese would consider this an unfriendly act by the French and that if Prisdang went to Cambodia, it was at his own peril: "if he [Prisdang] likes to go into the priesthood he could do so in Battabong[13] [sic] (where a murder could be committed without leaving any trace of evidence or be known to the world at large)."[14] It comes as no surprise that Prisdang disappeared and lived incognito until 1896, when he resurfaced on a ship bound for British Ceylon (Sri Lanka) to become a monk. No sooner had he arrived and enrobed in Colombo when he sparked controversy by proposing that King Chulalongkorn, as "the last independent reigning Buddhist sovereign," be considered the highest ecclesiastical authority under whom monks in Ceylon, Burma, and Siam should unite. But that is another story.[15]

MOTIVATED SOURCES, MULTIPLE TRUTHS

I have only begun to delve into the varied sources written by Prince Prisdang about the moment of his exile and the reasons he fell out of favor with King Chulalongkorn. These comprise his heartfelt letters expressing anguish and anger about his relationship to king and country.[16] They also include a crucial memorandum, written in 1891 for the British, which was critical of Siam's weak political institutions and the king's inability to administer impartially. Importantly, the document reveals the prince's real politik position regarding European colonialism, no doubt based on his experience as a diplomat in Europe, as France and Britain descended upon Siam's neighbors. He suggests to Swettenham that Siam's ruling officials—were they forced to choose—preferred colonization by the British over the French.[17] Another key source is Prisdang's autobiography written while he was in his late seventies and published in 1930, five years before he died "destitute" and "unnoticed" in Siam in his mid-eighties.[18]

In addition, I refer to contemporaneous official correspondence between British authorities in Siam and London, which attempts to decipher the politics behind Prisdang's extrusion from Siam. These letters are salacious in their gossipy detail and allege that Prisdang, born to an imbecile, owed his career to King Chulalongkorn. Despite this good fortune, Prisdang led a profligate life at home and abroad. They accuse him of fleeing ignominiously with his adulterous lover—a widowed, elite Siamese woman—after pilfering funds from the Royal Post Office. She allegedly stole

---

[13] Battambong is a Cambodia province along Siam's eastern border.

[14] Anonymous [Prisdang], "Confidential," in *Two Views of Siam*, 59.

[15] Anne M. Blackburn, *Locations of Buddhism: Colonialism and Modernity in Sri Lanka* (Chicago: University of Chicago Press, 2010), 167–86.

[16] NA, K.T. 6.26/2, Phraworawongthoe phraongchao Prisdang.

[17] Anonymous [Prisdang], "Confidential," 49–79.

[18] Prisdang, *Prawat yo*. See also Sumet Jumsai, "A Postscript," in *Prince Prisdang's Files on His Diplomatic Activities in Europe, 1880–1886*, ed. M. L. Manich Jumsai (Bangkok: Chalermnit, 1977), 267.

her family jewelry and escaped incognito, dressed as a boy. These accusations, most of which are suspect, stem from British officials in Bangkok who undoubtedly received the information in confidence from Siamese officials, who in turn had reason to destroy the prince's reputation. I treat all these sources with suspicion; they are motivated by and faithful only to their particular, contingent impulses.

Prisdang defends his decision to flee in a number of ways. One year into his exile, Prisdang appeared in British Malaya, where Resident Swettenham persuaded the prince to write a confidential memorandum for the foreign office in London. In this and in his autobiography, written nearly four decades after his exile, Prisdang points to the overt political cause of the falling-out: he believed he offended the king by breaking protocol when he led a group of high-ranking officials to petition the king for a constitutional, rather than an absolute, monarchy. Both the content of the petition and the process by which it was created and delivered to King Chulalongkorn (as a public document rather than as private correspondence between the king and Prisdang) earned him the king's lasting enmity. These documents defend his exile as political in nature and therefore honorable. By this point, Prisdang considered himself a political refugee. In his private letters, he points to more complex personal causes for his exile, but these would not serve him well abroad, where he needed a sympathetic audience among British colonial officials.[19]

The 1891 memorandum pushes the political rationale for his exile even further than his autobiography. It is an exposé, written for imperial Britain's representative in Southeast Asia. It bared all and spared nothing regarding King Chulalongkorn's decline from a principled and reformist leader to an autocrat who exercised absolute power, encouraged nepotism, and engaged in favoritism based on the influence of consorts and queens. In his memorandum, Prisdang claims that his critique (which had to have been leveled prior to his exile) of polygyny generally, the king's polygynous relations particularly, and the powerful, extra-institutional influence of women in the Inner Palace caused the rift between the king and Prisdang. However, in private Thai sources written by Prisdang to defend himself against accusations of adultery, he claims to have had several wives. In other words, Prisdang's records, like those of the British and Siamese governments, bring us no closer to the elusive truth.

As if these were not sufficient causes to leave Siam, the prince also hints at, but refuses to name, another reason for his departure. He maintains in his autobiography that he fled in 1890 for the political reasons outlined above, but in his preface he discusses stories that he refused to detail because "it might harm me."[20] His autobiography teasingly hints at an "incident," but refuses to divulge its core: five tantalizing pages—78 through 82—of the narrative are missing, as if Prisdang changed his mind and ripped them out just before his autobiography went to press. Yet, he remarks on the missing pages in the text, purposefully revealing their absence. As he hastily edited the volume so it could be printed in time for his seventy-eighth birthday, he worried that this section "described [things] too tersely. Readers would misunderstand it, so I cut out the entire section from pages 80 to 82,[21]

---

[19] These alternative reasons for his departure are the subject of my forthcoming book, *Bones Around My Neck*.

[20] Prisdang, *Prawat yo*, 39–40.

[21] The discrepancy in page numbers may have to do with his original pagination versus that of the final printed version. He may also have decided at the last minute to take out additional pages.

and preserved that to place in one of the other two volumes later."[22] His decision to alert his reading public about the excised pages, rather than simply removing them and suturing the narrative seamlessly together so readers would never have guessed at their existence, is inexplicable. However, by writing enigmatically about his exile, he suggests that by 1930 self-censorship offered a politically astute and safe way to gesture at an injustice that might, if fully revealed, breach cultural or political norms.

Ultimately, it remains a mystery why he fled Siam in disgrace, feared for his life, and lived in exile for twenty years. A descendant of Prisdang, Professor Sumet Jumsai [Chumsai], relays anecdotally (without citing a source) a livid exchange (in letters) between Prisdang and the king as the prince left. In it, the prince accuses the king of not keeping his promises, and scornfully pleads that in his next life he not be born into the royal family. The king, infuriated, ordered all the highest ranking royal officials to bar the prince from returning to Siam: "As long as this country is mine, do not allow Prince Prisdang to step foot on it again."[23]

It seems the king's alleged command was obeyed, and only after he died in 1910 was Prisdang, by then the abbot of Dippaduttarama Temple in Kotahena (British Ceylon), allowed to return to Siam to attend the funeral. By order of Rama VI (r. 1910–25), he was forcibly disrobed in 1911. Siamese officials made it impossible for to return to his temple in Ceylon. Ironically, given that he could not leave Siam, it was rumored that the minister of the capital, *Chaophraya* Yomarat, planned to imprison him for unlawfully fleeing the kingdom in the first place. Facing official censure, harassment, and blacklisting, Prisdang could not find a decent or sustainable livelihood. He briefly translated documents as a clerk at the Ministry of Foreign Affairs, but was laid off. He then became the editor of The Siam Observer, until he was fired for defamation. The prince developed a reputation for being an irascible bohemian with a sharp wit and volatile personality. One anecdote has him posting a sign outside his residence that barred entry to dogs and man, revealing that he had become, in his old age, a gloomy misanthrope.[24] He died in 1935, three years after witnessing the coup that overthrew the absolute monarchy. It is unrecorded, however, how he felt about the establishment, finally, of a constitutional form of government.

EARLY THAI AUTOBIOGRAPHY

Before he passed away, Prisdang published his autobiography as a way to have the final word about his role in Siam's history. On a steamy day in Bangkok in February 1930, Prince Prisdang Chumsai presided over the ceremony he arranged to celebrate his seventy-eighth birthday. With ill-fitting dentures that caused his speech to slur, he handed number eleven of the one hundred copies of his autobiography to Prince Damrong Rachanuphap.[25] One can only imagine the false pleasantries that

---

[22] Prisdang, *Prawat yo*, 41.

[23] Sumet Jumsai, *Wang tha phra* [Tha Phra Palace] (Bangkok: Krung Siam, 1971), 24; Bunphisit Srihong, "Samphanthaphap rawang phrabat somdet phra julajomklao jaoyuhua kap phra-ong jao prisdang jak lakthan chanton su khamtham to nakwichakan lae nak-khian prawatsat-rathasat" [The relationship between King Chulalongkorn and Prince Prisdang: From primary evidence to questions by scholars and writers of political history] *Ratthasatsan* 32, no. 3 (2011), 13.

[24] Anuman Rajadhon, *Fun khwamlang*, vol. 2 (Bangkok: Suksit Sayam, 1968), 61.

[25] The dates in his autobiography are confusing: the publication page states it was 1930, but the signature page lists 1928. He signs the concluding page and dates it 1924. The "schedule"

may have been exchanged between these two elderly gentlemen as the former political exile and reviled Prisdang required Damrong, one of the most celebrated and powerful men in Thai history, to sign the "Warranty Certificate" on the first page of the book. Peculiarly, Prisdang obliged each recipient to sign their copy underneath his signature, which was less an autograph than a contract that would confer upon the recipient permission to receive the second and third proposed volumes of the autobiography. The signatures must also have served as a validation for Prisdang: face-to-face confirmation that the invitees at his birthday ceremony would read and know his side of the story. If Prince Damrong's presence is any indication, then one can imagine that others from Siam's political and royal elite also attended. Prisdang staged a political and discursive event meant to end the speculation about his loyalty to Siam and to King Chulalongkorn. His chosen vehicle to avenge his omission from Thai history: an autobiography.

In its pages, Prisdang centers his life story on his efforts on behalf of Siam and King Chulalongkorn, to whom he pledged personal loyalty. His bitterness erupts when explaining that, despite his fervent patriotism, the king disavowed Prisdang, who then became persona non grata. By narrating his own history—the treaties he negotiated, the diplomatic breakthroughs he brokered, and the personal favors he performed for the king—Prisdang staged his return to the center of Siam's history, as the king's man. His desire was hardly radical. It required that he express his regrets about breaking protocol when he helped draft the 1885 petition and that he totally disavow the politically immoderate memorandum to the British written in 1891—the memo is never publicly or privately claimed by Prisdang. By the time he penned his autobiography in 1930, Prisdang did not want to change or disrupt history, but craved acknowledgement for his primary role in it. On an emotional level, the renegade royalist wanted back into the good graces of the king and history. His is the first Thai autobiography that embraces nearly an entire life, from cradle to near-grave, in an attempt to set the historical record straight and earn pride of place again in Siam's history.

Autobiographies were a rarity in Siam in the 1920s. It is unclear when the first recognizable autobiographies in Thai were published. There are several reasons for this, including the difficulty of preserving and collecting ephemeral texts and, more importantly, the issue of how one defines autobiography (or "life writing," as I explain later).[26] Biography, by contrast, has a longer and more solid presence in Thai historiography, in which the history of the royal family, especially that of the king, is often conflated with the history of the kingdom. The kingdom's traditional royalist

---

inserted as a loose-leaf page into the autobiography does not list a date but suggests he actually had the ceremony when he was seventy-nine in 1930. Prisdang, *Prawat yo*, 37, 41–42.

[26] Prisdang's book is a case in point regarding preservation. Although the tradition of giving gifts of books at ceremonies is much older, Prince Damrong is credited with initiating in 1901 the custom of handing out commemorative volumes at funerals as a way to reprint valuable manuscripts, some copies of which would go to the royal library. The autobiography of Prince Prisdang was one of the beneficiaries of Prince Damrong's scheme. When *Luang* Anaek Nayawathi (*Momratchawong* Narot Chumsai) passed away in 1968, the director of the National Library suggested that *Luang* Anaek's son, Manit Chumsai, consider reprinting Prince Prisdang's autobiography, which was rare. Manit requested the copy from Prince Damrong's library to print as a cremation volume for his father, who was Prisdang's nephew. Saved by this odd chain of events, Prince Prisdang's autobiography resurfaced as a cremation volume. On the tradition of cremation volumes, see Grant Olsen, "Thai Cremation Volumes: A Brief History of a Unique Genre of Literature," *Asian Folklore Studies* 51 (1992): 279–94.

history is compiled from semi-biographical accounts of the achievements of various monarchs as recorded in manuscripts and chronicles. Scholars have read back the conflation of monarchical biography and "national" history as early as the reign of King Ramkhamhaeng of Sukhothai, who some uncritically argue composed the first Thai autobiography in the eponymous late-thirteenth-century stone inscription.[27]

The Thai term for autobiography, *attachiwaprawat,* is defined in Thai dictionaries as a history that one writes or provides orally about oneself. Etymologically, it breaks down into at-ta, meaning self or oneself, which has both a Pali and Sanskrit root; *chiwa,* which more abstractly refers to life, existence, living, and vitality; and *prawat,* which refers to modern forms of history and historical writing.[28] Its first appearance in dictionary form as *attaprawat* occurred in the 1952 English-Thai dictionary by the leftist publicist So Sethaputra.[29] Having no shorthand Thai term for what he was writing in the 1920s, Prisdang merely refers to it as "history of oneself" (*prawat khong ton-ton eng*).

A history and analysis of life writing—a category that encompasses diaries, memoirs, letters, autobiographies, and other forms of writing that involve the construction of self and the narration of an individual life—in Thai studies has yet to be written, but a review of these kinds of texts extant in Siam by the 1920s reveals the uniqueness of Prisdang's contribution not just to Thai history, but to narrative style, subjectivity, and affect in Thai social life.[30] There are several types of life writing that were composed by Prisdang's near contemporaries, but his was among the earliest to offer a retrospective prose account that sought to make sense of his own existence.[31]

---

[27] Pathamon Kotrakunsin, "Kansuksa wikhro wiwatthanakan lae khunnakha khong sarakkhadi attachiwaprawat samai ratchakan thi 5 ratchakan thi 9" [An analytical study of the evolution and value of autobiography from the fifth through the ninth reigns] (master's thesis, Kasetsat University, 2007), 3; Laksanaying Rattasan, "Ngankhian choeng prawat khong thai nai samai rattanakosin rawang pho.so. 2325–2475" [Thai biographical writings from the Ratanakosin Period, 1782–1932] (master's thesis, Chulalongkorn University, 1976), 30. What few details the epigraph offers about the king's life are genealogical and brief compared to the achievements of the king as a political ruler. The inscription's authenticity is a matter of debate in any case. See, most recently, Mukhom Wongthet, *Intellectual Might and National Myth: A Forensic Investigation of the Ram Khamhaeng Controversy in Thai Society* (Bangkok: Matichon, *Sinlapawatthanatham* Special Issue, 2003).

[28] None of the earliest Thai dictionaries has an entry for *attachiwaprawat,* though they do have variations of the root, *atta.* See: Jean-Baptiste Pallegoix, *Dictionarium linguae Thai* (Paris: jussi Imperatoris impressum, 1854); Dan Beach Bradley, *Dictionary of the Siamese Language* (Bangkok: 1873); or George Bradley McFarland, *Thai-English Dictionary* (Stanford: Stanford University Press, 1944).

[29] So Sethaputra, *New Model English-Thai Dictionary,* Library Edition, vol. 1 (Bangkok: So Sethaputra, 1952), 106. So's earliest dictionary dates from 1940, but I have yet to locate a copy so cannot confirm whether *autobiography* exists in that version. In the Thai-English version, *atta-prawat* is simply translated as *autobiography.* So Sethaputra, *New Model Thai-English Dictionary,* vol. 2 (Bangkok: Thai Watthanaphanit, 1965), 1038.

[30] The phrase "life writing" was coined in the 1970s by feminist literary scholars, who critiqued the narrow definition of autobiography as the province of male writers, and insisted on the recognition of forms of writing outside the established canon. Life-writing materials included informal and unpublished sources in addition to formal published sources that describe an individual life. Barbara Caine, *Biography and History* (Hampshire: Palgrave Macmillan, 2010), 66–69.

[31] Philippe Lejeune, *Le pacte autobiographique,* cited in Philip Holden, *Autobiography and Decolonization: Modernity, Masculinity, and the Nation-State* (Madison: University of Wisconsin Press, 2008), 18.

Forms of life writing by Siamese royal elites and commoner intellectuals began to appear at the turn of the twentieth century, the same era that scholars generally agree that a literate bourgeois middle class emerged in Siam.[32] Thai language periodicals appeared in print by the 1870s and included short stories, not just of Buddhist Jataka tales but also of translations of Western literature and Thai fictional narratives.[33] Siam's first novels followed in the 1920s and 1930s. This literary efflorescence marks a time of self-reflection for individuals as well as their relationship to their king and country because of the transformations demanded by the intensity of that period's encounter with Western education, imperialism, and individuals.

It was also the era in which the first Siamese students, including Prisdang, began to study abroad.[34] Their letters home and daily journals often served as a form of life writing.[35] Several commoners, including most importantly K. S. R. Kulap Krisananon (1835–1922?) and Narin Phasit (1874–1950), produced histories, biographies, and other works that rivaled and challenged official, royal accounts. They used a technique by which they would insert autobiographical details into texts about radically different topics. Kulap's 1905 biography of important noble families, including an important monk patronized by the kings Mongkut and Chulalongkorn, began with an autobiography of Kulap himself.[36] The book caused a stir for its faulty information about the monk, but it has yet to be analyzed as a sly way to attract the monarch's attention to Kulap's life story.[37] Narin utilized a similar technique: he wrote a four-volume autobiography as a kind of intertextual commentary in writings on other topics published between 1920 and 1928.[38]

---

[32] See: Nakkharin Mektrairat, *Kanpathiwat sayam pho so 2475* [The Siamese Revolution of 1932] (Bangkok: The Foundation for the Social Sciences and Humanities, 1992); and Scot Barmé, *Woman, Man, Bangkok: Love, Sex, and Popular Culture in Thailand* (Lanham: Rowman and Littlefield, 2002), 1–11.

[33] Benedict R. O'G. Anderson, "Introduction," in *In the Mirror: Literature and Politics in Siam in the American Era,* ed. and trans. Benedict Anderson and Ruchira Mendiones (Bangkok: Duang Kamol, 1985), 12.

[34] Prisdang was the first Thai royal family member to graduate from a university abroad. He graduated from King's College London, with a degree in civil engineering in 1876.

[35] See for example, Prince Wachirunnahit, *Jotmaihet raiwan* [Daily Journal] (Bangkok: Samnakphim Bannakit, 2550/2007). He died in 1894, and his no-doubt edited daily journal was published later as an example to Siamese youth.

[36] K. S. R. Kulap Kritsananon, *Mahamukkhamattayanukun wong: waduai lamdap wong trakun khunnang thai thangsin nai phaendin sayam* [History of the great ministerial families: Genealogies of all the Thai noble families in the Siamese Kingdom] (Bangkok: Siam Praphet, 1905). For a discussion of the autobiographical content and the high-level investigation caused by the monk's faulty genealogy, see Craig J. Reynolds, *Seditious Histories: Contesting Thai and Southeast Asian Pasts* (Seattle: University of Washington Press, 2006), 55–77. See also Laksanaying, [Thai biographical writing], 35.

[37] According to Laksanaying, Kulap inserted his biographical material in a different biography of *Chao Phraya* Bodindecha (Sing), written in 1898. Kulap included details about his ancestors as well as himself. See: Laksanaying, [Thai Biographical Writing], 35; P. Wacharaphon, "K. S. R. Kulap," in *Khon nangsuphim* [Journalists] (Bangkok: [unknown publisher], 1963); and Thongchai Winichakul's essay in this volume (chapter 2).

[38] Peter Koret, *The Man Who Accused the King of Killing a Fish: The Biography of Narin Phasit of Siam, 1874–1950* (Chiang Mai: Silkworm Books, 2012). Narin included autobiographical snippets in books with titles such as *Narin Seeks Financial Assistance for His Ordination* (1920)

Clearly, Thai life writing appeared in many guises before it was called autobiography. Prince Prisdang's autobiography is thus not chronologically the first, but it is arguably uniquely self-centered, non-didactic, and structured as a continuous rather than episodic narrative of a whole life. He had no intention to teach readers moral lessons through a recounting of his mistakes, but rather sought to present his perspective, claim his place in Thai national history, make confessions, and air grievances. A brief comparison with a contemporaneous autobiography is instructive. Prince-Patriarch Vajiranana (1860–1921) began to compose his autobiography in 1915, but failed to finish it by the time he died of tuberculosis in 1921. Prince Damrong stepped in to complete and publish the autobiography in 1924. On the face of it, the prince-priest shares a great deal in common with Prince Prisdang. They were roughly contemporaries: Vajiranana was born in 1860 and Prisdang in 1852. Both came of age during the long reign of King Chulalongkorn, and imagined a life-long career devoted to king and country. Both enrobed as Buddhist monks for substantial periods of time—Vajiranana for life and Prisdang for fifteen years. Neither appear to have had children. Although Prisdang fails to mention it in his autobiography, both men allegedly had problems with extravagance and amassed debts; both were threatened with lawsuits by foreigners attempting to collect on these debts; and both preferred, or at least were comfortable with, socializing with Europeans.[39] However, Prince Vajiranana repented his behaviors and, in typical fashion, discussed his youthful mistakes in order to deploy them as Buddhist parables.

Craig Reynolds explains in the introduction to his translation of Prince Vajiranana's autobiography: "The moralizing tone is cloying in places, but we must keep in mind the genre of this writing. The purpose of a life, with the model of the Buddha's life in mind, is to instruct, to set an example, and the writing of a life must perforce be tendentious."[40] Sulak Sivaraksa talked about this internal contradiction between the Western notion of biographical writing and Thai Buddhist autobiography, which de-emphasizes the individual except when she or he stands as an exemplar of an abstract Buddhist ideal.[41] Confessions of mistakes serve a didactic function, and lives are not necessarily accounted for in chronological order but, instead, are ordered according to lessons from that individual's experience. In other words, their narratives are anecdotal rather than holistic. Truth relates to moral truth rather than the degree of correspondence with real life events (conventional truth). As a consequence, the Thai genre tends to be politically and socially conservative: Thai Buddhist biographies don't criticize parents or the royal family, and they don't mention personal shortcomings unless they teach a life lesson to the reader. For

---

and *The Statement Regarding the Samaneri of Nariwong Temple* (1928). Peter Koret, personal communication, September 16, 2013.

[39] NA, K.T. 6.26/1, Phraworawongthoe phraongchao Prisdang. The file includes a grievance against Prisdang dated October 9, 1890 by Mr. Meisner, a German in Bangkok, who had been alerted that Prisdang left the country. Meisner wanted the Siamese government to pay Prisdang's outstanding debt of about one thousand baht. It speaks to the suddenness and unplanned nature of Prisdang's decision to flee into exile and might not be indicative of an extravagant nature.

[40] Prince-Patriarch Vajiranana, *Autobiography: The Life of Prince Patriarch Vajiranana*, ed. and trans. Craig J. Reynolds (Athens: Ohio University Press, 1979), xlix.

[41] Sulak Sivaraksa, "Biography and Buddhism in Thailand," *Biography* 17, no. 1 (Winter 1994): 6–7.

instance, Prince Vajiranana mentions that he was a prodigal spendthrift in his early adolescence. He loved to shop for European-style clothing and disdained Chinese and Indian tailors. He drank alcohol and gambled, fished, shot game, and engaged in other decidedly non-Buddhist behaviors.[42] This sets up the narrative that leads to and contrasts with a life of detachment as a monk.

There is difference in form as well as function between Prince Vajiranana's and Prince Prisdang's autobiographies. The timeline of the former's narrative ends abruptly in 1882, when he was only twenty-two years old and firmly committed to the monkhood. It is tempting to surmise that his story covers the period during which he could safely explore (and express his involvement in) the temptations of the mundane world. This may be unfair because "by definition the end of the story cannot be told, the bios [life narrative] must remain incomplete" when the person writing it remains alive.[43] Even so, stopping the narrative at age twenty-two when the protagonist lives into his sixties is unusual. Prisdang finished his first volume by 1930, when he was deep into his seventh decade, and it covered his life from birth until age seventy. He never completed volumes two or three, though he drafted their tables of contents.

If Prince Vajiranana's incentive for writing his autobiography entailed a Buddhist didactic mission, what motivated Prince Prisdang? Prisdang's forward acknowledges autobiography as a Western cultural practice, but also claims a perverse engagement with Thai Buddhist frameworks of merit-making. For example, he refuses to follow the tradition of letting others make merit for him after he dies. He wants to "take care of my own corpse" and "hand out my own history before I die and rot" so he can hear what people have to say.[44] In fact, he provides an immediate opportunity for merit-making to those who received his autobiography: "I wish that the recipients of this history receive good deeds in the form they can see with their eyes, and feel with their hearts." More specifically, he hopes to use part of the donations he receives at his ceremony to buy new dentures, which is "the good deed that the donors will see with their eyes."[45]

He also writes his own history because if he didn't, "all this outlandish and unexpected knowledge would certainly lie sterile, pointless, and remain in the dark." Moreover, not telling it would allow "those arrogant know-it-alls" to "concoct a story to lead the young and innocent by the nose in a pointless direction." He also believed no one else could possibly write it—not just because they could not do his life justice, but because no one knew him well enough, given that he spent nearly forty years abroad, and that those who once knew him were either dead or were so old that they "are not worth knowing or refuse to acquaint with me nowadays." Prisdang writes his own history so that anyone reading it might …

> … either laugh, think it serves me right, find it pitiful, or even praise it. [I write] because there are people who deem themselves to be soldiers, students, scholars, politicians, and philosophers, who [think they] know it all and have seen it all,

---

[42] Vajiranana, *Autobiography*, 21–24.

[43] James Olney, "Autobiography and the Cultural Moment: A Thematic, Historical, and Bibliographical Introduction," in *Autobiography: Essays Theoretical and Critical*, ed. Olney (Princeton: Princeton University Press, 1980), 25.

[44] Prisdang, *Prawat yo*, 39.

[45] Ibid., 41–42.

who condemn me as dangerous, turbulent, crazy, and so on—whatever they can come up with. I don't mind they accuse me of being crazy; it gives me advantage over being normal. As for the ones who don't know who Prince Prisdang is, they will have a chance to get to know me before I die.[46]

His motivations are diverse and seep between the cracks of the stated rationale. Georges Gusdorf, a theorist of autobiography, pertinently argues that a gap exists between the "avowed plan of autobiography, which is simply to retrace the history of a life, and its deepest intentions, which are directed toward a kind of apologetics or theodicy of the individual being." In other words, when Prisdang writes his autobiography,

> he is not engaged in an objective and disinterested pursuit but in a work of personal justification. Autobiography appeases the more or less anguished uneasiness of an aging man who wonders if his life has not been lived in vain, frittered away haphazardly, ending now in simple failure ... So, autobiography is the final chance to win back what has been lost.[47]

Prisdang writes to avenge history and the contemptible, invisible corner to which it has relegated him. It follows that the people he invites to read this story are important.

Unlike individuals who write private diaries and letters, Prisdang wrote for a (limited) public audience of his contemporaries who attended his "life extension" ceremony, held at his home on Bangkok's Si Phraya Road, in 1930. He did not send out invitations, but the schedule for his ceremony states: "At 5pm, high-ranking royalty are invited to a private ceremony to pour holy water from the conch shell onto the prince's hands ..."[48] Friends, relatives, and the Supreme Patriarch, who gave the sermon, were also invited. As noted earlier, the presence of Prince Damrong is an indication of the high-caliber group of officials and royals who were likely in attendance.[49] The book's cover page similarly notes that the autobiography was published for "relatives, friends, and beneficiaries." He wanted them to know his version of the past.

CONCLUSION

Prisdang wrote his autobiography in his twilight years as a lonely, frequently sick, and relatively impoverished man. His autobiography was not an objective, accurate recollection of the past for history's sake; he even cites the wrong year for his birth in one place, and the dates of publication and the ceremony are misaligned. Still, it helps to understand that Prisdang is "engaged in a literary exercise," in which

---

[46] Ibid., 38.

[47] Georges Gusdorf, "Conditions and Limits of Autobiography," in *Autobiography: Essays Theoretical and Critical*, 39.

[48] "Kamnotkan," in Prisdang, *Prawat yo* (looseleaf insert, no pagination). It is essentially a schedule announcing the ceremony.

[49] Access to additional copies of his autobiography besides the one published as a cremation volume for M. R. Narot Chumsai (see above, fn. 28) would help identify attendees, since Prisdang insisted on numbering the copies, and compelled recipients to sign for their copy. No copies other than the one signed by Prince Damrong have been found.

he performs and constructs his identity through the narration of his own life.[50] He writes with a sense of historicity both of his place and that of Siam in the wider world. He tells his story in a range of ways that cannot always be reconciled with historical truth, and does not offer his biographers access to some inner core that would, like a encryption key, let them decipher his audacious life as an exiled diplomat, or as an alleged-adulterer-turned-abbot. Gusdorf noted that autobiography "cannot recall the past in the past and for the past—a vain and fruitless endeavor—for no one can revive the dead; it calls up the past for the present and in the present, and it brings back from earlier times that which preserves a meaning and value today..."[51] In other words, life writing is a historically situated practice of self-representation.[52]

Prince Prisdang writes to set the historical record about himself straight, and to give his point of view, which contrasts starkly with that provided by Siam's ruling elite, whose opinion came to represent that of the Thai state and its official history. Prisdang's life story contributes to understandings of the turn of the twentieth century, when his country and social peers witnessed dramatic shifts in fortune regarding their future as both colonized and imperial actors. Prisdang unabashedly broke with social norms and convention by writing about his emotive, subjective experiences and the king's private and sexual life, and by consciously choosing autobiography as the literary vehicle to tell his story. Unsurprisingly, the scholarship on Thai biography and autobiography is either unaware of his book, or purposefully shuns it because it does not fit into the otherwise gentile model of autobiography and biography.[53]

His conflict with the monarch goes to the heart of problems that continue to beset Thailand today regarding the sacred cultural authority of the king and the forms of self-policing it necessitates. Prisdang's decision to flee the country in 1890 resulted in part from behavior and speech that broke cultural taboos (which soon thereafter were transformed into codified criminal law—the defamation law of 1900). Prisdang's defiance, however, was paradoxically unwitting. He immediately and persistently regretted offending the monarch, apologized obsessively, and even wrote his autobiography to serve as a vehicle of self-redemption vis-à-vis this unintended offence. But monarchical authority, bolstered by princes and other official elites, brokered no challenges. Without institutional checks, the power of the monarchy encouraged competition among an ever-shifting entourage of men (often through female relatives in the palace) to win royal favor through offering the "best" intelligence about events in the kingdom. This funneling of power insulated the monarch from data and opinions that would challenge his authority. It encouraged rumors so powerful that some individuals who found themselves out of favor preferred exile to the relentless social harassment they faced within Siam.

Prisdang's drama places in high relief the subjective experience of politics in Siam and the emotional and behavioral norms for members of the ruling class regarding deference to hierarchy and expression of dissent. Power and control were

---

[50] Caine, *Biography and History*, 98.

[51] Gusdorf, "Conditions and Limits of Autobiography," 44.

[52] This phrasing comes from Jing M. Wang, *When 'I' Was Born: Women's Autobiography in Modern China* (Madison: University of Wisconsin Press, 2008), 3.

[53] See: Sulak, "Biography and Buddhism in Siam"; Pathamon, [Evolution and value of autobiography]; and Laksanaying, [Thai biographical writing].

exerted through ephemeral forms of social disciplining, not through law or other sources accessible to historians. The tools of social control used against Prisdang included gossip, rumors, and "influence"—extra-institutional methods that disciplined lapses in emotional expression. He was accused of all manner of social crimes including committing adultery in a Buddhist temple, insanity, status transgression, and disloyalty. Never publicly condemned, Prisdang instead suffered disgrace based on rumor and innuendo that followed him to the grave.[54] These forms of emotional control constructed and reinforced Siam's existing social and political hierarchy by casting out those who breached its limits. Prince Prisdang—the royal family's black sheep—was written out of history, and regarded as a traitor to the nation and his family.

Prisdang's autobiography offers a unique opportunity to explore the underbelly of Siam's political elite at a crucial moment in its modern history. It presents an alternative history of the construction of royal power: one that provides insights into the outrageous politics of *lèse majesté* that rankles Thailand's democracy in the twenty-first century. The mystery behind his expulsion from Siam is less important than what it exposes about the cultural practices bolstering Siam's power structure. Prisdang's life story sheds light on the process by which cultural norms about proper speech and obeisance to hierarchy were translated into rigid, codified law that served not to democratize power or protect the truth or the population, but instead to reify a particular political and social hierarchy. Certain speech acts and behaviors became not just blasphemous but treasonous in this new poetics of subversion regarding monarchical power and Siamese nationalism. Like many others then and now, Prisdang in 1930 very publicly highlighted his act of self-censorship of the "incident" that catapulted him out of Siam forty years earlier. As such, his conflict with the monarch goes to the heart of problems that continue to beset Thailand today regarding the sacred cultural authority of the king and the forms of self-policing it necessitates.

---

[54] For example, Prisdang recalls in his memo to Swettenham that the French ambassador asked a Siamese official what Prisdang had done to cause him to leave his post. His reply was that Prisdang had done nothing wrong but had gone insane and run off with a woman.

CHAPTER FOUR

THE PLOT OF THAI ART HISTORY: BUDDHIST SCULPTURE AND THE MYTH OF NATIONAL ORIGINS

Maurizio Peleggi

Like other graduate students in Cornell University's Southeast Asia Program from the late 1960s throughout the 1970s, Craig Reynolds had the opportunity to attend the "Breezewood Seminar." This was the informal name for the spring study retreat that took place in a private mansion-cum-museum sited in the countryside north of Baltimore, Maryland. It was "an imposing border-country house built over more than a century, set atop a hill, that indeed caught the breeze under the tall elms," as portrayed in the reminiscence of another Cornell scholar who was regularly in attendance, the late David K. Wyatt.[1] Breezewood was the residence of Alexander Brown Griswold (1907–91), a *sui generis* figure and self-taught student of Thai art history and epigraphy. Griswold embodied the Orientalist dimension of the neocolonial relationship that in the second postwar period bonded Thailand to the United States.

The Breezewood seminars took place in a high-ceilinged gallery in the west wing of the mansion, where Griswold had assembled a sizable collection of Thai antiques that he later bequeathed to the Walters Art Gallery in Baltimore.[2] By the mid-1960s, Griswold was acknowledged as an authority on Thai traditional art, sculpture in particular. A prolific writer, Griswold developed some original insights on copying as the orthodox mode of image-making in Buddhist visual culture, and proposed a controversial periodization of northern Thai (Lanna) sculpture. At other times, however, Griswold trod the path laid out by Prince Damrong Rajanubhap, whose much celebrated paternity of Thai historiography has tended to obscure his responsibility for founding Thai art history, shared with George Cœdès. Griswold's appraisal that the "profound originality of Sukhodayan art lies not in the invention

---

[1] David K. Wyatt, "Alexander B. Griswold and Thai Studies," *SEAP Bulletin* (1984): 13, http://seap.einaudi.cornell.edu/sites/seap.einaudi.cornell.edu/files/1984_SEAP_Bulletin.pdf, accessed October 28, 2014.

[2] Hiram W. Woodward, Jr., et al., *The Sacred Sculpture of Thailand: The Alexander B. Griswold Collection, The Walters Art Gallery* (London: Thames and Hudson, 1997).

of meaningless new forms, but in harmonious eclecticism" clearly echoed Prince Damrong's earlier claim that it was by borrowing and blending "the good and the beautiful features of various different styles" that "the characteristic style of Sukhodayan Buddhist art was formed, whose qualities are unsurpassed by any other period."[3] This standard view of the character and value of Sukhothai religious sculpture was restated even by UNESCO World Heritage, on whose coveted list Sukhothai was inscribed in 1991, along with the associated monumental sites of Si Satchanalai and Khamphaengphet: "The great civilization which evolved in the Kingdom of Sukhothai absorbed numerous influences and local traditions; the rapid assimilation of all these elements forged what is known as the 'Sukhothai style.'"[4]

Although the kingdom of Sukhothai only began to emerge from the mist of the past in the 1830s, by the 1920s it had secured a central place in the modern historical narrative of Siam/Thailand. Yet if the vegetation-enshrouded monumental ruins were unquestionable testimony of Sukhothai's past glory, the documentary evidence for reconstructing its history was epigraphic, sourced from stone inscriptions that were systematically dated and deciphered in the early 1920s by George Cœdès.[5] In his grand historical overview, *Les états hindouisés d'Indochine et d'Indonésie* [The Indianized States of Indochina and Indonesia] (first published in 1948), Cœdès wrote that, in Sukhothai, "between 1250 and 1350, the Siamese were able to develop their own characteristic civilization, institutions, and art."[6] Corrado Feroci, the Italian sculptor and art educator, and a naturalized Thai with the name Silpa Bhirasri, expressed this idea even more emphatically: "Every important civilization has a golden age when material, intellectual, and spiritual progress simultaneously reach a high level. The Sukhothai period was the golden age of Thailand, and the determining factors were national independence and religion."[7]

---

[3] A. B. Griswold, "The Sculpture and Architecture of Siam," in *The Arts of Thailand: A Handbook of the Architecture, Sculpture, and Painting of Thailand-Siam,* ed. Theodore Bowie (Bloomington: Indiana University, 1960), 88; Prince Damrong Rajanubhap, *Monuments of the Buddha in Siam,* trans. Sulak Sivaraksa and A. B. Griswold (Bangkok: Siam Society, 1973; repr. Bangkok: Diskul Foundation, 1982), 19. This volume contains the translation of the last two lengthy chapters (Ch. 8, "*Phutthasasana nai prathet sayam*" [Buddhism in Siam], and Ch. 9, "*Phuttha chedi nai sayam prathet*" [Buddhist monuments in Siam], of Prince Damrong's *Tamnan phra phutthachedi* [History of Buddhist Monuments] (Bangkok: cremation volume, 1926), together making up almost half of it. See also fn 12, below.

[4] UNESCO World Heritage List, "Historic Town of Sukhothai and Associated Historic Town," http://whc.unesco.org/en/list/574, accessed October 28, 2014.

[5] See: George Cœdès, "The Origins of the Sukhodayan Dynasty," *Journal of the Siam Society* 14, no. 1 (1921): 1–11; and *Recueil des inscriptions du Siam. Première partie: inscriptions de Sukhodaya* [Collection of inscriptions of Siam. Part One: Inscriptions of Sukhothai] (Bangkok: Bangkok Times Press, 1924). Before leaving Bangkok for Hanoi in 1929, Cœdès published a second volume of translations of inscriptions found in Siam, ones written in languages other than Thai; see: *Recueil des inscriptions du Siam. Duexième partie: Inscriptions de Dvaravati, de Çrivijaya et de Lavo* [Collection of inscriptions of Siam. Part Two: Inscriptions of Dvaravati, Srivijaya and Lavo] (Bangkok: Bangkok Times Press, 1929).

[6] George Cœdès, *The Indianized States of Southeast Asia,* ed. Walter Vella, trans. Susan Brown Cowing (Honolulu: East-West Center Press, 1968 [trans. of *Les états hindouisés d'Indochine et d'Indonésie*, third edition, Paris, 1964]), 222.

[7] Silpa Bhirasri [Corrado Feroci], *An Appreciation of Sukhothai Art* (Bangkok: Fine Arts Department, 1968), 3.

In this art historical narrative, what Austrian art historian Alois Riegl (1858–1905) termed *Kunstwollen* (artistic volition)[8] matched will to power as the converging forces prompting the rise of Sukhothai as the first instantiation of the Thai nation—an instantiation that, as argued by Feroci, possessed all the foundational marks of a mythic golden age. The emplotment of artistic volition fueled by Buddhist piety as a major theme in the narrative of Siam/Thailand found essential support in the aesthetic qualities of Sukhothai's bronze sculpture: supple Buddha images in seated, reclining, standing, and—most characteristically—walking postures; and with oval faces, hooked noses, arched eyebrows, and lowered eyelids. These combined Khmer, Burmese, and Sinhalese motifs into a distinctive style that not only exceeded the sum of its parts, but achieved such a perfection as to warrant the ultimate recognition of "classic"—arguably the most loaded term in the vocabulary of (Western) art history.

Following the proposition that "we identify an artwork in relation to the artwriting describing that artifact,"[9] this essay examines the discursive representation of the Buddhist statuary of Sukhothai as "the greatest achievements of T[h]ai art."[10] I am concerned here not with the validity of this virtually unanimous appraisal, but with its formulation and circulation, as well as its function in supporting the myth of Sukhothai as Thailand's golden age, when the "national" political and cultural institutions came into being. The "plot of Thai history," based on the chronological and political continuity of the Sukhothai-Ayutthaya-Bangkok kingdoms has admittedly been decentered since the 1990s, due to the twin trends of cultural localism and historiographic localism, ironically reviving the polycentric historical geography of premodern Siam espoused by King Chulalongkorn in his inaugural speech to the Antiquarian Society (*borankhadi samoson*), delivered in December 1907.[11] And yet, the centrality of Sukhothai in the Thai collective imaginary as the kingdom's first "capital" remains arguably undisputed.

PLOTTING THE HISTORY OF THAILAND'S ART

"Art history" as a scholarly concept was imported from Europe and localized in the Thai intellectual landscape in the early twentieth century, but it did not achieve the status of an academic discipline until the 1960s. Its first articulation dates to the second half of the 1920s, with the publication in 1926 of Prince Damrong's *History of*

---

[8] See also: Margaret Olin, *Forms of Representation in Alois Riegl's Theory of Art* (University Park: Pennsylvania State University Press, 1992); and Margaret Iversen, *Alois Riegl: Art History and Theory* (London and Cambridge, MA: MIT Press, 1993).

[9] David Carrier, *Artwriting* (Amherst: University of Massachusetts Press, 1987), 138. Carrier employs the single term "artwriting," generally spelled as two separate words, "to refer to texts by both art critics and art historians" (ibid., 141, fn. 1).

[10] Alexander B. Griswold, *Towards a History of Sukhodaya Art* (Bangkok: Fine Arts Dept, 1967), 1.

[11] "The Antiquarian Society Speech of King Chulalongkorn," trans. Chris Baker, *Journal of the Siam Society* 89, nos. 1–2 (2001): 95–99. For the Thai text of this speech, see National Archives of Thailand, comp., *Chotmaihet phraratchaphithi ratchamangkhala phisek ro.so. 126, 127* [Documents on the royal jubilee celebrations, 1907–1908] (Bangkok: Fine Arts Dept., 1984), 18–25. In his speech, King Chulalongkorn mentioned Sukhothai without any particular emphasis as just one in a long list of Thai city-states, starting chronologically with one called Hang Hang or Chang (p. 97).

Buddhist Monuments,[12] followed two years later by Cœdès's *Les collections archéologiques du Musée National de Bangkok* [The Bangkok National Museum's archaeological collections].[13]

The most prominent antiquarian of his age, Prince Damrong followed in the footsteps of his father, King Mongkut, whose alleged discovery in 1833 of King Ramkhamhaeng's stone inscription and other artifacts first placed Sukhothai in the collective historical imagination. Damrong had a keen disciple in his nephew, Vajiravudh, whose attempt to map Sukhothai's monumental topography based on the descriptions of the city provided by inscriptions influenced later archaeological investigations, including Cœdès's.[14] The artifacts that Damrong and interior-ministry officials collected during inspection tours of the kingdom's provinces (including several small Khmer bronzes) were displayed in the atrium of the ministry's building, standing as markers of the cultural richness as much as territorial boundaries that demarcated the territory under the ministry's authority.

Prince Damrong also oversaw, at King Chulalongkorn's request, the assemblage of fifty Buddha images in the cloister of the newly built Wat Benchamabophit—a project in which elite antiquarianism combined with the devotionalism attributed to earlier and similar assemblages, such as Wat Phra Chetuphon's. In his own account of this undertaking, Damrong wrote that the "old and beautiful images" were selected as representative of different styles, and "displayed in such a way that the public might acquire knowledge of Buddhist iconography." Elsewhere, he explained that images were installed in the cloister "for public worship and as models for people to copy when making new images."[15] Yet the images in Wat Benchamabophit were not arranged according to a chronological sequence—the dominant regime of nineteenth-century museum presentation.

Siam's declaration of war on the Central Empires in October 1917 led to the departure of Oscar Frankfurter, the German director of the Wachirayan Library. To replace him, Prince Damrong personally selected Cœdès, who since 1911 had been attached to the École française d'Extrême Orient (EFEO) headquarters in Hanoi (of which he later became the director). Given the close working relationship the two entertained since Cœdès's arrival in Bangkok early in 1918, the establishment of Thai art history must be regarded as a joint undertaking. Damrong's firsthand knowledge of the monumental remains scattered throughout the kingdom, as well as of textual sources, was married to Cœdès's mastery of epigraphic records in Pali, Sanskrit, Khmer, and Thai. Crucially, the formulation of this art-historical classification was concurrent to the creation in 1924 of the Siamese Archaeological Service (under Cœdès's direction), and was even more intimately linked to the reorganization of the Metropolitan (later National) Museum (*phiphithaphan sathan samrap phra nakhon,*

---

[12] The volume was originally printed as a cremation volume for Prince Damrong's mother with the title *Tamnan phutthachedi sayam*. It was later republished in a revised version under the title *Tamnan phra phutthachedi.*

[13] Cœdès's monograph, *Les collections archéologiques du Musée National de Bangkok*, was published as volume XII in the *Ars Asiatica* series (Paris and Brussels: G. Van Oest, 1928).

[14] Crown Prince Vajiravudh, *Ruang thiao muang phra ruang* [Account of a journey to the land of Phra Ruang] (Bangkok: Bamrung Nukunkit, 1907). This volume has been often reprinted as a cremation volume, the first time in 1928, with an introduction by Prince Damrong.

[15] Maurizio Peleggi, "Royal Antiquarianism, European Orientalism, and the Production of Archaeological Knowledge in Modern Siam," in *Asia in Europe, Europe in Asia*, ed. Srilata Ravi, Mario Rutten, and Beng-Lan Goh, (Leiden: IIAS, 2004), 133–67.

literally, "museum for the royal capital"), which was officially inaugurated on November 10, 1926.

The museum served as a model project intended to promote Siam's reputation as a country with a distinctive civilization, as well as the ability to conserve, study, and interpret its cultural properties on behalf of the domestic and international public. This objective was openly articulated in King Prajadhipok's speech at the museum's inauguration: "Objects of artistic and historical interest bear an important part in recounting the history of the nation; they exhibit the successive stages of its progress and civilization, and at the same time indicate the mind and character of the people. For this reason, among others, it is desirable that they be preserved."[16] In the Bangkok Museum—housed, then as now, in the Wang Na, or Palace of the Front— sacred images (*phra rup*) and other devotional objects (*khong saksit*) that, according to popular religiosity, were the carriers of supernatural powers, acquired a new epistemic status as material evidence of the nation's historical unfolding.

This synergy between a museological project and an art historical or, as Donald Preziosi has it, museographic classification was by no means unique; indeed, "in a substantive manner the theoretical and methodological discourse of the new discipline of art history is in a variety of ways itself an *artifact* of museological practices, a product of all that the museum as an epistemological technology affords."[17] But even though a "museum," comprising a variety of objects (coins, ceramics, fabrics, and royal paraphernalia), had been installed in the Front Palace as early as 1886, a clear vision for it was articulated only in the second half of the 1920s under the directorship of Cœdès, whose declared aim was "to create a truly national museum devoted to the arts and archaeology of Siam."[18] This objective was pursued by transferring to the museum selected artifacts from monasteries, the Metropolitan (later National) Library, the Ministry of Interior, and Prince Damrong's and the king's personal collections. These items were classified into distinct periods, and exhibited according to contemporary curatorial standards.

As I discuss in detail elsewhere,[19] the now canonical classification of Thailand's antiquities sketched by Prince Damrong and refined by Cœdès into eight chronologically sequential, if partly overlapping, periods or schools—Dvaravati, Srivijaya, Lopburi, Chiangsaen, Sukhothai, Uthong, Ayutthaya, and Rattanakosin— bears the following characteristics. Conceptually, the classification conflated art history with political history by assimilating the fortunes of a period or school of art to the rise and fall of the kingdom or principality after which it was named; methodologically, it relied on epigraphic sources for dating, and turned to the artifacts' stylistic features as clues to gauge their historic dating as well as the ethnic origins of their makers.[20]

---

[16] *Bangkok Times*, November 13, 1926, 5.

[17] Donald Preziosi, "In the Temple of Entelechy: The Museum as Evidentiary Artifact," in *The Formation of National Collections of Art and Archaeology*, ed. Gwendolyn Wright (Washington: National Gallery of Art, 1996), 167 (emphasis in the original).

[18] Cœdès, *Collections archéologiques*, 17.

[19] Maurizio Peleggi, "From Buddhist Icons to National Antiquities: Cultural Nationalism and Colonial Knowledge in the Making of Thailand's History of Art," *Modern Asian Studies* 47, no. 5 (2013): 1520–48 (esp. 1540–48).

[20] As Cœdès explains, "Epigraphy furnished the historical background and a few reliable dates as guideposts. The minute study of the evolution of artistic forms established a relative chronology of the monuments, which the epigraphic evidence corroborated." See: George

Turn-of-the-century archaeology subscribed to theories of racial anthropology that held biological factors responsible for physical, behavioral, and cultural differences among populations. The author of the very first scholarly publication on Siamese sculpture, Alfred Salmony, then the deputy-director of the Museum of East Asian Art in Cologne before his migration to the United States, opined: "From such works of art as are found on Siamese soil it is often impossible to discover the racial affinity of their authors. This fact renders any historical classification by style especially difficult, whereas the European investigator is accustomed to look upon monuments as manifestations of a single race in its own particular habitat."[21] Salmony accordingly concluded: "There is, therefore, no such thing as a Siamese sculpture with separate and distinct stylistic epochs—*only a sculpture in Siam* ... One preponderate occurrence set the final and definite stamp upon it ... the immigration of the Thai."[22]

The Damrong-Cœdès art-historical classification sought, in fact, to trace the ethnic lineage of Siam's antiquities as part of the wider project of documenting the kingdom's monumental landscape. In this classification there are three periods, or schools (the term employed by Cœdès), that predate the political and cultural ascendancy of the Thais towards the end of the thirteenth century: Dvaravati, Srivijaya, and Lopburi. Under the label "Dvaravati" were classified the oldest antiquities that had been discovered in Siam by the 1920s: stone and bronze Buddha images, bas-reliefs, and votive tablets influenced by the Indian art of the Gupta period, dating from the sixth to the eleventh centuries, and originating from the area of Nakhon Pathom, whose early inhabitants were Theravada Buddhists of Mon ethnicity.[23] "Srivijaya," a name Cœdès derived from epigraphic sources as that of a kingdom centered in southern Sumatra, was employed to classify stupas and Hindu and Buddhist bronze images from Peninsular Siam, which bore stylistic similarity to the religious sculpture and architecture of eighth- to thirteenth-century Java. Despite the geographical location at the crossroads of the Malay world, the ethnic paternity of these works was more difficult to establish, in part because of the significant stylistic variety of the Srivijaya School. Finally, the label "Lopburi," derived from an outpost of the Angkor empire, qualified religious images and monumental remains in the Khmer styles of the eleventh to fourteenth century (i.e., Baphuon, Angkor Wat, Bayon), sited in, or recovered from, an area that spanned the lower Chaophraya River valley through the northeastern plateau.

The first manifestation of ethnic "Thai" artistry was assigned to the Chiangsaen period/school. Prince Damrong employed "Chiangsaen" as an umbrella term for the architecture and bronze sculpture of the northern kingdom of Lanna (centered in Chiangmai), from before the Thai conquest in the mid-thirteenth century through Burmese domination during the sixteenth to eighteenth centuries, up until the incorporation of Lanna by the Bangkok (Rattanakosin) kingdom at the end of the

---

Cœdès, *Angkor: An Introduction*, ed. and trans. Emily Floyd Gardiner (Hong Kong: Oxford University Press, 1963), 68.

[21] Alfred Salmony, *Sculpture in Siam* (London: Benn, 1925), 1. The book was concurrently published in a French edition as *La sculpture au Siam* (Paris and Brussels: G. Van Ouest, 1925).

[22] Salmony, *Sculpture in Siam*, 45.

[23] Knowledge of the Dvaravati culture has expanded considerably since the 1940s, when major archaeological discoveries were documented by Pierre Dupont's seminal study *L'archéologie mône de Dvaravati* (Paris: Publications de l'EFEO, 1959).

nineteenth century. Cœdès stated in his monograph that the Chiangsaen School had exerted the deepest influence on the evolution of Siamese statuary, and identified seven characteristics of the Buddha images produced by this school, as mediated by both the Burman kingdom of Pagan, and the sculpture of eastern India in the period of the Pala dynasty (eighth to twelfth centuries).[24]

Prince Damrong prefaced the examination of Sukhothai art in *Tamnan phra putthachedi* with a summary of the Buddhist revival in thirteenth-century Sri Lanka, and its importation into mainland Southeast Asia by reordained local monks. The monks, he said, brought back home from the South Asian island stricter monastic rules and knowledge of the Pali canon, as well as "a large body of Sinhalese superstitions." The localization of Sinhalese Buddhism was thus presented by Damrong as the *sine qua non* for the kind of Buddhist art that was produced in Sukhothai: "The dynasty of Pra Ruang came to power at Sukhodaya at about the same time that Sinhalese Buddhism was making rapid gains in Siam. That is why all the Buddhist cetiyas [*chedi*] of the Sukhodaya period belong to the Sinhalese Hynayana school." As for images, "the most important objects of worship in the Sukhodaya period," Prince Damrong distinguished among three periods on stylistic grounds: archaic, middle, and later. The latter period's image type, dating from the reign of Lithai (1347–c.1368), and exemplified by the famed Buddha Chinarat in Phitsanulok's Wat Mahathat, "was much imitated in the North as well as the South, but few of the imitators can match the original in beauty."[25]

While agreeing with Damrong's appraisal, Cœdès placed emphasis not on Sinhalese sculpture and architecture as the model the Thais emulated, but on Khmer statuary as the model from which they sought to move away:

> It was in Sukhothai, and in the flourishing cities of this small kingdom free from Cambodian domination, that during the second half of the thirteenth century the Thai artists produced the classic type of the Siamese Buddha, of which the Chinarat in Phitsanulok is the most accomplished specimen. This [type] appears, at least with regard to the Buddha image's facial features, to go in the opposite direction of the Khmer type of Lopburi by exaggerating certain characteristics of the Thai type of Chiangsaen: the arched eyebrows, hooked nose, small mouth, and very elongated face.[26]

As Cœdès suggested explicitly elsewhere, these stylistic characteristics, as well as the use of bronze as a medium for sculpture in the round and of stucco for relief, instead of the stone that was favored by the Khmers, might be seen as a "perhaps unconscious" artistic reaction by the newly independent Thais against their former dominators.[27]

---

[24] Cœdès, *Collections archéologiques*, 30.

[25] Prince Damrong, *Monuments of the Buddha*, 17–18, 22.

[26] Cœdès, *Collections archéologiques*, 32.

[27] George Cœdès (with Jean Boisselier and M. C. Subhadradis Diskul), *Arte Thailandese* (Rome: L. del Turco, 1964), 55. *Arte Thailandese* is the Italian-language version of the catalogue of a traveling exhibition that touched several European cities during 1964–65, translated from the original French, *Trésors d'art de Thaïlande. Catalogue de l'exposition au Musée Cernuschi* (Paris: Presses Artistiques, 1964).

Cœdès also took issue with noted Anglo-Ceylonese art historian Ananda K. Coomaraswamy, who, in his topical *A History of Indian and Indonesian Art* (1927), dated the appearance of "the classic Siamese type" to the turn of the second millennium CE. Cœdès countered that it was impossible to speak of "Siamese" art before the thirteenth century, for the polished images admired by Coomaraswamy could have hardly been created by "tribes" that were then still subject to Khmer authority, and were depicted in an Angkor Wat bas-relief as exhibiting the demeanor of *"véritable sauvages."* [28] By invoking the notion of savagery, Cœdès clearly distinguished the still barbaric *twelfth*-century Thais from the "Hinduized" (i.e., civilized) Khmers who ruled over them, and highlighted by contrast *thirteenth*-century Sukhothai as the birthplace of Thai civilization.

Cœdès's concern with the shifting power relations between the Thais and the Khmers might also be the reason for his addition of an eighth art school to the seven originally proposed by Prince Damrong. Cœdès named this school Uthong, after the principality whose last, eponymous ruler was believed to have founded the kingdom of Ayutthaya, and he employed it to classify Buddha images that had been recovered in the Chaophraya basin, but were reputed on stylistic grounds to be anterior to the Ayutthaya school. Uthong's supposed historical role as *trait d'union* between Sukhothai and Ayutthaya was thus translated in art historical terms into the transitional Uthong style, whose stylistic features blended, according to Cœdès, the Lopburi school's "Khmer" style and the Sukhothai school's "Thai" style.

As for the sculptural production of the Ayutthaya school, Cœdès excluded it entirely from his monograph (though not from the museum) on the grounds of its mediocrity.[29] Whatever its aesthetic motivations, such a damning appraisal must also be seen as the inescapable consequence of the canonization of Sukhothai statuary as "classic." According to the historicist law of the progression, maturation, and decline of art styles, this definition entailed that the subsequent style must mark a corruption or involution of the classic ideal. Jean Boisselier, a French student of Thai and Khmer art of the generation after Cœdès's, has this to say about Sukhothai Buddha images: "These works attained an unsurpassable peak in religious sculpture; beyond it, image makers could only lapse into conventionality, affectation, or caricature."[30] Cœdès's "Oedipal" theory that Sukhothai's plastic arts marked a more or less conscious rejection of the Khmer style by their former vassals diverged greatly, however, from the assimilationist perspective of Prince Damrong. The prince redoubled Thailand's founding myth through the myth of the Thais' intrinsic adroitness at appropriating, and inventively adapting, foreign cultural elements.[31] This myth underwent a revival at the time of the Thai media's enthusiasm for globalization in the early 1990s.

---

[28] Cœdès, *Collections archéologiques*, 28–29.

[29] Ibid., 33–35.

[30] Jean Boisselier, *The Heritage of Thai Sculpture*, trans. James Emmons (New York and Tokyo: Weatherhill, 1975), 132.

[31] A similar theory about the "the special skill of harmonizing objects from foreign countries [being] unique to the Yamato people" was articulated in contemporary Meiji Japan by the art historian and nationalist ideologue Kakuzo Okakura. See: Stephan Tanaka, "Imaging History: Inscribing Belief in the Nation," *Journal of Asian Studies* 53, no. 1 (1994): 32.

When the Tai became rulers of Sukhodaya, which had been founded by the Khmer long before, both Mahayana Buddhism and the Brahmanical religions were already established there, as well as the use of Khmer language and script ... The Tai knew how to pick and choose. When they saw some good feature in the culture of other peoples, if it was not in conflict with their own interests, they did not hesitate to borrow it, and adapt it to their own requirements. For example, they took a Khmer script and adapted it to produce one that would be suitable for the Tai language.[32]

Damrong's reference to the invention of the Thai script is most significant, for Cœdès himself had dated the Ramkhamhaeng inscription to 1292,[33] thereby confirming its status as the oldest extant specimen of Thai writing, and, hence, the single most important piece of evidence in support of the historical myth of Sukhothai as the cradle of Thai civilization. While there is no reason here to retrace the controversy concerning the inscription's alleged fabrication that erupted in the late 1980s,[34] it is worth noting that the controversy was definitely sealed by the inclusion of the inscription in 2003 on the register of the UNESCO Memory of the World Program (launched in 1992). The program's website states that the Ramkhamhaeng inscription, "not only records the invention of Thai language scripts that are the foundation of the modern scripts used in Thailand by sixty million people, its rare detailed description of the thirteenth-century Thai state of Sukhothai also reflects universal values shared by many states in the world today. Those values include good governance, the rule of law, economic freedom, and religious morality—in this case, Buddhism, one of the world's major religions."[35] Art patronage, admittedly, goes unmentioned in the list of "universal values" of which Sukhothai is taken to have been a notable example. However, since Sukhothai's sculpture is predominantly Buddhist,[36] it might be assumed that art patronage is included among those universal values.

---

[32] Prince Damrong, *Monuments of the Buddha*, 4–5.

[33] George Cœdès, "Notes critiques sur l'inscription de Rama Khamheng," *Journal of the Siam Society* 12, no. 1 (1918): 1–27; and "Nouvelles notes critique sur l'inscription de Rama Khamheng," *Journal of the Siam Society* 17, no. 3 (1923): 113–21. See also Cœdès, *Recueil... Première partie*. Before Cœdès's work, translations had been attempted by Père Schmitt (also in French) and Adolf Bastian and Francis Bradley (in English). The most recent English translation is that by A. B. Griswold and Praset na Nagara, *Journal of the Siam Society* 59, no. 2 (1971): 178–228 and reprinted in their *Epigraphic and Historical Studies* (Bangkok: The Historical Society, 1992), 241–90.

[34] See James R. Chamberlain, ed., *The Ramkhamhaeng Controversy: Collected Papers* (Bangkok: The Siam Society, 1991).

[35] See: http://www.unesco.org/new/en/communication-and-information/flagship-project-activities/memory-of-the-word/register/full-list-of-registered-heritage/registered-heritage-page-8/the-king-ram-khamhaeng-inscription/#c187113, accessed September 20, 2013. The phrasing in this document—"good governance" and "economic freedom"—uncannily echoes the neoliberal vocabulary discussed by Kasian Tejapira in Chapter 9 of this volume. Other documents from Thailand included in UNESCO's Memory of the World Register are the Archival Documents of King Chulalongkorn's Transformation of Siam (inscribed in 2009), the Epigraphic Archives of Wat Pho (inscribed in 2011), and—most recently and intriguingly—the Minute Books of the Council of the Siam Society (inscribed in 2013).

[36] See M. R. Subhadradis Diskul, *Hindu Gods at Sukhodaya* (Bangkok: White Lotus, 1990). The late Prince Subhadradis, a renowned art historian who studied in Paris under Philippe Stern, was a son of Prince Damrong.

REVISING THE PLOT

The first proposal of a revision of the Damrong–Cœdès art historical periodization was advanced by Reginald Le May—ex-British consul in Chiang Mai turned Siam government adviser turned art connoisseur and antiques collector—in a lengthy study published in 1938, which he presented as "a connected history of the different forms of Buddhist art which have flourished in Siam from the early years of the Christian era up to the end of the sixteenth century." Building upon the archaeological discoveries of the intervening decade, Le May proposed a nine-fold periodization that linked more closely artistic styles to the ethnic groups from which they had originated.[37] In reviewing Le May's book, Cœdès pointed out that he had not intended his own classification as definitive (he made no mention of Prince Damrong's contribution), and benevolently criticized Le May for improving rather than questioning it.[38] In fact, Le May tried to disentangle art history from political history by suggesting that the Thai school of Chiangsaen may have predated the Sukhothai school, and hence that "the artistic development of the Tai [Thais] did not necessarily correspond with the period of their independence." At the same time, however, he acknowledged that only the Sukhothai school had produced the "ideal" form—at least in "Siamese eyes": "In Siam itself, the importance of the new school of doctrine and art combined was made manifest at once, and within a hundred years practically the whole country had accepted and adapted the Sukhothai ideal to its own immediate needs."[39]

Le May employed a botanical analogy to explain the Sukhothai style's relatively short efflorescence after its geographical diffusion that followed the imposition of the Sukhothai kingdom's suzerainty over Peninsular Siam:

> Once the Tai had firmly established their dominion over the country from Sawank'alok in the north to Nakon Sritammarat in the south, the *national* art which was formed out of a coalescence of all the earlier forces and currents quickly blossomed and as quickly faded, just as we see the brilliant, scarlet blooms of the Flamboyant tree suddenly burst upon us in April in all their glory and then, within one short month, fall to the ground and wither away. It would seem as if, stability once attained, all impulse to create died, and a dead conventional form was soon evolved which has lasted till the present day.[40]

---

[37] Reginald Le May, *A Concise History of Buddhist Art in Siam* (Cambridge: Cambridge University Press, 1938), xi. The nine stylistic periods are: (1) Pure Indian (i.e., imported): up to the fifth century CE; (2) Mon-Indian (Gupta): fifth to tenth centuries; (3) Hindu-Javanese: seventh to twelfth; (4) Khmer and Mon-Khmer transition: tenth to thirteenth; (5) Tai [Thai] (Chiangsaen): eleventh to fourteenth; (6) Tai (Sukhothai): thirteenth to fourteenth; (7) Khmer-Tai transition (Uthong): thirteenth to fourteenth; (8) Tai (Lopburi): fifteenth to seventeenth; and (9) Tai (Ayutthaya): fourteenth to seventeenth.

[38] Review published in *Journal of the Siam Society* 31, no. 2 (1939): 192–201. To stress the point, Cœdès recounted (193–94) that one day, in Bangkok's Sampheng district, he had been approached by a Chinese antiques dealer who offered to sell him two Buddha-statue heads said to be in, respectively, the Dvaravati and Uthong styles—a marketing ploy, Cœdès cheekily remarked, that the dealer was unlikely to change after the publication of Le May's book.

[39] Le May, *A Concise History*, 108, 128-29.

[40] Ibid., 143.

Ironically, the rise of Ayutthaya in the second half of the fourteenth century was assumed to have caused the Thai "creative genius" to subside, even though Le May's appraisal was not as dismissive as Cœdès's, for he saw some merit in the earlier products of the "National School." Still, the "dead conventional form" that furnished the template of the Ayutthaya school's later production unequivocally bespoke the exhaustion of the Thai *Kunstwollen*.

Looking at the Sukhothai images with a sculptor's eyes, and from the aesthetic perspective of Hegelian Idealism, Corrado Feroci argued in a public lecture in 1948 that "by understanding the human form from life, and by endowing that form with a wonderful religious spiritualism, the Thai genius came to create one of the finest styles of Buddhist sculpture ever produced."[41] Feroci's questionable elucidation of the Sukhothai Buddha images as combining spiritualism with naturalism—in spite of their stylized, androgynous forms—informed the standing Buddha image (markedly more masculine-looking than the Sukhothai Buddhas) he sculpted in 1957 for the state-sponsored celebrations of the 2,500th Buddhist year.[42] That same year, at least according to a somewhat dubious account, a large plaster image cracked open, while being moved within Bangkok's Wat Traimit, to reveal a solid-gold image that was conveniently identified on stylistic grounds—without, however, the support of archaeological evidence—with a golden image (*phuttharup thong*) mentioned in the Ramkhamaheng inscription as being located in the middle of the city of Sukhothai.[43]

Feroci espoused further on the subject of Sukhothai sculpture in a booklet published a decade later in the Fine Arts Department's "Thai Culture Series," where he accounted for the appearance of the new style by reference to the "special circumstances" prevailing at Sukhothai in the second half of the thirteenth century:

No free people of the past have been ethically united without a common belief; for the Thai this belief was, as it is now, that of Hinayana Buddhism … The creation of a new style is possible only under special circumstances such as those prevailing at Sukhothai … The Sukhothai images of the Buddha, whether sitting, walking, or reclining, all have a particular undulating and soaring character, which seems to render immaterial the heavy bronze of which they are made. Yet this spirituality does not destroy the sculptural qualities of the statues. The human forms, simplified and idealized, are exquisitely modeled, and there is not disharmony between the abstract idea and its material realization.[44]

---

[41] Corrado Feroci, "The Aesthetics of Buddhist Sculpture," *Journal of the Siam Society* 37, no. 1 (1948): 43–44.

[42] Promsak Jermsawatdi, *Thai Art with Indian Influences* (New Delhi: Abhinav Publications, 1979), 103. For an image of Feroci's life-size statue of the Buddha, see Damrong, *Monuments of the Buddha*, ill. 27 (no pagination). In 1981, a 52-foot-tall (15.85 m) cast of this statue was installed in the park in Phutthamonthon (literally, "Buddha's mandala"), a ceremonial district in Nakhon Pathom province whose development had been initiated by Phibun Songkhram for the 2,500th Buddhist year (the park measures 2500 *rai*, equivalent to about 400 hectares or 990 acres). Phibun took on the organization of the 1957 celebrations as a self-promoting stunt, causing the young King Bhumibol to distance himself from the event. The king presided over the unveiling of the statue, whose installation marked the completion of the park, whose realization had resumed after a thirty-year hiatus in 1976—the year of political restoration and the launch of the ideological campaign centered on national identity and national heritage. See below, fn. 57.

[43] Griswold and Praset, *Epigraphic and Historical Studies*, 273, 513.

[44] Silpa Bhirasri [Corrado Feroci], *An Appreciation of Sukhothai Art*, 5.

In the mid-1950s, A. B. Griswold published two articles by which he claimed a place in the discipline of Thai art history as its first American student. In these articles he partly followed and partly challenged the prevailing scholarly consensus. The imagery of Sukhothai he introduced to the American public as "nothing less than an artistic revolution, as speedy and as thorough as any revolution in Buddhist art has ever been—excepting only that ancient revolution in which aniconic symbols gave way to the 'anthropomorphic' image." Thus authoritatively presented, Thai sculpture was redeemed of its apparent "dreadful monotony," and placed on the same level as other Asian artistic traditions that were then better known in America, such as China's or Japan's—an enticing proposition, especially for art collectors and museum curators. Concurrently, in addressing Thai art history cognoscenti, Griswold rejected the "myth" that the northern Chiangsaen school had represented the earliest artistic expression of the Thais, this primacy belonging, in his opinion, unquestionably to Sukhothai.[45]

Griswold's second article was later expanded into a full-length monograph with a preface by Coedès, *Dates Images of Northern Siam,* where he espouses the distinction between an image's "type" and "style." The former reflects iconography, and thus shows little, if any, change through time (as is the case, one may note, with other kinds of religious imagery, e.g., Russian Orthodox icons); and the latter results, by comparison, from the craftsman's skills and creativity. With regard to iconography, opined Griswold, the Sukhothai sculptor "invents nothing really new. But in style he is brilliantly original … The modeling has a trance-like quality; the gilded contours flicker, the silhouette leaps like a fire. From an aesthetic point of view the result is an astonishing invention; but in the eyes of orthodoxy it was no more—or rather no *less*—than a copy."[46] Glossing on the label of "classic," Griswold introduced a sub-classification of Sukhothai statuary: pre-classic (thirteenth century), high-classic (fourteenth to mid-fifteenth centuries), and post-classic styles (from the end of the fourteenth century—overlapping with the high-classic style). High-classic Buddha images, wrote Griswold (with arguably an echo of Feroci's), "are like visions seen in ecstasy."[47]

In 1967, Griswold produced the most detailed study of Sukhothai art to date to mark the inauguration of the Bangkok National Museum's new wing.[48] Also, in the mid to late 1960s, the monumental sites of Sukhothai and its sister towns, Si Satchanalai and Khamphaeng Phet, were the object of government initiatives

---

[45] See: A. B. Griswold, "The Buddhas of Sukhodaya," *Archives of the Chinese Art Society of America* 7 (1953): 5–41 (quote, 17); and his "Buddha Images of Northern Siam," *Journal of the Siam Society* 41, no. 2 (1954): 95–162. In the latter article (143, note 17), Griswold wrote with characteristic assuredness that "the erroneous formula … 'Early Chiangsaen art, plus Sinhalese artistic influence, equals Sukhodaya art'" should be reversed into "'Sukhodaya plastic influence, reacting on Indian Pala iconography, produces the Northern Thai Lion Series.'"

[46] A. B. Griswold, *Dated Buddha Images of Northern Siam* (Ascona: Artibus Asiae, 1957), 22–24 (emphasis in the original). Griswold's reflections on copying were developed in a number of his writings; besides those already cited above, see "Imported Images and the Nature of Copying in the Art of Siam," in Ba Shin, Jean Boisselier, and A. B. Griswold, eds., *Essays Offered to G. H. Luce,* vol. II (Ascona: Artibus Asiae, 1966), 37–73.

[47] Griswold, *Dated Buddha Images,* 23–24 (quote, 22).

[48] Griswold, *Towards a History of Sukhodaya Art.*

(approval of a comprehensive conservation plan, excavations, and restorations) as well as a visit by UNESCO experts.[49] By proposing a reign-by-reign reattribution of specific images and monumental remains, the monograph sealed Griswold's reputation as the paramount expert on Sukhothai art. Nothing in the book could, however, prepare the reader for the author's conclusions:

> The school of Sukhodaya was active for nearly 400 years, perhaps longer. It did not come to a sudden end, but gradually lost its identity. Its artists, with their superb technique, must have been the envy of both Ayudhya and Lan Na: both put them to frequent use ... Yet the Sukhodaya provinces themselves, in spite of all the vicissitudes, retained enough artists to cling to the old traditions to produce characteristic work as late as the seventeenth century. Even in the eighteenth ... the Sukhodaya craftsmen were still excellent ... execut[ing] with a perfection that would not have been unworthy of Lü Tai's [Lithai's] reign.[50]

This was a startling assertion, which contradicted the earlier theory of decline by proclaiming the longevity of the "classic" style of Lithai's reign not just beyond the fall of Sukhothai, but for such an extended period of time as to parallel the production of the Ayutthaya School. The stone Griswold metaphorically threw in the water of Thai art history was so large that it should have caused ripples as big as waves; in fact, nobody really took notice, and the Sukothai "golden age" of sculpture continued to be confined to roughly a century of duration.

Towards a History of Sukhodaya Art was the last of Griswold's creative contributions to the art history of Thailand even though he still contributed pieces to exhibition catalogues. By the late 1960s, he had embarked, in tandem with Prasert na Nagara, on the project of "Epigraphic and Historical Studies," published in the *Journal of the Siam Society* from 1968 onwards, to which he dedicated his best energies over the following two decades.

CONCLUSION

Renowned art historian Piriya Kraikrish, who acquired much notoriety in Thailand for suggesting the Ramkhamhaeng inscription to be a nineteenth-century forgery perpetrated by King Mongkut, has lamented recently that Thai art history has made little progress since its inception in the 1920s.[51] Regardless of whether one agrees with Piriya, it is certainly true that the discipline's royal genealogy, its continuous dependence on a textual discipline like epigraphy for dating artifacts, and the still dominant concern of its practitioners for questions of style, have shielded it from the disciplinary upheaval of the last three decades that goes under the name of "new art history" (alas, no longer so new). Little attention has likewise

---

[49] Maurizio Peleggi, *The Politics of Ruins and the Business of Nostalgia* (Bangkok: White Lotus, 2002), 40.

[50] Griswold, *History of Sukhodaya Art*, 60.

[51] Piriya Kraikrish, "Re-Visioning Buddhist Art in Thailand," *Journal of Southeast Asian Studies* 45, no. 1 (2014): 113–18.

been paid to the historiography of Thai art history.[52] As an astute scholar of the history of (Western) art history points out,

> From its beginnings, and in concert with its allied professions [connoisseurship, archaeology, museology, etc.], art history worked to make the past synoptically visible so that it might function in and upon the present; so that the present might be seen as the demonstrable *product* of a particular past; and so that the past so staged might be framed as an *object of historical desire*: figured as that from which a modern citizen might desire descent.[53]

The re-establishment of the Bangkok "national" museum in the mid-1920s, and the concomitant formulation of an art historical classification as the combined product of epigraphy, archaeology, and museology, reflected a growing national, as well as international, interest in Siam's past. Within the museum's rooms, Siam's historical landscape, as configured post facto by the territorial boundaries demarcated at the turn of the twentieth century, was mapped out spatially as well as chronologically. But the idea of an ethnically homogenous Thai *chat* (from Sks. *jati*, etymologically related to the Latin *natio* via the Greek cognate, *genos*) also necessitated racially inflected cultural origins. Sukhothai was thus envisioned, both historically and art historically, as the particular past of which present-day Thailand was the demonstrable product, the golden age of the archetypical Thai nation to which modern Thais should look as the source of their identity. This idea has been restated lately by two archaeologists, Charles Higham and Rachanie Thosarat, who argue that "with the establishment of Sukhothai, and the dynasty of which Ramkhamhaeng was a member, we encounter a society within which any modern Thai would have felt at ease."[54]

Thailand's past, so staged, was initially framed as an object of historical desire—that is to say, nostalgia—by King Vajiravudh's lamentation on the ruins of Sukhothai as the neglected legacy of "our Thai nation" (*chat thai rao*).[55] *Luang* Wichit Watthakan, the chief Thai nationalist ideologue in the 1940s and 1950s, in a public lecture on "Sukhothai Culture" (the neologism *watthanatham* was Wichit's coinage), also praised King Ramkhamhaeng's achievements—from the invention of the alphabet to the construction of roads, canals for irrigation, and religious monuments—opining: "Thailand was a strong and vibrant nation in the Sukhothai period ... and in the time that has elapsed since then we should have made great progress ... [But] it was not possible, since we cast off our fundamental culture."[56]

---

[52] Besides my two articles cited above, see Rungrot Thammarungruang, *Prawat naeo khwamkhit lae witthikhon khwa wicha prawatisat silpa thai* [Historical perspectives and methodological approaches concerning the discipline of Thai art history] (Bangkok: Muang Boran Publishing, 2008), Chap. 3.

[53] Donald Preziosi, "Art History: Making the Visible Legible," in *The Art of Art History: A Critical Anthology,* ed. Preziosi (Oxford: Oxford University Press, 1998), 18 (emphasis in the original).

[54] Charles Higham and Rachanie Thosarat, *Prehistoric Thailand: From Early Settlement to Sukhothai* (London, UK: Thames & Hudson, 1998; Bangkok: River Books, 1998), 215.

[55] King Vajiravudh, *Thiao muang phra ruang* (Bangkok: Bamruang Nukunkit, 1909).

[56] Scot Barmé, *Luang Wichit Wathakan and the Creation of a Thai National Identity* (Singapore: Institute of South-East Asian Studies, 1993), 160–61.

This nostalgic framing of the past reached its climax in the 1980s with the restoration—and not infrequently reconstruction—of the ruins of Sukhothai as well as of Sisatchanalai (the site of the kilns that produced the Sawankhalok wares) and Kamphraeng Phet (Sukhothai's walled outpost), under the Fine Arts Department's project of Historical Parks (*utthayan prawatisat*). Inaugurated with great pomp in November 1988, after a decade of nationally and internationally funded interventions, as part of the celebrations for King Bhumibol's achievement of the longest reign in Thai history, the Sukhothai Historical Park epitomizes the nationalist manipulation of heritage, particularly at the critical time of the legitimacy crisis of the late 1970s, and of the consequent (re-) creation of political myth, which is an ideological vehicle for a ruling group that is being challenged, or for an opposition group, to support its claim to power.[57] The restoration and recreation of the ruins of the "first Thai capital" amounted to the revival of the myth of Sukhothai as Thailand's golden age, a revival ironically supported also by the controversy that erupted over the Ramkhamhaeng inscription's authenticity, which provided a rallying focus for the defenders of national identity.

In addition to being displayed in temples as devotional icons, and in museums as artistic masterpieces, the androgynous Sukhothai-style Buddhas figure prominently also as cultural icons in the vacuous neo-traditional painting. Paintings in this genre were much sought after by nouveau-riche and corporate art collectors during the mid-1980s through mid-1990s as a commodified expression of the new capitalist classes' yearning for the alleged non-materialist, spiritual Thai soul—a quintessential instance of false consciousness. As openly articulated by the website of a royal foundation, neo-traditional art "has been a most effective catalyst for arousing patriotism and creating a sense of Thai unity . . . [for] it conforms to national cultural policy and values and ... it reinforces a desire to return to the roots of Thai civilization ... [and] to embrace the fundamental values of the Thai Buddhist tradition."[58] Such a trite definition, verging on involuntary self-parody, should not come as a surprise, for myth, as Ginzburg notes, is by definition a foretold tale, a narration whose content is already known.[59]

---

[57] Peleggi, *The Politics of Ruins*, 7–8, 21–24, 40–44. The argument made here is that Thailand's heritage conservation policy in general, and the Historical Park projects in particular, were responses to the legitimacy crisis that followed the student massacre at Thammasat University on October 14, 1976, and the consequent flight of thousands of leftists to the outer provinces. Once there, they temporarily joined the clandestine Communist Party of Thailand before returning to civilian life as a result of the amnesty offered to the insurgents in 1978.

[58] http://rama9art.org/artisan/6decade, accessed October 29, 2014. The "Rama IX Art Museum," a website that features Thai art from 1946 to 2006 (managed by the eponymous foundation, and created on the occasion of King Bhumibol's diamond jubilee), distinguishes three subject matters in neo-traditional art: "imagined indigenous space ... , rural scenes related to a nostalgic yearning for a lost past or cultural heritage, and the glorification of monarchical leadership and the accomplishments of the Royal Family. Typical of neo-traditional painting are scenes of Traiphum Phra Ruang ... [and] Buddhist subjects, such as Lotus Blooming in the Triple World, Toward Nirvana, Bhuddabhumi, (Celebrating the Holy Relic)... Scenes of the Lives of the Buddha (*thosachat*) are [also] favorite subjects ..."

[59] Carlo Ginzburg, *Occhiacci di legno—Nove riflessioni sulla distanza* (Milan: Feltrinelli Editore, 1998), 70.

PART II

POLITICAL AND BUSINESS CULTURE

CHAPTER FIVE

REPUBLICANISM IN THAI HISTORY

Patrick Jory

Prachathipatai ... *ratthaban thi mi chao mueang*
pen yai. Pen chue ratthaban thi mi
prathanathipodi pen hua na khu kap ratchathipatai
ratthaban thi mi phra racha pen yai[1]

Democracy ... A government dominated by
the citizens; the name for a government
headed by a president; the opposite of
monarchy, where the government is
headed by a king

One of the themes that runs through the scholarly work of Craig Reynolds is an interest in dissident, outsider figures in Thai history. It is out of respect for his work in this area that I have chosen to discuss the history of a political idea that, given Thailand's dominant royalist political culture today, counts as the most seditious—a culturally foreign, almost unthinkable idea for Thai people to entertain: republicanism.

Despite the general decline and fall of most of the world's monarchies over the last century,[2] significant sections of Thai society still cling to a staunch monarchism that not only situates the king at the apex of the political system, but privileges a feudal conception of social hierarchy. How do we explain this stubborn attachment to a pre-modern political institution despite Thailand's wholehearted embrace of other forms of modernity? Part of the answer has to do with the longevity of the current monarch, who, after coming to the throne in 1946, is now the world's longest ruling king—indeed, he is the world's longest continuous holder of any political office. Another factor has been the hegemony of the political bloc of the military, the bureaucracy, the judiciary, and the Bangkok elite, formed in the 1950s, which regards

---

[1] *Pathanukrom* [Dictionary] (Bangkok: Textbooks Bureau, Ministry of Religious Affairs, second ed., 1927), 428.

[2] Benedict Anderson, "Rachathipatai samai mai priap thiap radap lok" [Monarchy in Comparative Global Perspective] *Fa Dio Kan* 10, 1 (January–March 2012): 59–78.

the monarchy as guaranteeing its political and economic interests. A crucial reason has been the success of the education system and the mass media, both monopolized by the state, in protecting a version of Thai history that posits the monarchy as the saviour of the nation, a narrative that Thongchai Winichakul has usefully termed "royalist nationalism."[3] The expansion since World War II of Western scholarship on Thailand, dominated by the United States, rarely questioned the centrality of the monarchy to Thai nationalism.[4] Moreover, in line with its support for Southeast Asian nationalism, such scholarship generally accepted the royalist orthodoxy that the Thai kings, especially Mongkut and Chulalongkorn, had saved the country from colonial rule.[5] Western scholars usually saw the principal obstacle to "democracy" in the period in which they were writing as the military. A final, and by no means insubstantial, reason for the lack of critical scholarly attention to the monarchy has been the *lèse majesté* law, which formally protects the king, queen, crown prince, and regent from slander, and, in effect, outlaws any criticism of the monarchy whatsoever.[6] This law is the strictest in the world and in recent years has been enforced frequently.[7]

Given this combination of factors, one might think that republicanism is a stranger to Thailand. Yet despite the political, legal, and cultural obstacles to the expression of republican views today, the country has a long history of republican thinking. Indeed, it is one of the oldest in Southeast Asia—both in the narrower meaning of the desire to limit monarchical rule as well as in the more radical sense of abolishing the monarchy altogether and replacing it with a presidential system. The aim of this essay is to argue that, in contrast to the prevailing view that republicanism is alien to Thai political culture, republican thinking in Thailand, in fact, has a tradition that dates back at least to the late nineteenth century. It will identify the moment when republicanism first appeared and trace its development over approximately the last 130 years.

---

[3] Thongchai Winichakul, "Prawatisat thai baep rachachatniyom: jak yuk ananikhom amphrang su ratchachatniyom mai rue latthi phor khong kradumphi thai nai patchuban" [Royalist Nationalist History: From the Colonial Era to the New Royalist Nationalism], *Sinlapawatthanatham* [Art and Culture Magazine] 23, no. 1 (November 2001): 43–52.

[4] There are some exceptions—especially in the aftermath of the October 6, 1976, massacre of students and the rightist coup, in which the monarchy was heavily implicated. See, for example, Benedict Anderson, "Studies of the Thai State: The State of Thai Studies," in *The Study of Thailand: Analyses of Knowledge, Approaches, and Prospects in Anthropology, Art History, Economics, History, and Political Science,* ed. Eliezer B. Ayal (Athens: Ohio University, Center for International Studies, 1978), 193–247; and Anderson's "Withdrawal Symptoms: Social and Cultural Aspects of the October 6 Coup," *Bulletin of Concerned Asian Scholars* 9, No. 3 (July–September 1977): 13–30. Both essays are reprinted in Benedict R. O'G Anderson, *Exploration and Irony in Studies of Siam over Forty Years* (Ithaca: SEAP Publications, 2014).

[5] See, for example, David K. Wyatt, *The Politics of Reform in Thailand: Education in the Reign of King Chulalongkorn* (New Haven: Yale University Press, 1969); and Wyatt's *Thailand: a Short History* (New Haven, CT: Yale University Press, 1984). The latter work has for many years been the standard English language reference book for Thai history.

[6] See: David Streckfuss, *Truth on Trial in Thailand: Defamation, Treason, and Lèse-Majesté* (Oxon: Routledge, 2011); and Soren Ivarsson and Lotte Isager, eds., *Saying the Unsayable: Monarchy and Democracy in Thailand* (Copenhagen: NIAS Press, 2010).

[7] The effectiveness of the *lèse majesté* law has been enhanced by the new Computer Crimes Act, enacted after the 2006 coup, whose main target is on-line criticism of the monarchy.

EARLY REPUBLICANISM

One of the impediments to establishing the legitimacy of republicanism in modern Thailand is its obviously foreign origins. Unlike the earlier European precedents of republicanism in ancient Greece and Rome, or in the Italian city states of the later Middle Ages, the Thai historical tradition and the particular school of Buddhist thought that helped shaped Thai political thinking appear to have little to offer.[8] The real origin of republican thinking in Siam/Thailand dates to the latter part of the nineteenth century. It coincides with and was stimulated by, on the one hand, the imminent threat posed by the European colonial powers to the independence of the kingdom of Siam, and, on the other hand, the centralization of power by the Siamese monarchy under King Chulalongkorn.

The first official expression of the desire to limit the powers of the Thai monarchy appears in a petition submitted by a group of princes and royal officials attached to the Siamese embassies in London and Paris in 1885.[9] It came at a time of acute political crisis on mainland Southeast Asia. Britain was in the process of defeating the Burmese, Siam's centuries-old enemy, in the third Anglo-Burmese war, which would result in the annexation of the remaining areas of Burma not yet under British administration and the abolition of the Burmese monarchy. At the same time, after two decades of expanding French influence, Vietnam lost the last vestiges of its sovereignty following the defeat of its tributary overlord, China, in the Sino-French War of 1884–85.

While maintaining a superficially respectful tone, the petition was written in unusually blunt language. Noting the perilous situation in which Siam now found itself, and with an acute understanding of the current global situation, the petition set out in logical fashion the argument why the only chance that Siam had of saving its independence was to change its system of government. Concessions and

---

[8] This is not to say that a republican tradition in Buddhism and ancient India more generally could not be found if one looked hard enough, or, perhaps more importantly, if there was a contemporary political agenda that could stimulate such a search. The Buddhist theory of "elective kingship" set down in the Buddhist scripture the *Aggañña Sutta* explains the origin of the institution of kingship as deriving from a mythical time when the people *elected* the first king. He was given the title of *Mahasammata*, or the "Great Elect." After the 1932 overthrow of the absolute monarchy, Thai conservatives looking to give Thai kingship a "democratic" origin made reference to this theory; see Prince Dhani Nivat, "The Old Siamese Conception of the Monarchy," *Journal of the Siam Society* 36, no. 2 (1947): 91–106. Two decades after the establishment of the Republic of India, J. P. Sharma published *Republics in Ancient India c. 1500 B.C.–500 B.C.* (Leiden: E. J. Brill, 1968), which argued that India had a long and proud history of republican institutions. Some of the sources on which he based his argument, the Pali canonical scriptures and the Jatakas in particular, were well-known in the Thai Buddhist tradition (see my "A History of the Thet Maha Chat and its Contribution to a Thai Political Culture," PhD dissertation, Australian National University, 1998). Indeed, according to Sharma, there is "little doubt" that the Sakya clan from which the Buddha came was a "non-monarchical political community" (189). I am unaware, however, of any similar Thai endeavor to search its ancient political and traditions for republican precedents, let alone any attempt to celebrate them. I thank my colleague, Adam Bowles, for drawing this work to my attention.

[9] *Chaonai lae kha ratchakan krap bangkhom thun khwam hen jat kan plian plaeng ratchakan phaen din ror. sor. 103 lae phra ratchadamrat nai phrabat somdet phra chula chorm klao chao yu hua song thalaeng phra borom rachathibai kae khai kan pokkhrong phaen din* [The Princes and Royal Officials Offer their Opinion on Reforming the Administration of the Kingdom, 1885, and King Chulalongkorn's Speech Announcing the Correction of the Government of the Kingdom], Cremation Volume, Phra Anurakphubet (Tem Bunyarattaphan), Wat Makut Kasatriyaram, February 10, 1970.

compromises would not satisfy the great powers for long, as Japan had found out. Siam was in no position to compete with the Europeans militarily. The costs of expanding its armed forces were prohibitive, and obtaining the necessary military hardware from the Europeans would be problematic. Even if Siam defeated the Europeans in one battle, it would be unlikely that such victories could be sustained indefinitely, while defeat would bring demands for reparations and worse. Agreeing to become a buffer state between the regions controlled by the great powers was to risk having Siam's sovereignty reduced to a narrow strip of territory, where problems of law and order would inevitably provide the pretext for further European intervention. Awarding the Europeans trade benefits would not satisfy them for long. Treaties with the European powers were no guarantee of protection, as China had learned. Improving travel and communications meant that engagement with the Europeans would only increase in the future. And Siam could not hope for justice under international law, since those laws were written for the benefit of European powers and equal protections were denied to Asian countries, as Japan had found out.[10]

Quite apart from these outward threats to Siam's survival, however, the petition also explicitly acknowledged the weakness and backwardness of the present Thai system of government. Siam had both "good" and "bad" customs. Resisting the Europeans was not only unfeasible, but would obstruct the progress of Siam and its citizens and ensure the continuation of those "bad" customs. The concentration of power in the hands of the king and members of the royal family was dangerous. Justice and progress could only come to Siam with a European-style constitution.[11]

Having outlined the external threat to Siam and the country's internal backwardness, the petition presented a set of seven demands:

(1) that the kingdom's system of government be transformed from an "absolute monarchy" to a "constitutional monarchy," along the lines of countries in Europe and Japan;

(2) that a cabinet government should be established such that the administration of the country would be in the hands of senior officials appointed by the king, and that clear rules of royal succession would be put in place;

(3) that bribing officials should be outlawed and officials paid an adequate salary;

(4) that the people should be treated equally under the law;

(5) that customs or laws that were criticized by the Europeans and which obstructed the progress of the country should be abolished;

(6) that freedom of thought and speech and of the press be allowed; and

(7) that a meritocratic system of educated officials of the royal government be established.[12]

The petition also displays the embryo of a nationalist vision for the kingdom: "The heart of this proposal is to reorganize the country along European lines ... so that the people feel that oppression and injustice have ended and so they will love their country and realize that Siam belongs to them, and that they must look after

---

[10] Ibid., 8–19.

[11] Ibid., 12–13; 20, 23.

[12] Ibid., 23–25.

and care for it … "[13] There was "no other way" but to reform Siam's system of government according to the European model.

King Chulalongkorn's response to this radical proposal, which represented a sharp critique of his record of administration, and, indeed, a veiled attack on his authority, was seemingly measured. He replied that he was fully aware of the threat to Siam's independence, and of the constitutional systems in Europe that limited monarchical power. He agreed that Siam needed government reform. But he rejected the central demand for a constitutional monarchy. He argued that he was not an oppressive monarch like "those one reads about in the history of Europe, who had to be pressured to moderate their authority," and he was well aware of the dangers of oppressive rule, having seen it for himself in other countries. The main reason he could not agree to reduce royal power, he claimed, was the lack of qualified officials.[14]

In the aftermath of the petition's presentation, Prince Prisdang,[15] the leading figure behind the proposal, was demoted and eventually went into exile, returning only in 1911, after the death of Chulalongkorn.[16] The potential threat posed by the class of Western-educated aristocrats and nobles was partially neutralized by the court's co-opting of some of them into the system of royal administration, which expanded rapidly following the great reforms of royal administration introduced in 1892. In fact, the trend to absolutism that had so worried the drafters of the 1885 petition actually accelerated.

Yet it was an absolutism that was subject to the interests of European powers, most significantly the British. After the 1893 Paknam incident, which had almost led to the loss of the Siam's independence to the French as the drafters of the 1885 petition had predicted, the king appointed large numbers of European (especially British) "advisors," many of whom had served in other European colonial administrations, to overhaul the royal administration. Despite Siam's nominal independence, the royal administration in Siam was comparable to the colonial administrations that were being set up in British Burma and Malaya, the Dutch East Indies, and French Indochina, presided over by resident commissioners. The term "advisor" belies the preponderance and influence of Europeans over Siam's internal administration. The case of the Belgian international lawyer Gustave Rolin-Jacquemyns, who was appointed "General State Advisor," is illustrative. Rolin-Jacquemyns had been a one-time minister of the interior in the Belgium government and had had experience in the brutal colonial administration of the Belgian Congo, which was a virtual fiefdom of King Leopold II. Between 1892 and 1901, the crucial period of royal administrative reorganization, Chulalongkorn employed Rolin-Jacquemyns to oversee most of the major reforms. Such was his influence in the

---

[13] Ibid., 26.

[14] "Phraratchadamrat torp khwam hen khorng phu thi ja plian kan pokkhrong jor. sor. 1247" [King Chulalongkorn's Reply to Those Who Want to Change the System of Government], Chai-Anan Samudavanija and Khattiya Kannasut, eds., *Ekasan kan mueang kan pokkhrong thai phor. sor. 2417–2477* [Thai Political Documents, 1874–1934] (Bangkok: Social Sciences and Humanities Textbook Foundation, 1975), 76–81.

[15] On Prince Prisdang, see Tamara Loos's essay in this volume (chapter 3).

[16] B. J. Terwiel, *Thailand's Political History: from the 13th Century to Recent Times* (Bangkok: River Books, 2011), 205, fn 13.

kingdom that, as he remarked in a letter to an acquaintance, "all the important affairs of all departments pass through my hand."[17]

Thus, a symbiotic relationship developed whereby the monarchy granted the Europeans commercial and diplomatic concessions, the right of extraterritoriality, and almost half of the kingdom's territory[18] in return for their acquiescence to Siam's nominal independence. In this respect, the Thai monarchy can be seen to have become, as Carl Trocki has argued for traditional rulers in colonial Southeast Asia more generally, an "indigenous collaborator" with European imperialism.[19] In a similar vein, Kullada regards Siam in this period as having joined Pax Britannica, and that Siamese absolutism, and resistance to it, needs to be seen within this context.[20]

Criticism of absolutism, at least that which has entered the historical record, did extend outside elite circles, but not very far. It appeared in the emerging private print media, and was voiced by a new social group that Nakharin has referred to as "bourgeois commoners" (*phra kradumphi*).[21] Born close to but outside the aristocracy and the nobility, they had received a good, usually Buddhist, education, and often had studied English and other foreign languages. Some of them had traveled overseas and worked for European concerns. The most famous of them was Thianwan (1842–1915). Although a commoner, he was supposedly descended from a noble family of Ayutthaya. His uncle was the supreme patriarch, Sa (1813–99). As a teenager, Thianwan had worked as a petty trader, as well as on a ship trading with cities on the China coast.[22] He was ordained as a monk and studied at Wat Bowonniwet, where sons of the royal family had habitually been educated. After leaving the monkhood he returned to trading, including more stints of overseas travel. Upon his return he started working as a lawyer. He was deeply impressed by Western culture, and in his clothes and self-presentation he affected the manners of a Western gentleman. It was through his legal practice that he encountered his first problems with the royal government, which eventually led to his imprisonment for seventeen years on a contempt charge.

In prison Thianwan began to write about and propose reforms regarding the Thai kingdom. It is said that it was while in prison that he proposed the

---

[17] Walter E. J. Tips, *Gustave Rolin-Jacquemyns (Chao Phraya Aphai Raja) and the Belgian Advisors in Siam (1892–1902): An Overview of Little Known Documents Concerning the Chakri Reformation Era* (Bangkok: White Lotus, 1992), 203.

[18] Specifically, the territories of the left bank of the Mekong that later became "Laos," three provinces of the western part of Cambodia, and the northern Malay provinces.

[19] Carl Trocki, "Political Structures in the Nineteenth and Early Twentieth Centuries," in *The Cambridge History of Southeast Asia: Volume Two, Part One: From c.1800 to the 1930s*, ed. Nicholas Tarling (Cambridge: Cambridge University Press, 1999), 89. Later, a Maoist version of this view was put forward by the Communist Party of Thailand that since the second half of the nineteenth century Thailand had become a "semi-feudal, semi-colonial" state; see the discussion of this point in Craig J. Reynolds, *Thai Radical Discourse: The Real Face of Thai Feudalism Today* (Ithaca: Cornell Southeast Asia Program Publications, 1987), 149–69.

[20] Kullada Kesboonchu Mead, *The Rise and Decline of Thai Absolutism* (London and New York: Routledge-Curzon, 2004), 8.

[21] See Nakharin Mektrairat, *Kan patiwat sayam phor. sor. 2475* [Siam's 1932 Revolution] (Bangkok: Fa Dio Kan, 2010), 25–26.

[22] Walter F. Vella, "Thianwan of Siam: A Man who Fought Giants," in *Anusorn Walter Vella*, ed. Ronald D. Renard (Honolulu: Southeast Asia Papers, 1986), 78–91.

establishment of a constitutional system for Siam.[23] In 1898 he was released, and two years later he began publishing a journal, *Tunlawiphak photchanakit* (Words of Judgment), with a print run of around one-thousand copies.[24] In his journal he criticized what he saw as the evils of his time, including government corruption, poor education, gambling and other vices, slavery, polygamy, the lack of freedom of speech and freedom of the press, and, especially, problems with the existing system of government. He regularly decried the rapacity of government officials and the corruption within the legal system. Most significant was Thianwan's advocacy of a parliamentary system, with the United States and Japan being the most appropriate models. Not even the 1885 petitioners had gone that far:

We ought to prepare the day
For the people to voice their wishes
In a parliamentary system
If we wait too long
We shall fall behind the times

Let us be truly civilized and not tarry
Let us hurry to establish a parliament
And get the people to unite
And move on to freedom without delay
To care for our land and help our princes[25]

Thianwan's real influence is difficult to assess, but the fact that the literary-minded Crown Prince (later King) Vajiravudh (r. 1910–25) felt the need in 1905 to pen a sarcastic parody of Thianwan's demand for a parliament, depicting the chaos that would befall Siam if a parliamentary system were adopted, suggests that Thianwan's ideas were important enough in Siam's emerging public sphere for the future king to go out of his way to discredit them.[26]

Another source of criticism of the monarchy's autocratic rule was the Western-owned Thai-language press. One of the earliest of these publications was the magazine *Sayam Samai* (The Siam Times), run by an American missionary, Samuel J. Smith, between 1881 and 1885, for the purposes of spreading the Christian message. The significance of a mainstream publication run by a Westerner was that, under extraterritoriality laws, foreigners residing in Siam were not subject to prosecution by the Thai courts. That exclusion provided one of the few outlets for public criticism of the royal government. Besides the strident line of its American missionary publisher, local Thais, both elite and commoners, writing anonymously, could take advantage of *Sayam Samai*'s special legal status to criticize the royal government. Apart from articles devoted to Christian evangelism, the magazine harshly criticized what it saw as the many problems plaguing Siamese society, among them slavery, exploitation of the peasants, excessive taxation, and the corruption that characterized

---

[23] Ibid., 80–81.

[24] Chris Baker and Phongpaichit Pasuk, *A History of Thailand* (Cambridge: Cambridge University Press, 2005), 107.

[25] Ibid., 84. Given Thianwan's relationship with the royal authorities, the sincerity of the last line might be questionable.

[26] Ibid., 90.

the relationship between Chinese tax farmers and royal-government officials. *Sayam Samai* attributed these problems to Siam's absolutist system of government. Whoever was the head of government, it argued, should rule only with the consent of the people. The magazine offered examples of alternative systems, such as that of France, which had transformed itself from an absolute monarchy to a presidential system with a parliament.[27]

THE MATURING OF REPUBLICANISM

The seeds of republican thought were thus sown in Siam by the late nineteenth century, though its extent was limited to an educated, mainly Bangkok-based elite and a small but increasingly influential bourgeois class. International events in the first decade of the twentieth century fertilized those seeds. Japan's emphatic victory over Russia in 1905, and the revolution that erupted in Russia that year, led to the establishment there of a constitutional monarchy. (Tsar Nicholas II had visited Siam, and enjoyed close relations with Chulalongkorn.) Constitutional revolutions also brought an end to absolutist regimes in Persia in 1906, and the Ottoman Empire in 1908. In Portugal, the oldest colonial power in Southeast Asia, a revolution overthrew its monarchy in 1910, and transformed the country into a republic. But the most significant event of all for Siam was the Chinese Revolution of 1911, and the abolition of China's two-millennia-old imperial monarchy. Chinese revolutionary thought was already influential among Siam's large and rapidly growing Chinese community, which, if counted together with the assimilated Sino-Thais, made up perhaps half of Bangkok's population.[28]

In 1907, Sun Yat Sen had sent a colleague, Wang Ching-wei, to Siam to set up a branch of the Chinese Revolutionary Alliance, acting under the front of the Chung-hua Association. Sun himself visited Bangkok in 1908. Chinese-language newspapers espousing revolutionary ideas were founded during this period, and a Thai-language edition, *Jinno-sayam Warasap* (Siamese-Chinese Good Words), was also published for assimilated Chinese who had been educated in Thai and could no longer read Chinese.[29] In 1908, the Chino-Siam Bank was set up to receive deposits from local Chinese rice millers and merchants, but it also helped fund revolutionary activities.[30] Sun Yat Sen's doctrine of the "Three Principles of the People" (Nationalism, Democracy, and Welfare of the People), first enunciated in 1905, was translated into Thai and circulated in Siam.[31] Monarchies with which Siam enjoyed ancient relations were being toppled one by one and republican ideas were gaining a wider circulation as a consequence.

The culmination of this decade of international revolution was Siam's failed anti-monarchical coup in 1912 led by a group of junior military officers, the so-called

---

[27] Kullada, *Rise and Decline of Thai Absolutism*, 108–10.

[28] Baker and Pasuk, *A History of Thailand*, 102.

[29] G. W. Skinner, *Chinese Society in Thailand: An Analytical History* (Ithaca: Cornell University Press, 1957), 156–59.

[30] Ibid., 158.

[31] The Thai translation was "*latthi trairat*"; see Natthaphon Jaijing, "Jak 'khana ror. sor. 130' thung 'khan ratsadorn': khwam pen ma khong khwam khit 'prachathipatai' nai prathet thai" [From the 1912 Group to the People's Party: The Origins of "Democracy" in Thailand] *Sinlapawatthanatham* [Art and Culture Magazine] 32, 4 (February 2011): 89–92.

Kabot ror. sor. 130. The causes of the attempted coup, later referred to as a "revolution" in a memoir by two of its leading participants,[32] are subject to debate. An incident in 1909 in which some army officers were flogged on the orders of then Crown Prince Vajiravudh over a dispute involving some royal pages had caused strong resentment within sections of the army. The armed forces had expanded rapidly in recent decades. The junior and middle-ranking officers were drawn almost exclusively from the ranks of commoners, while commanding officers were mostly from the aristocracy. Bitterness at this barrier to career advancement was growing. There is also the possibility that ambitious members of the aristocracy dissatisfied with the new king advanced the chances of a coup.[33] Even so, the proximate cause seems to have been a budget crisis in 1908 that resulted in cutbacks to recruitment and promotions in the army and navy after a period of sustained expansion.[34]

The conspirators were led by Captain *Khun* Thuayhanphitak, otherwise known as "Mor Leng," a Thai of Chinese descent who served in the army's medical division. Meetings of the conspirators would begin with a lecture by Mor Leng, who, in unusually strong language, condemned what he saw as the most egregious evils associated with the absolute monarchy, including favoritism, the king's oppression and exploitation of the people, and royal profligacy. There were strong appeals to national sentiments. Potential conspirators were told that the backwardness of Siam's current absolute monarchy was holding back the progress of the nation.

Mor Leng's lectures also outlined the structures, advantages, and disadvantages of different forms of government: absolute monarchy, "limited monarchy," and a republic. He explained that countries where the people had brought the monarchy under constitutional rule or who had abolished it altogether, as in Europe or America, were making progress and had become more civilized because the people were now "free." He noted that Asian countries, too, were following this example: Japan, Turkey, and even China. Only Siam retained this "barbaric" system of rule.[35] On the republican form of government, he wrote:

> A republic is a country in which the monarchy has been abolished. Instead there is a committee [*thi prachum*] to govern the country strongly. The head of the government of the country is the President. The people or citizens all become the same class [*trakun*]. No one is allowed to be inferior or superior to anyone else, like in those countries with political systems that divide the people up into different classes making the feudal lords the highest class, then the nobility who are appointed by the king, then the commoner class and the low-class people, such as slaves. Put simply, the king elevates his own people to the highest level like angels and suppresses the people to become the lower class, like animals. Even those who are raised up to the nobility are just like the slaves of the king. This division of humanity into lower and upper classes means that people do not receive justice equally. Those in the higher classes are proud and arrogant and look down on the lower classes or oppress and exploit them at their pleasure.

---

[32] The Thai term was *"patiwat"*; see 2nd Lt. Rian Sijan and 2nd Lt. Net Phunwiwat, *Patiwat ror. sor. 130* [The 1912 Revolution], ed. Natthaphon Jaijing (Bangkok: Matichon, 2013).

[33] Especially the king's brilliant younger brother, Prince Chakrapong, director of the Military Academy and Minister of Defence; ibid., 156–57.

[34] Kullada, *Rise and Decline of Thai Absolutism*, 123–25.

[35] Ibid., 161–71

In a republic these social divisions have been abolished, and all the people are pushed into one class. Everyone possesses the same freedoms. There are no high-class or low-class people. [...] For this reason the people of all countries all want to change their form of government into a republic. At this time almost all countries around the world, large and small, are republics. For example, the countries on the American continent are all republics. In Europe, France and Portugal are republics. France was the first to begin this form of government. Portugal just changed last year. At this moment in China they are fighting fiercely to change its system of government to a republic.[36]

At a number of meetings a vote was held among the leading conspirators as to what they would do with Siam's monarchy. While some proposed a "limited monarchy" (i.e., a constitutional monarchy), the leading conspirators are said to have favored a republic.[37] Some reports claim that the conspirators had even drawn ballots to decide who would be the one to kill the king. It was the person who "won" the ballot, *Luang* Sinatyotharak (Yut Khongyu), who betrayed the plot to the head of the army, Prince Chakraphong.[38]

Despite the amateurish nature of the movement's organization, its half-baked plans for assuming power, and its members' limited political awareness, the plot appears to have been more than just a foolhardy adventure by a few discontented officers. The movement was said to have involved perhaps as many as three thousand people.[39] While its leadership was made up of mostly army and navy officers, some of those from the army were from units stationed outside Bangkok, as far away as the northern provinces. There were also some prominent civilians involved. The discovery of the plot captured international attention. The March 6, 1912, edition of *The New York Herald* ran the headline "Siam Has Caught Republic Fever," while another New York paper, *The Sun*, announced the news this way: "Want Republic in Siam."[40] After the plot was uncovered, three hundred people were arrested by the authorities and more than one hundred of them were sentenced to long prison terms, a number that was eventually reduced to twenty-three individuals. Even if the movement had been motivated by the career self-interest of the conspirators, or, indeed, was part of a deep court intrigue triggered by an unpopular monarch, it demonstrated the growing popularity of republican ideas

---

[36] Rian and Net, *Patiwat ror. sor. 130*, 251–52.

[37] Kullada writes, "Whenever a vote was taken, [those who advocated a republic] always won …" Those conspirators of Chinese descent are said to have favored establishing a republic, suggesting both the influence of Chinese revolutionary thinking and perhaps a heightened sense of resentment at official discrimination against the ethnic Chinese in Siam. See: Kullada, *Rise and Decline of Thai Absolutism*, 170. Natthaphon writes that the leadership favored a republic, but, following the increase in the numbers of members, at the last meeting before the planned coup those who favored a "limited monarchy" had a "slight majority." See Natthaphon Jaijing, "Sayam bon 'thang song phraeng': nung sattawat khong khwam phayayam patiwat ror. sor. 130," *Sinlapawatthanatham* [Art and Culture Magazine] 33, 4 (February 2012): 80.

[38] Yuth Khongyu later took part in the failed 1933 Boworadet rebellion against the People's Party, and was imprisoned, where he hung himself; see Rian and Net, *Patiwat ror. sor. 130*, 9.

[39] Baker and Pasuk, *A History of Thailand*, 111.

[40] "Miscellanea," in *Patiwat ror. sor. 130*, ed. Natthaphon, 330–31.

among a new, expanding, and increasingly politically influential class. Kullada refers to that class as "bourgeois bureaucrats"—educated commoners who entered the royal bureaucracy created by Chulalongkorn's great administrative reforms, but who were now finding their careers blocked by members of the aristocracy who held a monopoly on senior positions by birthright.

Following the successful coup against the absolute monarchy by the People's Party in 1932, the organizers of the 1912 plot received an official pardon from the new regime.[41] Moreover, the organizers were honored by Pridi Phanomyong as the forerunners of the 1932 revolution and, according to two of the leading conspirators, Rian Sijan and Net Phunwiwat (who wrote a memoir of the 1932 plot), were the inspiration for Pridi's own revolutionary ideas.[42] The 1912 plot thus entered the historical record as the first organized republican movement against Thai absolutism.

Another gauge by which to measure the influence of republicanism in Siam during this period are the measures taken by the government to shore up support for the monarchy. King Vajiravudh responded to this shock to his authority so early in his reign by attacking his enemies' ideas. The king penned a series of articles in the press criticizing the ethnic Chinese, whom he regarded as the most dangerous source of republican ideas. In one of his most famous articles, "The Jews of the East," which was obviously influenced by European anti-Semitism as well as European "anti-Sinicism,"[43] the king predicted that the problems caused by the Chinese in Siam would lead to their suffering the same fate as befell the Jews in Russia.[44] Vajiravudh condemned the turn of events in republican China as producing disorder and violence, and ignoring the voice of the people. The king took aim at those Thais who were either copying the "habits" of the Chinese or else "imitating the West" in demanding political reforms along the lines of political systems used in Western countries.[45] These criticisms can be seen as the first expression of a conservative argument mobilized to defend the monarchy that remains popular today, which depicts republicanism and political liberalization more generally as antithetical to the Thai nation. The king attempted to take the wind out of the sails of the republican-minded nationalists by situating the monarchy at the ideological heart of Thai nationalism, most famously through his coinage of the slogan "Nation, Religion, King," modeled on the British motto "God, King, and Country."[46] "Only those who are loyal to the King of Siam," the king wrote, "can be considered real Thais."[47]

The state education system gave the monarchy a powerful instrument by which to instil the value of loyalty to the monarchy in the class that represented the greatest

---

[41] Natthaphon, "Sayam bon 'thang song phraeng,'" 90.

[42] Rian and Net, *Patiwat ror. sor. 130*, 13. On the political thinking of the conspirators and their contribution to the thinking of Pridi and the revolution of 1932, see Natthaphon, "Jak 'khana ror. sor. 130' thung 'khan ratsadorn,'" 80–99.

[43] Skinner, *Chinese Society in Thailand*, 160.

[44] Matthew Copeland, "Contested Nationalism and the 1932 Overthrow of the Absolute Monarchy in Siam" (PhD dissertation, Australian National University, 1993), 37–38.

[45] Ibid., pp. 38–39.

[46] Walter Vella, *Chaiyo! King Vajiravudh and the Development of Thai Nationalism* (Honolulu: University of Hawaii Press, 1978), 33.

[47] "Asvabahu" (penname of King Vajiravudh); excerpt quoted in *Sinlapawatthanatham* [Art and Culture Magazine] 33, 4 (February 2012), 11.

threat to it, the future "bourgeois bureaucrats." The new education curriculum introduced in 1910, the first year of Vajiravudh's reign, differs noticeably from the 1905 curriculum with its clear emphasis on patriotism and loyalty to the monarchy.[48] One of the most famous and long-lived civics textbooks in the new curriculum, *The Good Citizen* (*Phonlamuang di*), first used in 1911, taught the importance of swearing lifelong allegiance to the king. Loyalty to the monarchy was also the subject of a popular essay penned by Vajiravudh during the same period, "Stirring the Spirit of the Wild Tigers" (*Pluk jai sua pa*). In it he recalled the history of kings who had defended Siam's independence, and exhorted Thais not to let anyone impugn the reputation of the monarch: "if anyone is critical of the king we must fight them with all our energy, even at the cost of our lives. We must defend and protect the king who rules over and protects our nation."[49] Laws criminalizing criticism of the monarchy in Siam were introduced in the years leading up to the failed coup, with the first law enacted in 1900 and a revised version in 1908.[50]

Despite the absolutist state's rear-guard action against those demanding a constitutional system and the more radical republican fringe, international events and Siam's extraterritoriality laws meant that Vajiravudh's new royalist nationalism did not go uncontested. The Russian Revolution of 1917, the abolition of monarchies in Germany and Austria-Hungary the following year, and the end of the Ottoman Sultanate in 1922 demonstrated that, globally, the republican tide was rising. As Matthew Copeland has shown, the difficulty of prosecuting foreign-registered newspapers, even those shell publications that effectively were run by Thais, meant that in the 1910s and 1920s Siam enjoyed a lively, critical press. Indeed, this period represents the emergence of "political journalism" for the first time in Siam, and the backwardness of the absolute monarchy was a constant theme of those who practiced it.[51] Ideas from the European modern political lexicon, such as "equality," "socialism," and "feudalism," became more widely discussed. Examples from European political history were used to throw light on Siam's current predicament. Vajiravudh was likened to profligate European kings, such as England's Charles I or France's Louis XVI, before their violent overthrow and execution. The 1917 Russian Revolution was frequently commented on favorably for the way in which it had supposedly brought to an end the system of exploitation of the peasant masses by the royal family and corrupt officials. In the aftermath of US President Woodrow Wilson's famous 1918 "Fourteen Points" statement and the 1919 Paris Peace Conference, some newspaper columnists turned Vajiravudh's royalist nationalism on its head by representing the Siamese monarchy itself as the obstacle to national self-determination.[52] Siam was compared to other "slave states," such as colonized Burma and Cambodia, where a Europeanized elite looked down upon and exploited the Thai people, while the monarchy did the bidding of the European colonial

---

[48] Rangsima Khositangkun, "Naew khwam khit ruang nathi phonlamuang nai baep rian prathomsuksa (por. sor. 2435–2533)" [The Idea of the Citizen's Duty in Primary School Textbooks, 1892–1990] (master's thesis, Thammasat University, 1996), 51.

[49] Quoted in ibid., 4

[50] Streckfuss, *Truth on Trial in Thailand*, 87–93.

[51] Copeland, "Contested Nationalism," especially 51 ff.

[52] Ibid., 63–66.

powers.[53] In this counter-nationalism approach, the absolute monarchy was depicted as the real obstacle to the Thai nation's progress.

The popularity of republican ideas among the educated elite in Siamese society may be judged by the apparent ease and lack of violent resistance to the overthrow of the absolute monarchy by the People's Party in 1932. It is apparent in the blunt language of the famous "Declaration of the People's Party Number 1," issued on the day of the coup, and believed to have been drafted primarily by the French-trained lawyer Pridi Phanomyong:

[...] The king's government does not govern the country for the people, as in other countries. The king's government treats the people like slaves (called "serfs" or "servants"), or like animals; they are not treated like people [...] In no other country in the world are the feudal lords given as much money as they are here, except the Czar and the Kaiser, who have already been dethroned by their nations [...]

You the People should know that this country belongs to you, not to the king as you have been deceived into thinking. [...] In fact, the money that has been collected by the feudal lords should have been used to develop the country and provide employment [...] but the feudal lords have not done this. They will continue to suck your blood. Whatever money is left they will send it out of the country and prepare to leave when the country goes into decline, leaving the people starving. This is their wickedness.

[...] On the question of the head of state, the People's Party does not wish to seize the throne. It will invite this king to continue in his office as king, but he must be placed under the law of the constitution governing the country. He will not be able to act of his own accord without receiving the approval of the House of Representatives. The People's Party has informed the king of its wish. We await his reply. If the king refuses the invitation or does not reply by the deadline, selfishly believing that his power has been reduced, then he will be judged to be a traitor to the nation. *It will be necessary to govern the country as a republic* [prachathipatai]; *that is, the head of state will be a commoner appointed by the House of Representatives for a fixed term of office* [...][54]

The 1932 overthrow of the absolute monarchy is now regarded as representing the beginning of Thai "democracy." But as the highlighted sentence from the declaration shows (see above), the term *"prachathipatai"*—normally translated today as "democracy"—when used in the People's Party's first public announcement actually conveyed the meaning of "republic," that is, a state *without* a hereditary monarchy in which the head of state is appointed for a fixed term. In fact, as Nakharin has pointed out, in the original 1932 draft of the declaration, the Thai word *"prachathipatai"* was followed by the English translation, "republic."[55] This was not a

---

[53] Ibid., 178–79.

[54] Emphasis added. See: "Prakat khana ratsadorn chabap thi 1" [People's Party Announcement No. 1] *Sathaban pridi phanomyong* [Pridi Phanomyong Institute], http://www.pridi institute.com/autopage/show_page.php?h=11&s_id=19&d_id=19, accessed July 9, 2013.

[55] Subsequent publications of the declaration, such as the well-known 1975 collection of Thai political documents edited by Chai-anan Samutwanit and Khattiya Kannasut, omitted the

political sleight of hand. In official dictionaries from this period, both Thai-to-Thai and Thai-to-English, the common translation of the Thai word *prachathipatai* was "republic."[56] Before 1932, Pridi himself had taught his law students that there were two types of "democracy": a country with a president as the head of government, as in France, or a government in which executive authority lay with a committee, as in the Soviet Union.[57]

Another notable feature of the declaration is the strident language in which it was written. Not only are the king and "feudal lords" accused of being the root cause of all kinds of suffering experienced by "the people," but the declaration eschews the standard convention of using "royal language" (*rachasap*) when addressing or referring to royalty. In a kind of linguistic republicanism, the king is referred to using the same language as one would use when talking to commoners. Given that this first public announcement by the People's Party must have been designed to garner maximum public support during a politically critical period, the choice of words suggests that Pridi, at least, believed that republican ideals were widely accepted in those sections of Thai society whose support the People's Party needed the most.[58]

Within the People's Party itself there was dissension on the question of what would happen should the king refuse to submit to a constitution. The text of the official letter submitted to the king demanding a constitution (signed by *Phraya* Phahonphayuhasena, *Phraya* Songsuradet, and *Phraya* Ritthiakhane) stated that should the king refuse to submit to the constitutional form of government being offered by the People's Party, a new king would be chosen from among the other princes. According to Nakharin, this change from Pridi's more radical position regarding the declaration's wording was favored by senior military officers within the People's Party.[59] It is intriguing to speculate how close Siam may have come to formal republican rule if King Prajadhipok had refused to agree to the People's Party's demands. In the end, the king accepted its demands, and his signing of the provisional constitution of June 27 formally transformed Siam into a constitutional monarchy.

Yet the place of the monarchy within the new system was still uncertain. A permanent constitution introduced in December 1932 recovered some of the

---

English translation of *prachathipatai*; see Nakharin, *Kan patiwat sayam phor. sor. 2475*, 306, fn. 1. This latter omission was presumably made for reasons of political sensitivity, coming at a time when the King was increasingly politically active.

[56] Nakharin, *Kan patiwat sayam phor. sor. 2475*, 309, fn. 2. In the 1927 dictionary produced by the Ministry of Religious Affairs, the translation of *prachatipatai* reads: "*Ratthaban thi mi chao mueang pen yai. Pen chue ratthaban thi mi prathanathipodi pen hua na khu kap ratchathipatai ratthaban thi mi phra racha pen yai*" [A government dominated by the citizens; the name of a government headed by a president; the opposite of monarchy, where the government is headed by a king]; see *Patanukrom* [Dictionary], 428. The word *prachathipatai* is also translated as "republic" in C. Dansuputra, *Scholars' Siamese–English Dictionary: A Useful Manual for Students of Both Languages Containing More Than 13,500 Entries* (Bangkok: Amnuay Silpa School, 1936). My thanks to Sophie Viravong of the Thai collection of the National Library of Australia for drawing my attention to this reference.

[57] Natthaphon, "Jak 'khana ror. sor. 130,'" 93.

[58] The United States Legation in Bangkok had reported that "the movement has been very popular as the people are generally tired of the autocratic rule of the Royal Family." See: Benjamin Batson, *The End of the Absolute Monarchy in Siam* (Singapore: Oxford University Press, 1984), p. 240.

[59] Nakharin, *Kan patiwat sayam phor sor. 2475*, 309.

monarchy's lost powers. What accentuated the question of the monarchy's role was Pridi's introduction in March 1933 of his "Outline of an Economic Plan," which argued essentially for the implementation of a system of state control over the economy. The king, in his formal response to the proposal, condemned the plan as "communistic." It was also opposed by conservative factions, both within and outside the People's Party. The crisis caused by Pridi's economic plan led to the closing of parliament, the dissolution of the cabinet and the king's appointment of a new cabinet, and Pridi's own voluntary exile for a short period. The struggle between the People's Party and the forces loyal to the monarchy came to a head with the failed Boworadet Rebellion in October 1933, ending with the routing of royalist forces. The People's Party imprisoned over two hundred royalist supporters of the rebellion, including some princes, with many others going into voluntary exile. King Prajadhipok himself fled into exile before eventually abdicating in 1935. The People's Party appointed the young Ananda Mahidol as the new king, who was then being educated in Switzerland with his younger brother, Bhumibol. As a result, over the next decade Siam was without a resident king. This was the closest Thailand came to becoming an actual republic.

FROM LIBERAL REPUBLICANISM TO COMMUNIST REPUBLICANISM

The period leading up to the November 1947 coup saw the growth of liberal republicanism in Thailand. However, a number of developments toward the end of WWII brought this era to an end. The Phibun government's decision to ally with the Japanese and declare war on the Allies led to a fracturing of the ideological unity within the People's Party. Following Japan's defeat, Phibun's ill-fated decision created significant problems for Thailand's relations with the victorious Allied powers, including demands for reparations and war-criminal trials for some of the country's leading politicians. The country's economy also suffered greatly as a result of the war.

Perhaps most significantly, Pridi's decision in 1945 to reconcile with royalist forces by offering an amnesty for royalist prisoners incarcerated since the 1930s, and to rehabilitate the image of former king Prajadhipok (whose picture had been banned from being displayed due to his alleged involvement in agitation against the People's Party), allowed a regrouping of royalist forces. Yet the royalists never got over their suspicion of Pridi's real intentions toward the monarchy. Following the shooting death of King Ananda Mahihol in June 1946, rumors were stoked that Pridi had had the young king assassinated in order to bring about a republic. Royalist attempts to implicate Pridi in the king's death were a major factor behind the 1947 conservative coup that overthrew the government Pridi was backing and forced him to flee into exile. That coup marks the beginning of the restoration of the monarchy's political position under the leadership of the military's conservative faction. Later, during the Sarit dictatorship (1958–63), US support for the role of the monarchy in propaganda campaigns aimed at countering communist influence in Thailand helped seal the return of the monarchy to the apex of Thai politics.

Nevertheless, the decade following the death of King Ananda Mahihol was a perilous one for the Thai monarchy. Rumors of Bhumibol's involvement in his brother's assassination placed his future, and that of the monarchy, in question. According to Field Marshal Pin Choonhavan, one of the November 1947 coup leaders, the coup had been carried out to prevent Pridi's supporters from publicly naming the person who had killed the king, and thus gaining an advantage for establishing a republic.[60] As Natthaphon Jaijing has shown, records of the British and American Embassies reveal that there were persistent rumors throughout the 1950s that Phibun, Police Chief General Phao Siyanon, and the exiled Pridi and his supporters were considering using the circumstances surrounding the regicide as a political weapon against the royalists and as ammunition for establishing a republic.[61] However, with the onset of the Cold War and the United State's realization that the monarchy was extremely useful in propaganda campaigns against communism, US officials became increasingly wary of republican sentiments.[62]

By the end of the 1940s, with the liberal wing of the former People's Party in disarray, the only significant political group with a political platform openly advocating republicanism was the communist party. The origins of communism in Thailand go back to the late 1920s when its influence grew among the populations of ethnic Chinese and Vietnamese. The Communist Party of Thailand (CPT) was officially founded in 1942. It experienced growing popularity over the decade, partly as a result of Pridi's lifting of anti-Communist legislation between 1946 and 1948. By the end of the decade, with the communists' victory in China as well as the appearance of Marxist journals in Thai, such as *Aksornsan*, and the writings of Thai intellectuals, such as Supha Sirimanon and Kulap Saipradit, Marxism emerged as a mainstream vehicle with which to critique Thai society.[63] That communism implied republicanism was an article of faith among the royalists. As Somsak has argued, for the royal family and its supporters, "the threat of communism and the threat of republicanism were one and the same thing."[64] Pridi's attempt to introduce his economic plan in 1933 had been the catalyst for the government's decision to enact Siam's first Anti-Communist Act in the same year. The leaders of the royalist Boworadet rebellion later that year also cited Pridi's "communist policies" as one of the reasons for their actions and demanded that the monarchy be safeguarded by the government "for eternity."[65]

The first systematic analysis of Thai society from a Marxist perspective was Udom Sisuwan's *Thailand: A Semi-Colony*, published in 1950.[66] The book would provide the basic framework for the way the monarchy was viewed within Thai Marxism until the decline of the left in Thailand in the early 1980s. However, the books critique of the monarchy also represents a continuity with earlier liberal republican arguments discussed above. Udom argued that since the mid-nineteenth

---

[60] Natthaphon Jaijing, "Kan mueang thai samai jorm phon por phibun songkhram phai tai rabiap lok khong saharat amerika (phor. sor. 2491–2500) [Thai politics in the Era of Field Marshal Phibunsongkhram under the US World Order, 1948–1957] (doctoral thesis, Chulalongkorn University, 2009), 65.

[61] Ibid., 202–25.

[62] Ibid., 202, 221.

[63] See: Kasien Tejapira, "Commodifying Marxism: the Formation of Modern Thai Radical Culture, 1927–1958" (PhD Thesis, Cornell University, 1992), 290–94, 417–23; and Somsak Jeamteerasakul, "The Communist Movement in Thailand" (PhD Thesis, Monash University, 1993), 267–333.

[64] Somsak, "The Communist Movement in Thailand," iv.

[65] Ibid., 122.

[66] Aran Phromchomphu (Udom Sisuwan), *Thai kueng mueang khun* [Thailand: A Semi-Colony] (Bangkok: Mahachon, 1950).

century, with the coming of imperialism and capitalism, the feudal rulers of Thailand had had to adapt themselves to the new international situation. King Chulalongkorn's great administrative reforms essentially represented the monarchy's accommodation of the new status quo determined by European imperialism. These reforms not only enhanced the power of the "feudal class," but made it dependent on foreign capital. Since that time, Thailand had become a "semi-colonial, semi-feudal society." Udom's work also represented a break with the 1932 revolution and with Pridi himself. For Udom, 1932 represented not a revolution, but merely a coup d'état, since Thailand's status as a "semi-colonial, semi-feudal society" continued. "The feudal class has had its political rights restricted, but its vast economic influence has remained intact. The same is true for the imperialists' influence." As for the Thai people, they were still subject to "feudal and semi-feudal exploitation."[67] The book ended with a call to "overthrow imperialist influence and wipe out the remnants of feudalism."[68] Such a call naturally implied the ultimate objective of a republic. The analysis of Thai society provided by Udom's book became official doctrine for members of the CPT, and was influential among the Thai left for perhaps a generation.[69]

Following the political decline of the People's Party, the banner of republicanism in Thailand was not abandoned entirely but was taken up by the CPT. By then, however, the political environment both within Thailand and internationally meant that promoting republicanism involved far greater challenges than had been the case earlier. Republicanism in the first half of the twentieth century had been encouraged by a seemingly inevitable international trend toward republican forms of government, a publishing environment in Siam under the absolute monarchy in which newspapers advocating republican ideas took advantage of the protection afforded them by the extra-territoriality laws, and, after 1932, a political regime in the People's Party that was sympathetic to republican principles. By contrast, in 1952, a new anti-communist law was enacted and the government carried out a crackdown on communists and suspected communists. Following Sarit's 1958 coup and the establishment of a conservative military dictatorship, the campaign against communism intensified and communist activity was pushed further underground. With the escalation of the Cold War in Southeast Asia, the United States provided massive financial, military, and logistical support for the suppression of communism. The government embarked on an ideological campaign that placed the monarchy at the center of a new conservative nationalism, targeting not just the small, educated upper and middle classes, as in the days of the absolute monarchy, but now the entire nation.[70] To carry out this campaign, the new conservative dictatorship had at its disposal two key instruments of state propaganda: the education system and modern mass media. The result was that, after the ousting of the leaders of the military regime following massive student demonstrations in October 1973, the monarchy emerged as the key political player for the first time since the end of the absolute monarchy in 1932.

---

[67] Quoted in Somsak, "The Communist Movement in Thailand," 273.

[68] Ibid., 276.

[69] Ibid.

[70] Thak Chaloemtiarana, *Thailand: the Politics of Despotic Paternalism*, revised edition (Ithaca: Cornell Southeast Asia Program Publications, 2007).

The short-lived period of political openness between 1973 and 1976 saw the growing influence of Marxism among students, workers, and the rural population. Republican ideas became increasingly associated with an opposition to *sakdina*, or feudalism, a concept that was developed in and popularized by Jit Phumisak's *The Real Face of Thai Feudalism Today*.[71] The work was first published in 1957, then banned, and republished after the 1973 student uprising, going on to enjoy "immense popularity."[72] Although the work was unfinished and dealt almost entirely with the historical formation of Thailand's "feudal" system,[73] the republican sentiments of this emblematic text of the Thai Left in the 1970s should not be doubted. As Jit wrote in the introduction: "... The principal enemies that must be driven away with all urgency are the imperialists without and the *saktina* within."[74] Those sentiments appear again in the editor's note in the 1957 edition of the book, which explain that "this work is still unfinished ... We will come to the economic, political, and cultural role of the *saktina* today, and we end with *the means by which the People will liberate themselves from semi-saktina semi-colonial [conditions]*."[75]

The growth of the left in the 1970s and the increasing influence of the CPT on student politics attest to the enduring popularity of republican political thought. Thai society become increasingly polarized. The popularity of left-wing political parties and the frequency of strikes and demonstrations led to a violent reaction from the right. Royalist movements like Nawaphon, the Red Gaurs, and the Village Scouts were set up to protect the monarchy and fight "communism." By 1975–76, the leaders of farmers' associations were being frequently assassinated. In 1976, the secretary general of the Socialist Party, Boonsanong Punyadhoyana, was killed, and there were frequent attacks on other left-wing parties and their candidates.[76] The king himself was active in rallying violent forces to defend the monarchy.[77] The victory of communist forces in Vietnam, Laos, and Cambodia in 1975 and the establishment of three new socialist republics galvanized conservative forces in Thailand to ward off communism and save the monarchy. Following a massacre of students at Thammasat University by Nawaphon, the Red Gaurs, the Village Scouts, and pro-monarchy border police units on October 6 1976 the military seized power in a coup and ushered in a regime that would make the preservation of the monarchy its highest priority. The maximum penalty for *lèse majesté* was more than

---

[71] Jit Phumisak, *Chomna sakdina thai* [The Real Face of Thai Feudalism] (Bangkok: Chomrom Saeng Tawan, 1974). The 1957 version had a slightly different title, "The Real Face of Thai Feudalism Today"; see Reynolds, *Thai Radical Discourse*, 177.

[72] Reynolds, *Thai Radical Discourse*, 167.

[73] Ibid., 11–18.

[74] Ibid., 4. I used Reynolds's translation of *The Real Face of Thai Feudalism Today* and retained his transliteration of *saktina*. On Reynolds' distinction between *sakdina* and *saktina*, see: ibid., 152.

[75] Emphasis added; see: ibid., 143.

[76] See Pasuk Phongpaichit and Chris Baker, *Thailand: Economy and Politics* (Oxford: Oxford University Press, 1995), 306–11.

[77] On King Bhumibol's role in whipping up anti-communist sentiment, see Somsak Jeamteerasakul, "Rao su: phleng phra ratchaniphon kan mueang kap kan mueang pi 2518–2519" [We Will Fight! The King's Political Songs and Politics 1975–76], in *Prawatisat thi phung sang: ruam bot khwam kiao kap karani 14 tula lae 6 tula* [The History that Has Just Been Constructed: Collected Articles on 14th October and 6th October] (Bangkok: Samnakphim 6 Tula Ramluek, 2544), 115–48.

doubled to fifteen years[78] and state indoctrination programs identifying the monarchy as the central institution of the nation were intensified. As in earlier periods when the monarchy's authority was challenged, the vigor with which state propaganda emphasized the centrality of the monarchy to the Thai nation after 1976 was a measure of the perceived strength of the republican threat.

The real blow to Thai republicanism under the leadership of the CPT came with the collapse of the party in the early 1980s and the end of its jungle-based insurgency. The significance of this historic defeat was that it left Thailand with neither a Marxist critique of the monarchy nor the liberal one, which had more or less been extinguished by the 1950s. From 1980 to 1988, former commander of the army and palace favorite General Prem Tinsulananda held the prime ministership, ensuring royalist political control. Royalist indoctrination programs that had been ramped up in the aftermath of the 1976 coup continued apace. As a result, the monarchy achieved a position of ideological hegemony perhaps unmatched since early in the century. Indeed, the nature of the monarchy's popularity changed due to the expansion and increasing sophistication of the mass media, especially television, which penetrated the lives of the Thai populace in an unprecedented way. The monarchy's position in Thai society expanded beyond its relations with the politically influential elite and developed into a mass phenomenon, what Somsak has referred to as "mass monarchy."[79]

CONCLUSION

It is clear, then, that in contrast to the political and cultural hegemony that the monarchy currently enjoys, Thailand in fact has a long and continuous history of republican thinking dating back over a century. That this history is poorly acknowledged is due primarily to political and legal reasons—the hegemony of the monarchy and the military since the late 1950s, and the effectiveness of the *lèse majesté* law. The collapse of the Left in the early 1980s led to a hiatus in open expressions of republican thinking due to the absence of organized political support.

Yet the more liberal political climate of the late 1990s, the advent of a new media form—the Internet—and, most importantly, the Thaksin government's conflict with the palace starting in 2005, has opened up a space for the return of republican ideas. These ideas have been expressed in new academic journals, including *Fa Dio Kan* and *An* and their associated publications; in the debates on blogs, web boards, Facebook walls, and on YouTube sites, all of which run the gauntlet of the *lèse majesté* law; and, since 2007, the Computer Crimes Act. Many of the older familiar motifs of Thailand's republican history are discussed in these forums, including the comparison of Thailand's situation with the 1789 French Revolution or the 1917 Russian Revolution. There is renewed scholarly interest in the failed coup against the absolute monarchy in 1912 and the successful one of 1932.

Outside of intellectual circles, an increase in anti-monarchical sentiment can be seen in the "political schools" that have been set up around the country by the

---

[78] Streckfuss, *Truth on Trial in Thailand*, 105.

[79] Somsak Jeamteerasakul, "Mua nai luang prachuan pi 2525 lae khor sanoe wa duai sathaban kasat baep muan chon" [The King's Illness in 1982 and a Proposal about the Phenomenon of Mass Monarchy], http://somsakwork.blogspot.com.au/2007/11/2525-mass-monarchy.html, November 15, 2007, accessed August 21, 2013.

United Front of Democracy against Dictatorship (UDD), and expressions of republicanism among the radical wing of the Red Shirts. The struggle between a parliament of elected politicians and the political bloc made up of the military, the monarchy, the judiciary, and the Bangkok elite has stimulated a reconnection with Thailand's long republican tradition. It has also led to a re-examination of the meaning of "democracy," with both sides to the conflict claiming democratic credentials.

How widespread is republicanism in Thailand today? This is a notoriously difficult question to answer, given the constraints imposed by the *lèse majesté* law. Publicly admitting to republican views would constitute a criminal offense. No polls on the level of republican sentiment can be carried out, and research is exceedingly difficult on such a sensitive topic. Yet the absence of open expressions of republicanism—and, by contrast, the daily barrage of royalist propaganda—should not be taken as evidence of its lack of influence. Royalists certainly view the monarchy as being in great danger.[80] Since the 2006 coup, royalist forces have consistently and publicly invoked the fear that Thaksin and his supporters are a threat to the monarchy, yet in subsequent elections, Thaksin's political parties have easily and consistently outpolled his rivals. When the royalists managed to maneuver Abhisit Vejjajiva into the premiership in 2008, the new Democrat-led government made defending the monarchy one of its two top priorities, and the police department's top priority.[81] In 2010, the anti-censorship group Global Voices Advocacy reported that the Abhisit government had blocked over a hundred thousand websites, and that "almost all blocked websites were accused of breaching Thailand's infamous *lèse-majesté* law.[82]

David Streckfuss, an authority on Thailand's *lèse majesté* law, has documented the explosion in charges under the law since the coup of 2006. He claims that in 2011 there may have been as many as 170 political prisoners in Thai jails convicted of *lèse majesté*.[83] All this suggests that republican views have spread beyond intellectual circles. A more tangible expression of popular republicanism is the appearance of anti-royal graffiti in Bangkok following the crackdown on Red Shirts protesters in May 2010.[84] In a rally in downtown Bangkok on the anniversary of the September 2006 coup, thousands of Red Shirt protesters appeared to spontaneously break into the chant "*Ai hia sang kha, i ha sang ying*" [the (*expletive*) ordered the killings, the (*expletive*) ordered the shootings]—a reference to the alleged role of the king and

---

[80] Shortly after the 2006 coup, political scientist Thitinan Phongsudhirak remarked openly in a BBC interview that the coup was "nothing short of Thaksin versus the king." See: Kate McGeown, "Thai King Remains Centre Stage," *BBC News*, http://news.bbc.co.uk/2/hi/asia-pacific/5367936.stm, Thursday, September 21, 2006, accessed November 3, 2014.

[81] David Streckfuss, "The Intricacies of Lese-Majesty: A Comparative Study of Imperial Germany and Modern Thailand," in *Saying the Unsayable: Monarchy and Democracy in Thailand*, ed. Søren Ivarsson and Lotte Isager, (Copenhagen: NIAS Press, 2010), 134. The other priority was "fixing the economy."

[82] Pavin Chachavalpongpun, "Thailand's Massive Internet Censorship," *Asia Sentinel*, http://www.asiasentinel.com/index.php?option=com_content&task=view&id=2601&Itemid=164, accessed November 3, 2014.

[83] David Streckfuss, *Truth on Trial in Thailand*, 205.

[84] Serhat Ünaldi, "Working towards the Monarchy and Its Discontents: Anti-royal Graffiti in Downtown Bangkok," *Journal of Contemporary Asia* 44, no. 3 (2014): 377–403.

queen in the killings of Red Shirts the previous May.[85] With the expansion of Red Shirt networks, especially in the north and the northeast, the spread of the Internet, and the popularity of community radio stations run by Red Shirt sympathisers, it is difficult to imagine that republican sentiment has not grown in the aftermath of royalist attacks on pro-Thaksin governments. As this chapter has shown, there is a century-old tradition that provides fertile soil for such sentiments—even if the *lèse-majesté* law constrains their expression.

The political conflict in Thailand, now in its tenth year, has led to a re-examination of the meaning of "democracy," with both sides in the conflict claiming democratic credentials. Thailand's political system is officially referred to as, *"prachathipatai an mi phra maha kasat song pen pramuk,"* which is often inaccurately translated as "constitutional monarchy." The real significance of this term, however, is that it distinguishes the existing system from an older meaning of *prachathipatai* that associated "democracy" with republicanism. A central part of the history of democracy in Thailand, therefore, is the history of republicanism.

---

[85] Ibid., 378–79.

CHAPTER SIX

MADNESS, AUTHORITARIANISM, AND POLITICAL PARTICIPATION: THE CURIOUS CASE OF CHAM JAMRATNET

James Ockey

A new and lively pleasure is taken in the old confraternities of madmen, in their festivals, their gatherings, their speeches. Men argue passionately for or against Nicolas Joubert … who declares himself the Prince of Fools … there follow pamphlets, a trial, arguments; his lawyer declares and certifies him to be "an empty head, a gutted gourd, lacking in common sense; a cane, a broken brain, that has neither spring nor whole wheel in his head.[1]

Nai Thongdi Israchivin of Chiengmai told the court … Nai Cham repeatedly pretended to eat sun rays while at the Parliamentary Club, and once took off all his clothes with the exception of his underwear and lay in the sun to be baked. Nai Chardbutr Ruangsuwan, Khonkhaen MP … added that Nai Cham often carried a stick, and when asked the reason for this, would beat himself on the head with it.[2]

Cham Jamratnet, fondly known as *Khru* (teacher) Cham, devoted his life to the Thai parliamentary system. He contested the first indirect election in 1933, and remained involved in parliamentary politics up until the 1970s, winning election five times in all.[3] He was frequently evicted from parliamentary sessions, twice jailed for his political activities, and on several occasions had his sanity investigated—in the final instance, leading to his early release from prison. A controversial figure in his own time, today Cham is fondly remembered in his home province of Nakhon Sithammarat, where he was a long time MP (Member of Parliament). What do we

---

[1] Michel Foucault, *Madness and Civilization: A History of Insanity in the Age of Reason*, trans. Richard Howard (New York: Vintage Books, 1988), 36–37.

[2] "MPs Give Tribunal Details on Nai Cham," *Bangkok Post*, February 17, 1951, 1.

[3] He also won an additional by-election in 1970; see *Bangkok Post*, December 12, 1978, 3.

make of *Khru* Cham? What can his life tell us of politics, of society, and of madness in Thailand? I begin by examining Cham's life and some of his unconventional behavior, including that which led to the charges of madness. I then attempt to peel back the layers of complexity that made up *Khru* Cham, illuminating in the process something of the history of parliamentary politics, madness and psychiatry, and freedom and authoritarianism in Thailand.

THE LIFE (AND TIMES) OF CHAM JAMRATNET

Cham Jamratnet was born in 1898 in Nakhon Sithammarat. His father was a government official, so Cham went to the best schools. He graduated from *mathayom* (equivalent to high school, the highest level of education available in the provinces at the time) and obtained his *nak tham ek* degree (the highest qualification in Dharmic Studies available in the provinces) in the same year. He worked for a time as a teacher in Thungsung, becoming, for the first time, *Khru* Cham.[4] However, he soon decided to move on to a new position, in Bangkok, perhaps to live in the capital city.

Cham took a position as a brakeman on the railroad, assigned to the Thonburi-Phetchaburi cargo train. According to a friend of Cham's who also worked for the railroad,[5] he was unusually forthright in his ways, such as being willing to point out his supervisor's mistakes in a quite public fashion. His boss eventually retaliated, charging Cham with malfeasance for eating fruit taken from a cargo car, a common and accepted practice at the time. For this minor offense Cham had his salary cut by 25 percent, many times the value of the fruit, without being given a chance to speak in his own defense. Cham waited about two months before seeking revenge. Then he crawled across the top of a moving train to the caboose, where he challenged his supervisor to a fistfight on the spot, which turned into a brawl. Battered and bruised, Cham left the train and caught a passenger train back to Bangkok. His equally battered and bruised supervisor stopped at a station and telegraphed a report back to Bangkok before completing the journey, which, when received, marked the end of Cham's time as a brakeman.[6] While Cham no doubt practiced poor judgement in attacking his supervisor, he also demonstrated that he was willing to fight, in this case physically, for what he thought was right, putting his livelihood at risk. He would do the same many times throughout his political career. And he would later draw on his experience as a brakeman to expose corruption in the State Railroads of Thailand in speeches he made in the parliament.

After losing his job with the railroad, in 1930, Cham was hired as a teacher at Wat Chana Songkhram, near Sanam Luang, a position he held until 1932. During this period, he reconnected with a friend from Nakhon Sithammarat who had become a village scout leader (*luksua chaoban*) and, admiring the uniform, he decided to become a scout leader himself. Then, when the Promoters[7] carried out their

---

[4] Cham later began work on a degree in political science at Thammasat University, but did not finish, as his studies were interrupted by World War II. Interview with Janthip Jamratnet, Cham's daughter, in Nakhon Sithammarat, January 2003.

[5] Sawaeng Yensamut, "Khru Cham khon di muang nakhon," *Sinlapawatthanatham* 7 (July 1986): 36–43.

[6] Ibid. Sawaeng claims the unfair treatment that Cham received helped to build solidarity among railway workers, who would go on strike in 1934.

[7] The Promoters were a group of military officers and civilian bureaucrats who overthrew the absolute monarchy. Pridi was the leader of the civilian faction, and later organized the

successful coup against the absolute monarchy in 1932, Cham wanted to participate in what he saw as a progressive movement. The Promoters had printed leaflets to explain their actions and the new form of government, so Cham put on his scout uniform, went to the public relations department, and asked for a large pile of leaflets, which he took outside and distributed. He returned several times to restock, and ran other errands as well, in the process getting to know some of the leading Promoters, including Luang Thawin Thamrongnawasawat, a close friend of Pridi Phanomyong, the leader of the civilian faction. Cham's diligence was noted, and he was given a job as a civil servant, working closely with Pridi and staying in his compound. He also worked for a while in the secretariat for the new parliament.[8]

In 1933, the politically ambitious Cham decided to contest the first election in Nakhon Sithammarat. Unsure how to best campaign in this first indirect election, and with limited experience of his own, he created posters that extolled the achievements and sacrifices of his ancestors, a strategy that ultimately proved unsuccessful, as he was not elected.[9] Cham continued to work in the civil service through the mid-1930s, mostly in the Ministry of the Interior. In 1937, new elections were held, and Khru Cham went home to Nakhon Sithammarat to contest the election. Through his campaign techniques in this and later elections, we can discern much about him, about the political system, and about the electorate, at least in Nakhon Sithammarat.

NAKHON SITHAMMARAT ELECTION, 1937

In the 1937 election, Cham could appeal directly to the voters, so he decided he needed to be innovative. He sought to impress voters with his education, while also appearing to be poor, like them. Here his sobriquet of "khru" was a distinct advantage, as teachers lived among villagers and educated them. Cham decided to create election posters in the form of Thai-style poetry (*khlong*) that praised the 1932 revolution, extolled those who put down the Boworadet rebellion, and explained the purpose of the constitution and the rights and duties of all Thai citizens, rich and poor alike. And, of course, situated him as a teacher and leader in the new democratic society. The verse shown on the next page, praising the 1932 revolution, exemplifies his campaign-poster style.

Leaving its literary appraisal to the critics, or, perhaps better yet, to the voters, we see Cham attempting to convey to the people the historical importance of the change in government, something many may not have fully grasped. We also see him praising the party of the Promoters, Khana Rath, and declaring his loyalty to it. And we see him avowing his willingness to make sacrifices to represent the people of Nakhon Sithammarat. All this in verse, so that it might more easily be spread and remembered.

People's party, while Phibun was leader of the military faction. Luang Thawin was a close ally of Pridi. Each would later serve as prime minister.

[8] See: ibid., 40; and cremation volume for Khru Cham Jamretnet, B.E. 2522 [1979] (mimeograph copy provided by Janthip Jamratnet), 7.

[9] Sawaeng, "Khru Cham khon di muang nakhon," 40.

เปลี่ยนการปกครอง[10]
Changing the Governmental System

ครูน่ำจำรัสเนตร	นรเขตต้นครศรี
Khru Cham Jamratnet	of Nakhon Si
ธรรมราชสมรรถมี	มนเกื้อนุกูลไทย
Thammarat capably	Intending to advocate for Thailand
ยอมพลีชีวีอาตม์	สละขาดมิเยื่อใย
Is willing to sacrifice his life	Put aside relationships
มอบกายถวายใจ	กะประชานิกรกอง
Sacrifice his body and heart	for the public
เข้าพรรคคณะรักชาติ	คณะราษฎร์มันปอง
Joined a party that loves the nation,	Khana Rath, intending
เปลี่ยนการปกครอง	ลุสำเร็จและเสร็จสม
to change the governmental system	Focused on finishing and on completion
นับเป็นประวัติกาล	คุณซ่านนิยมชม
for all time	Convey praise for
พลีชีพปฐมบรม	ก็เพราะเพื่อประชาชน
the pioneering supreme sacrifice, of life	made for the people
ใช่ว่าจะหยุดยั้ง	เฉพาะครั้งมีหนึ่งหน
Certainly it will conclude	Specially, but once

Cham also sought to reinforce his rather tenuous link to the Promoters, in quite a clever fashion, since the People's Party actually had another candidate. As noted above, Cham had worked for the government, was studying at Thammasat University, and had come to know Pridi quite well, so Cham set out to use this connection. He had saved some money for his campaign, so before going to Nakhon Sithammarat, Cham went to Pridi and asked him if he would hold on to the money until Cham needed it, as he trusted Pridi and it would be more convenient than putting it in a bank account. Pridi agreed, and the money was left with him while Cham traveled to Nakhon Sithammarat and began campaigning. As part of the campaign, as we see in the election verse, Cham claimed to be an ally of Pridi and the Promoters, and a member of Khana Rath.

When Cham got to Nakhorn Sithammarat he told government officials and voters that he had Pridi's support. Lots of people doubted him, particularly government officials who knew the preferred candidate of Khana Rath. But he just kept repeating that he was close to Pridi, and that people would soon see that Pridi would provide support for his campaign. After his relationship with Pridi had

---

[10] Reprinted in Khru Cham Jamretnet's cremation volume, 11 (my translation).

become the subject of considerable discussion, Cham went to the telegraph office and sent Pridi a message asking him to send money. Pridi immediately sent him money; it was Cham's own money, of course, though no one in Nakhorn Sithammarat knew that. Cham kept quiet, correctly judging that the news would spread on its own.[11]

Khru Cham also played heavily on his religious background, making opposition to greed and corruption a major theme in his campaign.[12] More creatively, he played out the Jataka tale of Phrawet Sandon, or Prince Vessantara, who was famous for his generosity, giving away everything he had to any who asked of him. One morning Cham got dressed in fine Western-style clothes, including fashionable shoes and a hat. Then he went downtown to the market and made offerings at the shrine, stopping to talk with people, telling them he was going to campaign in a remote area. This aroused considerable discussion, just as Cham intended—why would he dress like that to go out in the mud and dirt of the outer city? He set off on foot, greeting people and chatting along the way. As he went, he handed out sweets to the children, and when he met poor people, he gave them a modest amount of money. Soon he had a small crowd following along, and eventually he ran out of money. For the next poor person he met, he took out his wallet, noted it was empty, and gave it to her, saying that she could sell it for a lot of money. The next person got the hat, the next his shirt. Eventually Cham had given away everything but his briefs. Then he turned around and retraced his steps back to the market, walking past the same people who had seen him leave that morning dressed in his finest clothes. Seeing a candidate for parliament wearing nothing but briefs was surprising enough to engender considerable discussion, which, of course, was exactly what Cham sought. Once the story of his giving away everything he had began to spread, people quickly made the connection to the legendary tale of Phrawet Sandon, making *Khru* Cham the talk of the electorate.

Appealing to his fellow poor, with associated connotations to the wealth and corruption of his rivals, can be seen in other campaign tactics *Khru* Cham developed.[13] One favorite campaign technique for many candidates in early elections was to rent a film projector to take a movie around to the different villages in the constituency. People would come to see the free movie, creating a large audience for the politician, who would speak before the film was shown and then depart. As the movie was a gift, this would also provide a sense of obligation that encouraged a vote for the candidate who provided it. The cost to rent a movie, projector, screen, sound system, and truck, and to hire people to set up all that equipment, was expensive, beyond the range of a mid-level civil servant like Cham. So, *Khru* Cham sought a means to counter this election tactic. After some thought, he purchased a large box of candles and began to follow the campaigns of candidates showing movies. As the movie could only begin after dusk, by the time the movie ended, many villagers found themselves having to travel some distance home, late at night, in the dark. So when the film was over, *Khru* Cham was there to hand out candles to

---

[11] See: Jongkon Krairoek, *Sinlapaluaktang* [The art of elections] (Bangkok: Thepnimit, 1968), 98; and Samnao Hiriotapata, *Phuthaen thi di det* [The outstanding MP] (Bangkok: Phadungsin, 1969), 63 and ff. Samnao added that Cham then went to government officials and asked them to provide him with a government vehicle and a sound system for use during his campaign, since he was Pridi's man, and they did (104).

[12] Samnao, *Phuthaen thi di det*, 76.

[13] Interview, Janthip Jamratnet, January 2003.

villagers, along with the message that he was, like them, a poor man who could not afford to provide expensive movies like the rich candidates. However, he could provide candles to light the darkness, and help the villagers find their way home. Nor did he ignore the symbolic aspects of providing a candle in times of darkness, nor, as one would expect from someone educated in the Dharma, the votary aspect of candles. Thus, through his cleverness, *Khru* Cham was able to neutralize and even capitalize on one of his rivals' most effective tactics.

Khru Cham was contesting an election as a candidate without the support of the government, without much money, and without prestigious titles or positions. Denied all those advantages, he turned to creative strategies, and to a kind of "man of the people" campaign style that proved effective. In fact, his style was so effective that he won a second election a year later after an early dissolution of parliament, while most of his colleagues were not reelected.[14] His ability to win elections by playing a clever but ordinary man tweaking those in power is revealing, and belies claims that having money or status were the only ways to gain power. It points instead to a society where a clever, common man willing and able to challenge authority was respected and admired, perhaps to the chagrin of those who did rely on status, authority, and wealth.

In 1937, then, Cham left the civil service and became a Member of Parliament, the representative for Nakhorn Sithammarat. He was proud to be an MP, for while his personal opinions might mean little, the expression of the will of the voters of Nakhorn Sithammarat, at least for Cham, gave him the support he needed to speak back to power. Ideologically, Cham did not fit any defined categories. He opposed instability, disorder, corruption, and the abuse of authority, and he consistently held to two clearly prioritized principles. First, he supported the Promoters, for he had been drawn into politics by their cause and remained loyal to them. Although he was friendly with Pridi and *Luang* Thawin Thamrongnawasawat, ultimately he followed Phibun more closely.[15] Second, in line with his election techniques, Cham insisted on being in the opposition, on speaking out for his fellow citizens against any injustices, especially those committed by the state. Thus Cham served a higher principle than loyalty to Phibun and the Promoters. This included speaking out against Phibun's regime when he was in power. Of course, opposition to quasi-military rule was not always simple or straightforward. And so, just as with his campaign techniques, Cham sought out clever ways to express his opposition.

Cham soon developed an original style of debate, drawing much attention from the national press and annoying his colleagues. This style is evident in a 1944 debate that took place soon after the Phibun government had been pushed from power and replaced by a Khuang Aphaiwong caretaker administration, in the hope that Thailand would be treated less harshly when the war ended. The caretaker government had the support of Pridi and others, as it seemed the best hope for Thailand in the short term. As both a supporter of Phibun and a committed opposition MP, Cham chose to take on this fragile government when the military's

---

[14] About half of the members of this parliament were reelected (forty-seven of ninety-two).

[15] *Khru* Cham Jamretnet's cremation volume, 9. While he was linked to Phibun, perhaps in part for the protection such an association afforded, Cham's politics were not the Cold War politics that would set Phibun against Pridi—which have come to dominate later analyses of this period—but were, rather, early 1930s politics. He was anti-aristocracy and in favor of popular sovereignty and democracy. Aristocratic ministers seem to have been a particular target for *Khru* Cham.

secret fund came up for debate. The secret fund—so-called because, while its amount was known, any disbursements were secret—had long been controversial and a source of political contention, most famously in 1938—under a government already tainted by a corruption scandal—when a group of Northeastern MPs, led by Tiang Sirikhan, successfully used the fund's notoriety to force a dissolution of parliament. In the 1944 special session called to pass the budget, the parliament took up a proposal to cut the secret fund. Cham rose to speak in opposition to the secret fund, and, as was his wont, focused on corruption. He pointed out that a secret fund could not be monitored, that the money could be spent on anything, perhaps even to purchase wedding gifts or to pay tennis ball boys. Moreover, he argued, if the funds were not being spent frivolously, there would be a lot of the fund remaining. He suggested that the secret fund be closed and transferred to the general fund, and, referring to the 1938 debate, said that the government could be "knocked out" over the issue. Told to stay on topic, he replied that this was a serious issue, not a joke, and that it had to be taken seriously. In any event, a parliamentary committee had already made the same proposal to cut the secret fund, and it passed easily. Thus, Cham's protest was meaningless, since the government agreed with him and he was arguing for something that had already passed.

Although the parliament approved the proposal to cut the secret fund, Cham remained dissatisfied. That afternoon, the parliament took up other aspects of the budget, including government office supplies. Cham rose to debate, and in the context of discussing office supplies, he repeatedly raised the secret fund as an example of problems in the budget, each time receiving a warning from the speaker for straying from the topic at hand. As the debate proceeded to the budget for the State Railways of Thailand, which called for a cut in the number of positions, Cham again rose—this time defending the railway employees, but also returning to his theme that the parliament had a need for full budget information. As before, this was his attempt to address the secret fund, but it was again averted by the president. Cham's defense of the SRT employees faltered when it was noted that only vacant positions would be cut and no workers would be fired, and the debate moved on.[16] While this example is relatively mundane, it marks a distinct style Cham would develop into an art form. He learned to push the rules of parliamentary debate beyond the edge until he provoked a reaction from the speaker, in this case, a fairly mild reprimand. His determination to pursue controversial issues even after the parliament had concluded difficult debates on those topics naturally made him unpopular with presidents of parliament.

As the war came to an end, Cham's antics in the parliament and his tendency to annoy authorities cost him dearly. After the war, in an effort to pacify the Allies, the Thai government charged a small number of leading politicians with war crimes, most importantly, former prime minister Phibunsongkhram.[17] Just eight people were charged and arrested, and all but one of them either top government leaders or key figures in the wartime propaganda apparatus. The exception, of course, was *Khru* Cham, by far the least politically important figure among those charged. Formally,

---

[16] See *Raingan kanprachum sapha phuthaen ratsadon* [Record of the meeting of parliament], *Samai 2, chut 3 phiset* [Session 2, set three special], December 1944.

[17] For a detailed account, see Angkhana Kiattisaknukun, "Khadi achayakon songkhram nai prathet Thai pho. so. 2488–2489" [War crimes trials in Thailand 1945–46] (MA thesis, Chulalongkorn University, 1990).

Cham faced two charges of encouraging pro-Japanese sentiment. First, he was charged with giving a speech in Nakhon Sithammarat in which he argued that because Britain and the United States had long oppressed both Thailand and Japan, and because Thailand was now in alliance with Japan, Thailand therefore had to support Japan against Britain and the United States. Second, in the introduction to a tract called "A Caution to Thai Friends," Cham encouraged Thais to join hands with the Japanese and fight against the United States and Britain.[18] That Cham was such a lesser figure relative to the others indicted led Sang Phatthanothai, a fellow inmate, to conclude that the government had charged Cham because it wished to prevent him from running again for parliament, an indication of the frustration he had caused through his contentious style.[19] In any event, Cham was not able to contest the election. According to Sang, Cham told the other prisoners that he was Hanuman, the monkey trickster from the Ramayana. Sang also tells us that Cham kept up a constant racket from the time he arrived, sometimes praying, sometimes singing, and, later, even weeping throughout his trial. While this may have annoyed his cellmates, Sang wrote that it noticeably lightened the previously gloomy atmosphere.[20] Eventually all the prisoners were freed, as the court decided that the law on war crimes had come after the events in question, and it could not be applied retroactively.

Cham returned to parliament after the January 1948 election. Judging from the extant leaflets, during his election campaign he had to overcome rumors that he was ineligible for a seat in parliament, presumably because he had been ineligible during the previous election. One of Cham's leaflets, a short poem, ends with "*Khru* Cham still is eligible to be a representative, as he was before, elect [him] for nation, religion, king, and constitution." Another leaflet argues that to vote for a weak candidate is to waste the vote and destroy the nation, and ends with "Absolutely do not believe the many rumors criticizing *Khru* Cham, please ask *Khru* Cham."[21] In the end, Cham's campaign techniques and his reputation were enough as he was again elected to represent Nakhon Sithammarat.

The ensuing term was characterized by some of Cham's most eccentric behavior, both inside and outside parliament, and thus some context may be useful in understanding his conduct. When he entered parliament this time, in 1948, it was during a period of economic and political turmoil, both nationally and internationally. In the wake of WWII, the international economy was still struggling toward recovery, and Thailand was burdened by war reparations in the form of a rice quota. Politically, communism had become the next great threat, and with the rise of Mao, increasingly the focus of concern shifted to peasants and rural insurgency. In Thailand, the elite had divided into three groups: the royalists, represented politically by the aristocratic leaders of the Democrat party, Khuang Aphaiwong, and brothers Khukrit and Seni Pramoj; Pridi loyalists, the only left-of-center group, with allies in the navy and the still armed Free Thai movement; and the Phibun group, strengthened by Phibun's release from prison, which dominated the army. The conflict quickly turned violent and reached a level of intra-elite violence

[18] Ibid., 92–93.

[19] Sang Phatthanothai, *Khwamnuk nai krongkhang* [Thoughts while in prison] (Bangkok: Khlangwitthaya, 1956), 590, cited in ibid., 93.

[20] Sang, *Khwamnuk nai krongkhang*, 591.

[21] *Khru* Cham Jamretnet's cremation volume, 14–15.

unmatched before or since in modern Thai history.[22] Initially, the Phibun and royalist factions joined together against the Pridi faction, engaging in both character and physical assassinations of Pridi and his top allies, including the assassination of three leading cabinet ministers in March 1949. The Phibun faction also turned on the royalist faction, forcing them from power, though they departed peacefully. Finally, the Phibun faction itself split in the mid-1950s, with former Phibun ally Sarit Thanarat joining with the royalists to expel Phibun and Phao Siyanon. Cham brought his oppositional style into the midst of this political violence when he entered parliament for the third time. And he did so with less support than previously, as he had had a falling out with Phibun, over Phibun's alleged marital infidelity.[23]

Khru Cham demonstrated his new aggressiveness early in the parliamentary term, questioning, in a variety of ways, the democratic credentials of the government. Led by Khuang Aphaiwong and the Democrat party, the government had limited legitimacy, despite winning the election, as it had been installed through a military coup the previous November. The government appointed a speaker, Kasem Bunsri, who quickly alienated many provincial MPs, as he was seen as condescending.[24] When the new government set out its policies in the first session of the parliament, *Khru* Cham rose to speak, during the debate on the communications policy, to challenge the portfolio of a member of the nobility, M. L. Udom Sanitwong. Cham, pointing, shouted "entrepreneurial minister [*ratthamontri sengli*], do you know what is going on in the Transport Association? It has corruption, but you pretend not to know. Therefore, the government should resign." He added that he [Cham] should not be dismissed as an "evil star," as 100,000 people had elected him, and yet, although he was a representative of the people, when he came on the train to Bangkok, he had to sit in the stairway, and "cling like a bat," then he proceeded to act out his clinging to the stairway. Eventually, the president called him to order, and the minister responded that he would not answer the interpellation, as Cham had called him an entrepreneurial minister, and it was not true.[25]

Cham's behavior spread to other provincial MPs, and, while none were as creative and outspoken, several were quite disruptive.[26] Just a week later, parliament was already inquorate, as government MPs failed to attend, to the frustration of the opposition. In the next session, on March 17, Cham pushed the speaker on a purely procedural motion until parliamentary police were called in to "invite" Cham out of the meeting. Cham insisted that if the speaker would just speak politely, he would

---

[22] Overall violence was higher in the 1970s compared to post-WWII, and perhaps in other periods, too, but the primary targets of that violence were the lower classes, as is typically the case, versus intra-elite conflict. In general, defeated elites are allowed to exit peacefully, whether to internal or external exile.

[23] Interview, Sookprida Bhanomyong, Bangkok, January 17, 2003.

[24] Kasem Bunsri's condescending attitude is apparent in the parliamentary record, thinly veiled at best.

[25] *Sayam Nikon*, March 4, 1948, 1. Cham was sometimes called *dao rai*, meaning evil star, or, perhaps better, ill-omen star, in the press. Pointing at someone is considered very rude in Thailand.

[26] In a meeting two weeks later, for example, MP Chuen Rawiwan had to be warned six times for the use of rough language, and when Cham acted out to the point of being removed by police, other MPs rose to his defense. See: *Sayam Nikon*, March 31, 1948, 1; and *Raingan kanprachum sapha phuthaen ratsadon* [Record of the meeting of parliament] 3/2491, March 17, 1948.

obey. Later, Cham visited Adun Detcharat, former chief of police, in the presence of reporters and complained to him about the behavior of the parliamentary police. He suggested Adun should return as chief of police. Adun listened, joked with him, and sent him on his way, happy.[27] The message of an aristocratic style of "democracy," where ministers and the speaker treated provincial and opposition MPs condescendingly, was made quite clearly, if obliquely, by *Khru* Cham and his allies.

The Khuang government lasted only until April, then resigned under pressure from the military and Phibun returned to power. Despite Cham's previous support for Phibun, however, he continued to act out against the undemocratic nature of parliament. While we cannot recount each event, some of his actions can be taken as representative. Perhaps the one best remembered came in July, at the beginning of Buddhist Lent. *Khru* Cham, a devout Buddhist, dressed in peasant clothing, climbed on the back of a water buffalo, and rode it down to the session underway in parliament. Many considered this a sign of disrespect toward parliament, Thailand's most important democratic institution. Cham's supporters claim it was intended to convey a message: that Cham was familiar with peasants and their way of life. Yet this does not explain the outrage MPs felt toward Cham at what they perceived as a slight. To fully understand the message Cham was sending, we have to look back to the previous senate, which had been called a "House of Buffalos,"[28] the buffalo being a symbol of both loyalty and stupidity. Nor was this Cham's first reference to buffalos. In a budget debate at the beginning of July, Cham had complained about the high rate of crime, noting that buffalos and cows had been stolen and the homes and gardens of people had been destroyed by criminals. He called for more money to be spent on electricity, to bring light to the people, which, he said, was extremely necessary.[29] Thus, Cham riding a buffalo to parliament can be seen as a powerful metaphor, one supportive of peasants and critical of servile government MPs. In the context of the Buddhist lent, with his colleagues coming to parliament in expensive automobiles, it can also be seen as a critical commentary on luxury and encouragement to pursue simplicity.[30]

Cham's frustration with the behavior of his fellow MPs seems to have peaked in December. At that time, Khukrit Pramot, former secretary-general of the Democrat party, who had quit the House of Representatives after complaining that he could not sit with opposition members who would vote themselves a pay raise, decided to join the Phibun cabinet—which would, of course, give him the pay raise even as he moved from the opposition to the government. Deeply frustrated by what they saw

---

[27] *Sayam Nikon*, March 31, 1948, 1.

[28] Pasuk Pongphaichit and Chris Baker, *Thailand, Economy, and Politics* (Oxford: Oxford University Press, 1995), 268. Royalists had made this accusation against Pridi supporters in the senate, but the term "House of Buffalos" stuck over the next decade or so as a more general description of loyal, powerless parliaments. In a debate in 1957, for example, one disrupted by Cham, an MP shouted out, "People's representatives, not buffalo representatives" (phuthaen ratsadon mai chai phuthaen khwai). See *Raingan kanprachum sapha phuthaen ratsadon, samai saman* [special session], April 1, 1957.

[29] *Raingan kanprachum sapha phuthaen ratsadon* 15/2491, July 1948, 1108–9. He was interrupted by the president on the grounds that he was criticizing the previous Khuang government, and thus his comments were deemed out of order.

[30] This is another well known and often told *Khru* Cham story, perhaps best told in Samnao, *Phuthaen thi di det* , 42–45. Other than details, the tale varies little from one telling to the next. Samnao also wrote that Cham carried a candle, symbolizing lighting a pathway through oppression, similar to his call for more electricity to bring light to the people.

as Khukrit's hypocracy, opposition MPs in a special session were highly critical of him. In the midst of the debate, Phibun rose and insisted that no vote of confidence was needed, and a motion was made to close debate. Opposition MPs objected vociferously, with Cham again at the forefront. After the motion was seconded and the vote was called, Cham rose to speak, before the vote could be taken. Under proper parliamentary procedure it was time for the vote, which Cham well knew, and the president of parliament ordered him to sit. Cham refused, shouting, "Let me speak, you are assassinating me."[31] The president again ordered him to sit and Cham still refused, so the parliamentary police were called in. Cham shrieked like a banshee, so that, according to *Sayam Nikon*, the parliament became "like a cemetery,"[32] and he fought with the police, shouting, "No, you cannot arrest me, we are representatives of Thailand, we must ask to speak, we will not yield, we must ask to speak ..."[33] Tables and chairs were overturned, one guard was cut in the struggle, and Cham was forced from the room. The next day the *Bangkok Post*, in a front page editorial, suggested tongue-in-cheek that a charm school be established for MPs, noting that, surely, if children can be taught to speak only when told, then MPs can, too.[34] Thus Cham's message, while symbolic, was conveyed through the press in a way that made his point quite clearly: Thailand's parliament was a cemetery of democracy where MPs were to speak only when and as allowed, or suffer the consequences, up to and including assassination.

By this time, Cham's symbolic speech had developed into a stylized pattern, as with a story, or, better yet, a play. He would goad the parliamentary president throughout the day, with long, rambling off-topic speeches, with demands that violated parliamentary procedure, and with attempts to reconsider topics already decided. As the speaker became increasingly frustrated, Cham would intensify his behavior, eventually reaching a denouement when parliamentary police were called, and Cham would make his metaphorical point clear, through actions that were well outside conventional behavior for the parliament, and often for society as a whole. For example, in November 1949, Cham introduced a bill on the rice trade. The government had its own bill it was introducing, and, of course, Cham's draft had no chance of being adopted. At the start of each session the parliament traditionally began with interpellations. Cham rose and asked to set aside the interpellations that day, and move forward his bill instead, because rice is the bread of life for the Thai people. Then he changed his mind and said they should do the interpellations after all, even set aside an entire day just for interpellations. The parliamentary president declared most of this out of order.

---

[31] At a time when politicians were literally being assassinated to shut them up, the hyperbolic use of the word "assassination" for shutting up MPs in parliament was quite bold, yet Cham did it frequently.

[32] *Sayam Nikon*, December 3, 1948, 1.

[33] *Raingan kanprachum sapha phuthaen ratsadon* 6/2491, special session, December 2, 2491 [1948], 557–59.

[34] *Bangkok Post* December 3, 1948, 1. The flavor of the editorial is evident in a reference to an earlier incident, with a different MP: "This is not the first report we have read of MPs forgetting their manners. There was the one a couple of months ago who kicked the government worker in the face. True, he removed his shoe to do it, but we still thought the act a trifle discourteous ... if an MP can be courteous enough to remove his shoe before kicking someone in the face, it is our contention that that MP can be taught that it is not polite to deliver the kick in the face at all." One of the editorial's references to Cham suggests that "That rebellious MP who was dragged by the guards from the Throne Hall [where parliament then met] can be taught as we teach children, 'to speak only when spoken to.'"

A few minutes later a motion to bring his rice bill forward was made and Cham again spoke. He began by saying that he was not speaking for the prime minister, but for all members, and for all citizens, who are the true lords of the Thai nation, again a reference to a servile parliament. He engaged in a long, rambling speech, referring to alleged plots and the corruption involved in bringing the government's bill forward. He was eventually cut off by the president, who asked him to stick to the subject. Cham followed with another long, rambling speech, which the president again had to interrupt; then after some suggestions for amendments were made, Cham again rose and said he wanted to withdraw the motion to advance his bill, since it was not going to get unanimous support, and he wanted the vote to be unanimous. Thus, much of the morning was wasted as Cham alternated between advancing his bill and withdrawing it. During the course of the day, Cham rose several more times to speak, with his rambling, off-topic speeches slowly revealing his theme: that "Field Marshal Phibun—oi—Prime Minister Phibun" rarely attended parliamentary meetings because of his righteousness, implying again that the (corrupt) parliament had no real power. The president repeatedly interrupted him to get him to return to the topic at hand. Cham responded that if the president continued in this vein, it would get "hot." He noted that poor people nationwide were suffering (*duatron,* a term that contains the word for "hot") over the problems with rice, and asked for mercy for "this child," meaning himself, that his mouth not be closed. He stated that MPs are leaders, that they should not be strangled or have their mouths closed. When warned that he was again off topic, he told the president, "Sorry father." Then he gave this interesting speech:

> I'm sweating all over. And I'm shaking all over. I'm sorry, let me take a short break. Let Mr. Phoem Wongthongluea speak for me. At the time that Mr. Khuang and you, Mr. President, were fighting like a couple of battling elephants, I called the police to come in and stop it, but they wouldn't come. But when the people speak, you have to call the police to come in and settle things, like this. This is not appropriate. I'm sweating all over because I want to speak for the poor people and those who are comfortable … It's so hot, I can't stay to speak, just a minute and I will come back and speak.[35]

And he walked out of the room. The president noted that the motion was effectively withdrawn. Cham returned a moment later, saying he had cooled off,[36] and was given his final warning. He was quiet for a time, then he raised the issue again. Then again.

Later in the day, having clarified his theme, and having goaded the speaker to the point of exasperation, Cham began his symbolic protest, which would lead to the denouement. It began as he again tried to raise issues that were out of order and was told to sit, but instead he reminded the president he represented all the people of Nakhon Sithammarat and that he had seniority in the parliament. Then came this exchange:

---

[35] The debate, including this speech, is in *Raingan kanprachum sapha phuthaen ratsadon* 7/2492, special session, November 24, 2492 [1949], 674–767.

[36] On some occasions Cham cooled off by jumping in the fountain outside parliament.

Cham:	Since the president doesn't understand nor care about my ideology, I will sit, whatever.
President:	Then go ahead and sit. I order you to sit.
Cham:	I ask to debate further. I have sat down.

[Cham sits on the floor]

President:	You can sit. I want you to sit. Sit there. Otherwise I will have the police take you out.
Cham:	I ask to continue the debate, according to procedure.
President:	No.
Cham:	You told me to sit quietly. Don't call the police in. I will sit quietly. I haven't finished speaking.
President:	Does anyone else wish to speak?

[Cham begins taking off his clothes, because of the heat]

Cham:	Sir, don't call the police in. I'm sitting. Sir, don't call the police in. I won't allow it.

[Cham sits in the middle of the floor; he removes all his clothes but his briefs]

President:	Take him out.

[Police come in and invite Cham out of the meeting]

Cham:	No! I won't go! I'm sitting! I'm being good already. Let me put my clothes on first. Don't break my hand. Don't do this. Let me put my clothes on first.
President:	Police, take Teacher Cham outside the meeting room. Don't let him return. Take him far away please.[37]

Cham's message has several parts, including references to a paternalistic government and a servile parliament, to suffering and oppression, and perhaps to the bravery necessary to face up to military authoritarianism "naked" of power and authority.[38] It also has the same pattern of badgering the leadership, leading up to a symbolic message and a denouement replete with eccentric behavior.

Cham's activities outside parliament continued in the same symbolic fashion. As with riding the buffalo into parliament, his public behavior was often thematically linked to his outbursts in parliament. In November 1950, Cham paid a visit to the Ministry of the Interior. As he was walking down the hall he saw a group of peasants sitting outside an office, waiting to meet with a ministry official. Nearby was a table with some pitchers of water for use by visitors. Cham picked up a couple pitchers, began shouting "communists" at the peasants, and threw the water at them. We see again the theme of heat and cooling off. And as before, it is the context that clarifies the message. With the Maoist revolution having succeeded in China, this is the period when the anticommunist movement shifted its focus to victimize the peasantry. Cham "cooled off" those peasants who had simply approached the

---

[37] Summarized and translated from *Raingan kanprachum sapha phuthaen ratsadon* 7/2492, special session, 674–767.

[38] As demonstrated by his reference to "Field Marshal—oi—Prime Minister Phibun," an allusion to Phibun's military power as the reason for his political position.

Ministry of the Interior for help—the same ministry that was responsible for local government, rural development, the police, and communist suppression. Instead of receiving assistance, however, the peasants were called communists and subjected to (Cham's) attack.[39]

Over this period, Cham's behavior was so bizarre that it drew considerable attention from the press, and, of course, among his colleagues. When the new Constitutional Court came into being, some of Cham's fellow parliamentarians decided to use the court to challenge his MP status on the grounds that he was of unsound mind.[40] In return, Cham asked the tribunal to fine his accusers 84,000 baht, "the equivalent of the number of priests who gathered to hear the first sermon of the Lord Buddha on Maka Buja Day."[41] When the Constitutional Court rejected the case, a special parliamentary committee was established to hear it. After some delay, the trial began, with most hearings open to the public and the press. As the hearing proceeded, Cham's bizarre behavior, and, of course, his symbolic protest, was replayed in the pages of the press.

Thongdi Isarachiwin, MP from Chiangmai, testified that Cham pretended to swallow the sun's rays, and had even taken off all his clothes but his briefs to soak in the sun at the parliamentary club.[42] He added that Cham had created his own political party, the Buddhist Party (*Phutphak*), with only one member. He noted that Cham had been repeatedly ejected from parliament for his conduct, for shouting out that the government should resign, and for exclaiming loudly that "Phibun is my father."[43] Chatbut Ruangsuwan, MP from Khon Kaen, told the court that Cham walked around with a stick, and when asked about it, hit himself in the head with it.

---

[39] *Bangkok Post*, November 7, 1950, 1.

[40] In fact, this looks like a publicity stunt throughout, as several of those who accused Cham had previously worked with him, or at least alongside him, in opposing the president of parliament and seeking to highlight the weakness of the parliament. With most of the sessions open to the public and press, the trial provided an opportunity to replay the same debates on the front pages of newspapers, and included both repetitions of the criticisms and explanations for the behavior, although the symbolic elements were not explained.

[41] "Nai Cham Turns Tables, Claims MPs Accusing Him Should Be Penalized," *Bangkok Post*, January 23, 1951, 1. Maka Buja (Magha Puja) Day commemorates the day when 1,250 *arahant* (perfected person) turned up simultaneously, without invitation, at Veruvana temple on the day of the full moon of the third lunar month. The Buddha gave a sermon establishing the rules for the monastic order, then ordained each of them to it. In the lunar calendar, Magha Puja Day follows in February or March each year, and would have been the next major Buddhist holiday at the time Cham made his request. (Either the writer or Cham must have been confused here, for 84,000 is an important numerological symbol in Buddhism, sometimes said to be the number of teachings of the Buddha, but it was not the number of *arahant* who appeared at the temple.)

[42] He would open his mouth wide as if experiencing a huge yawn, and then close it and swallow, as blatantly as possible. When asked, he would say that he was swallowing the sun, which was good for the health. As this was widely known as *yuk muud*, an era of darkness, accepting more light and more openness to create a more healthy society must be part of the message conveyed.

[43] "MPs Give Tribunal Details on Nai Cham," *Bangkok Post*, February 17, 1951, 1. While this last remark ostensibly indicates support for Phibun, it also highlights the paternalism in the relationship between the prime minister and the parliament, and perhaps is part of the explanation for Cham's "childish" behavior in parliament.

He added that Cham could often be seen playing with children outside the parliament.[44]

In the subsequent meeting, Phethai Chotinuchit, Yai Sawitchat, and Khlai La-ongmani testified similarly, recounting Cham's behavior in parliament, including his removal of clothing, and stating that a sane person would not so behave, and that Cham was not faking. Yai Sawitchat also told of a recent debate during which Cham came dressed in a peasant shirt, for an interpellation on the shortage of schools for children in some rural areas. When he was dissatisfied with the answer, he tore open his peasant shirt to reveal a red undershirt, beat his chest, and made a sound like crying.[45] Khlai La-ongmani, also a southern MP, complained that Cham acted in ways that brought embarrassment to people of the south, for instance, by singing *nora* (traditional song–dance routines) or acting out comedy films on the stairs of a train they shared, rather than sitting politely in their compartment. He also claimed that Cham made frightening faces at a foreigner on the train, leaving Khlai so embarrassed that he had to tell the stranger that Cham was not well. He also reported that Cham once prayed for an hour in the restroom of the train, that he rode a buffalo to a temple ceremony, and that Cham once brought an interpellation to him to sign that suggested turning the entire country over to Phibun alone.[46]

In the third session, Sakhon Klinphaka accused Cham of verbally abusing a female parliamentary official. Sakhon also complained about Cham's inappropriate behavior in parliament, behavior in which no sane person would consider engaging. Sakhon admitted, however, that he asked Cham privately about the behavior, and Cham answered that he wanted to create such a comedic fuss that it would be reported in the paper, so that people reading about it would say that Cham was clever and afraid of no one. The female parliamentary official also testified regarding Cham's verbal abuse, then complained that, one day, Cham arrived in a *samlo* (tricycle taxi) with a *kaen* (a traditional northeastern instrument) and had the driver play the *kaen* while Cham sang. Another parliamentary official reported that he had found Cham dressed only in briefs, in the reception room for foreign visitors, singing. Then, during the court proceedings, Cham sang the song, which praised Phibun as the savior of the nation (like Taksin of old), but the official denied recognizing it and claimed he had not paid any attention the first time.[47]

In later sessions, Cham was asked to respond to the many accusations. Regarding his behavior in parliament that led to his expulsion, Cham claimed it was intended to so anger members of the opposition that they would walk out and miss voting against the government of Prime Minister Phibun. He explained that he threw water on the peasants at the Ministry of the Interior because he thought they would assassinate the minister. And he responded that "eating the sun" was a cure for his stomach problems.

---

[44] Ibid. Perhaps a reference to the Khuang government coming to power through a military coup (the stick), then insisting on its democratic legitimacy, only to be forced from power (beaten about the head) by the same soldiers. I have found no other reference to this behavior.

[45] *Sayam Nikon*, February 26, 1951, 1. The symbolism here seems obvious, the peasant turning into a red as the government failed to take care of rural children.

[46] Ibid., 1, 10.

[47] "Cham wa jom phon ma thaen phrajao Tak" [Cham says field marshal (Phibun) comes in place of phrajao Tak (sin)], *Sayam Nikon*, March 5, 1951, 1, 10.

Perhaps more honestly, he admitted that his antics were an attempt to gain publicity, and observed that whereas some MPs amused themselves with billiards, he amused himself with jokes. He also asked the tribunal for a quick decision, as an election was underway and he wanted to return to Nakhon Sithammarat to campaign.[48] Later that year, Cham was declared "sane" by the parliamentary committee. There is no reference to the involvement of any mental health practitioners at any point during the committee's investigation, as the Thai state took it upon itself to determine sanity. The committee also delayed its decision until after the election, and Cham lost his seat.[49]

By 1952, there was little semblance of democracy remaining in Thailand. With Pridi loyalists and Democrat party royalists largely sidelined by the 1950s, the military had divided against itself. The navy had kidnapped Phibun, only to see the air force bomb the flagship *Si Ayutthaya*. Phibun leapt from the ship and survived. Subsequently, two army generals—Phao Siyanon, who had transferred to the police department, and Sarit Thanarat, who commanded the army—began to compete for power. Phibun was left with limited support, and his continued relevance depended on maintaining some rapport with the two competing generals. Thus, by 1955, Phibun decided that a return to democracy might benefit him, as he hoped to gain the support of the electorate to shore up his legitimacy. He announced the opening of a Hyde Park-style Speakers' Corner at Sanam Luang to facilitate political speeches, and scheduled elections for 1957.

The new Hyde Park quickly developed a core group of speakers, many of them with loose connections to Phibun, others with links to the Thai left. While it seemed the perfect venue for one like Cham, he was only an occasional participant; he seems, instead, to have been focused on winning the election, following his loss in 1952.[50] His most noteworthy participation in Hyde Park came at the time of the "Fasting Revolt" [*kabot odkhao*], perhaps the high point of the Hyde Park movement.[51] The Fasting Revolt began primarily as a protest against a proposal to have appointed representatives in the new parliament, although a range of other concerns were also raised. The strike began in two places—at Sanam Luang, site of the speeches, and, following a march, at Government House. On February 18, 1956, the day before the hunger strike began, Cham came to Sanam Luang and took the stage. He began by paying respect to a Buddha image, to Wat Prakaew, and to the audience. He then admitted that in the past he had been a deceptive "monkey," but asked that they pay close attention to his words. He then called attention to his beautiful sharkskin suit,

---

[48] See: "Tribunal Hears Nai Cham's Own Reasons for Strange Antics in Parliament," *Bangkok Post*, March 24, 1951, 1; "Nai Cham Tells Tribunal His Antics Publicity Acts," *Bangkok Post*, April 10, 1951, 1; and "Cham reng kamakon sopsuan hai set wa klai luaktang tong pai ha siang" [Cham urges tribunal to finish, says with elections nearing, he must go campaign], *Sayam Nikon*, March 12, 1951, 1. The latter also includes testimony of Cham's odd behavior at home in Nakhon Sithammarat, including hiding from his wife at his neighbor's home, and stating that the prime minister (Phibun) was bad, but the field marshal (also Phibun) was good.

[49] Thus, if it were a publicity stunt, it backfired, due to the delays the committee imposed.

[50] *Bangkok Post*, February 14, 1956, 1, reports that Cham's party, Thammathipat, was then campaigning in the south, employing a Hyde Park style—a full year ahead of the election. A *Deli Mei* reporter met him on a southern train about this time, on his way to campaign in Phatthalung. See: *Deli Mei*, February 25, 1956, 7; and *Deli Mei*, February 28, 1956, 7.

[51] James Ockey, "Civil Society and Street Politics in Historical Perspective," in *Reforming Thai Politics*, ed. Duncan McCargo (Copenhagen: Nordic Institute of Asian Studies, 2002), 107–23.

referred obliquely to political leaders, and asked why no attention was being paid to the high price of rice, to loud cheers.[52] Cham continued to speak at Sanam Luang during the days of the fast; on February 21, when the fasters were arrested and charged with inciting rebellion, Cham was arrested with them.[53] A week later, a hearing was held, and, before the judge arrived in the courtroom, Cham began creating a disturbance, shouting *"chaiyo"* (hurrah!), as if cheerleading, although no one joined his cheer. Later, one protester was released, Cham was sent for psychiatric evaluation at the hospital, and the rest were returned to the jail.[54]

Cham's extended campaigning in Nakhon Sithammarat in the lead-up to the 1957 election bore fruit, as he was reelected to parliament in the February election. He returned to his antics immediately during the new session. When called upon to swear the oath, he refused, quite loudly. Later, before finally taking the oath as required, he first promised he would be honest to Luangpho Ophasi perpetually.[55]

During the presentation of government policy, Hyde Park Movement party member Phi Bunnak sarcastically pointed out that the nation's high level of defense spending would not be necessary if the navy still had the *Si Ayutthaya* warship, at which point Cham shouted out a curse. Asked to withdraw his rude words, Cham replied, "I am angry that people would kill my father [Phibun] with the *Si Ayutthaya*." On a second request to withdraw his curse words, he replied, "I apologize, and withdraw my words, and please kill my father and kill the ship *Si Ayutthaya*."[56]

As the debate later drew to a close, Cham, as he had done in the past, set out to provoke the president of the parliament. As the president called a close to the debate, Cham called for a point of order. Told by the president that there was nothing out of order, Cham rose anyway and complained that the president had not looked to all sides of the parliament before declaring that there were no objections to closing the debate. Told to stop, Cham replied that if the president would discuss it with him, he would stop. When the president refused, Cham returned to his original complaint, pursuing it until the president called in the police, who came and asked Cham to leave. Instead, he quieted down, the police left, and he immediately began again. The president then berated Cham for damaging the honor of the parliament, and called the police back in, whereupon Cham again quieted down. Eventually, the president ordered the police to physically remove Cham. Later that afternoon, Cham returned and again complained that the president had not looked to all sides before closing the earlier debate, at which point the president retorted that Cham was acting as if he were drunk. Cham replied that he was not drunk, but was hurt, as if he had been punched in the nose by Kothang and Jamroen (two famous boxers).[57]

---

[52] In other words, a quite clear critique of wealthy politicians ignoring the plight of the poor. *San Seri*, February 19, 1956, 1 ff.

[53] The orders came from the Minister of the Interior, Police-General Phao Siyanon, on the grounds that the speakers had gone beyond the bounds of the law and, by advocating some of the same principles, were abetting the communist movement. See [3] SO. RO. 0201 6/36 box 3, *Kanjapkum phu kin lae od ahan prathuang duan mak* [Arrest of people who ate and fasted in protest, urgent] 4431/2499 (Ministry of Interior, February 24, 1956).

[54] *Deli Mei*, February 28, 1956, 1.

[55] Luangpho Ophasi is a well known monk from Nakhon Sithammarat who passed away two years earlier.

[56] *Raingan kanprachum sapha phuthaen ratsadon* 3/2500.

[57] Ibid.

Cham was reelected in December 1957, following the Sarit coup. However, this parliament, like the previous one, proved short-lived, and after Sarit abrogated the constitution and eliminated the parliament, Cham was sidelined from formal politics for over a decade. This did not silence him, however. When the king came on a royal visit to Nakhon Sithammarat, Cham dressed in his finest clothes, got a gift for the king, and, as a former MP, went to meet him. Upon meeting the king, Cham said that the king had raised up a giant (*yaksa*) in Field Marshal Sarit as prime minister, only to have him destroy the country. This led to the police taking Cham to the hospital for another psychiatric evaluation. When Cham's friend asked whether he would do it again, given the chance, Cham responded that next time he would give the king a papaya, to symbolize the corruption (*kinmuang*, literally, "eating the city") in the bureaucracy.[58]

With Sarit in power, Cham was charged with treason and placed in custody at Latyao prison, where he shared a cell block with those charged with being communists or communist supporters. Cham's lawyers urged him to plead not guilty by reason of insanity, and doctors were lined up who were willing to testify accordingly.

Cham's behavior at the prison was quite eccentric. First thing in the morning, when the doors to the courtyard were unlocked, he would move to the base of the flagpole in front of the hospital and, in a loud voice, produce a crow's call that would resound throughout the prison, waking prisoners still asleep. He would then proceed to meditate and to "eat the sun." Throughout the day, he was quiet, then at night, when the time came for lockdown, he would act up again, claiming to be ill, and forcing the guards to chase him around the compound, even taking refuge in mud puddles to escape, temporarily. This often led to him spending the night in the hospital rather than in a cell.[59] At one point, he became so incensed at being locked up that he picked up the table and slammed it into the toilet, breaking the table, then stuffed the toilet full of paper. Because of this behavior, Cham was put in chains for a time.[60]

Cham's trial, before a military tribunal, was among the first conducted in his cellblock, perhaps because he was expected to plead insanity. However, when he took the stand, he refused to use an insanity defense, claiming that he had always been perfectly sane.[61] He was sentenced to five years in prison. After the verdict, after the insanity plea was no longer in play, he behaved differently, so that his cellmates were left with mixed views on his sanity. He stopped his crow calls, stopped eating the sun, and spent more time reading and less time talking. He sought a transfer to a prison in Nakhon Sithammarat, which he soon received.[62]

After his release from prison, Cham ran for election one last time, in 1970, in a by-election in Bangkok. Although he won a seat, the parliament was abrogated shortly thereafter. At about that same time, he was attacked by unidentified

---

[58] Interview with a close friend of Cham's (name withheld), January 2003.

[59] Siwa Ronachit [pseud. Suwat Woradilok], *Jotmai jak latyao* (Bangkok: Prakai, 1978), 15–16.

[60] Ibid, 32.

[61] Ibid., 26–27. Suwat believed that Cham's pride prevented him from pleading insanity.

[62] Ibid., 16, 27, 35; interview, Thawip Woradilok, Bangkok, January 2003. Thawip expressed the opinion that Cham was not in full control of himself, but also said that he and others were unsure about Cham's actual state of mind, given the differences in his behavior when it was not beneficial for him to be insane.

hooligans in Bangkok and left paralyzed, living quietly thereafter at home in Nakhon Sithammarat. He passed away in 1978, at age eighty.[63] His legacy comes not in the form of a successful party or an ideology, and not in the bills he championed, for he spent his career in the opposition, deliberately; even when formally associated with a party, he largely worked on his own. Looking back at his career, this seems to stem from his desire to speak up for ordinary people and to speak back to power and authority, especially when that power was bullying the disadvantaged. He found creative ways to do that, even under authoritarian and dangerous circumstances. At the same time, he sought to make the parliament a place of and for the people, a place where an MP might play football with children, a tricycle driver might play the music of the countryside, and a representative might arrive on a buffalo rather than in an expensive car with an entourage of officials. Quixotic perhaps, for that time, yet admirable, nonetheless.

KHRU CHAM, MADNESS, AND POLITICS

Khru Cham lived a long, interesting, and eccentric life, one that took him in and out of parliament and prison, and included several evaluations of his sanity. In finding some meaning in his colorful life, we might also find meanings in politics, prisons, and madness in Thailand. Cham's mental health remained in question throughout much of his life. As noted above, some of Cham's cellmates thought him mad, others thought he was pretending. One of his colleagues in parliament, Jongkhon Krairoek, believed that Cham pretended to be mad for so long that he eventually became mad.[64] Cham's daughter said that he was always perfectly rational at home, that all his outbursts were in public, and that at home his wife often scolded him for his public demonstrations.[65] One of Cham's closest friends, who hosted him while he was undergoing psychiatric evaluation in Suratthani, believed that Cham was actually mad at that time.[66]

A doctor at the Suratthani hospital told me that, while the doctors agreed to certify Cham insane if he asked them to do so, they had doubts, suspected that he might be pretending, and thought the chances were about 50-50 whether he was mad or just pretending to be.[67] Of course, the experts' evaluations of Cham's madness were based on his abnormal behavior, and in that sense, his madness was socially constructed.[68] Abnormal behavior is assessed against what society deems normal, and there is no question that Cham acted outside of societal norms on many occasions. That does not necessarily make him insane, and, of course, Cham acted within societal norms far more often than he acted outside of them. It thus may prove useful to think carefully about those occasions when he acted outside societal norms, to discover the patterns and the purposes of his strategic if erratic behavior.

---

[63] The rather vague story of Cham being beaten by hooligans and the reference to the by-election are in his obituary; see: *Bangkok Post,* December 12, 1978, 3. Cham's daughter said that Cham eventually agreed to accept a declaration that he was insane, whereupon he was released early from prison. By the time he returned home, paralysis had already set in.

[64] Jongkon, *Sinlapaluaktang,* 104.

[65] Interview with Janthip Jamratnet, January 2003.

[66] Ibid.

[67] Ibid.

[68] See: Roy Porter, *A Social History of Madness* (London: Weidenfeld and Nicolson, 1987); and Foucault, *Madness and Civilization.*

Khru Cham's eccentric behavior began with his political campaigning, perhaps most notably in his emulation of Phrawet Sandon, for, surely, walking through the market wearing nothing but briefs stands outside societal norms. As we noted, Cham was contesting elections as a member of the opposition, with limited financial resources. He did so at a time when pro-government MPs often had access to government resources and wealthy candidates had large advantages in their ability to promote themselves effectively through providing goods and entertainment to voters. Under the circumstances, Cham had to be creative in his campaigning. In an interview with a reporter in 1957, he discussed his campaign techniques. He began by asking the reporter what people thought of his actions, to which the reporter replied that people thought he was crazy. Cham replied, "Exactly ... I'm very pleased with that. I invest only a little money, and campaign simply, but the benefits are extensive."[69] Cham went on to point out that his eccentric actions were a form of advertising, which stimulated interest in him. Cham carried with him a newspaper article that described some of his eccentric behavior, and showed it enthusiastically to people, as it demonstrated that he had enough importance to receive coverage in the national press, which he clearly thought beneficial to his election campaign.

Cham also claimed that people of all ages and places knew him and understood he was not crazy, and that even doctors had been unable to confirm he was crazy. He insisted that voters in Nakhon Sithammarat would not have elected him if he were truly crazy, because they were not crazy. The reporter notes that Cham was perfectly sane throughout the interview. Cham was, of course, delighted to be interviewed, and to discuss his craziness with the press in the midst of an election campaign. Last, we must note that when Cham's tricks were discovered, voters did not react with outrage, but, rather, with delight. Cham, like Hanuman, played the trickster, challenging wealth and power with his cleverness, and was greatly admired for it.

Explaining Cham's eccentricities in terms of campaigning may be straightforward. Explaining his behavior as an opposition MP is more complex, for here he was speaking to power, and only indirectly to voters. On the surface, getting expelled from parliament, on multiple occasions, for complaining that the president had not "looked in all directions" before closing a debate, would seem to serve no purpose. And yet, as a means of complaining that government MPs were unfairly advantaged by the president relative to opposition MPs, his tactics may have been effective, to some degree. In the aftermath, attempts were made to pacify Cham, and he, at least, debated quite frequently during this period. By fighting with parliamentary police, Cham also got his protests covered in the newspapers. My informal survey of the press during this period indicates that, among all MPs, only party leaders got more coverage than Cham. And last, the writer Samnao Hiriotapa claims that, at times, Cham *wanted* to be expelled, so that he could show the subsequent newspaper clippings to voters, as evidence that he was willing to fight, even literally, against the powerful on their behalf.[70]

Much of Cham's eccentric behavior, inside parliament and out, was full of symbolic meaning. Sometimes that meaning was quite clear; at other times it was more difficult to read, depending, perhaps, on how dangerous the speech was. When Cham sent brooms through the mail to government officials, or spent time publicly sweeping streets, his message of a need to clean up corruption was clear and simple

---

[69] *Deli Mei*, February 28, 1957, 7.

[70] Samnao, *Phuthaen thi di det*, 19–20.

to read. When he donned peasant clothing and rode a buffalo to parliament (one imagines him tying his water buffalo to a post amidst a line of expensive cars), most people read it as an expression of solidarity with the peasantry. By comparison, the reaction of his colleagues indicates that many of them received his other message, that the parliament was little more than a herd of water buffalos, loyal and not very astute. When Cham visited the Ministry of the Interior and threw water on the peasants there and shouted "communists," his message is more difficult to discern. (As noted above, it probably was a reference to the government's latest strategy of targeting peasants as communists, or at least as potential communists.) Cham never explained the symbolism behind this particular antic, claiming instead that he had simply been afraid that the peasants had come to assassinate the minister[71]—a neat reversal of the actual pattern of assassinations at the time, whereby the powerful killed the less powerful.

It is in these symbolic messages that we can see most clearly what Cham was doing: speaking to authoritarian power in a way that maximized attention while minimizing danger (risk). As related above, in a parliamentary session *Khru* Cham complained about the train service, saying he had had to cling to the stairway, hanging like a bat on the train, and acting it out as he spoke. The president of the parliament, tired of Cham's act, banged his gavel and asserted, "This is not a theater!"[72] He could not have been more wrong. With the authoritarian government controlling the parliament, it had become nothing but a theater, which Cham knew well. In an interview with a reporter in 1957, Cham said of his eccentric parliamentary behavior that he was merely acting out a drama (*sadaeng lakhon*). However, perhaps rather than the formal *lakhon*, Cham's style may be characterized as *likay*, a more populist and subversive form of theater. The key figure in *likay* is the clown, whose role is largely ad libbed. The clown occupies an unusual role, moving back and forth between members of the audience and actors in the play, seeking laughter through social commentary, including poking fun at the aristocracy in ways that would have been considered subversive in other settings.[73] King Vajiravudh, in particular, was dismissive of *likay*, calling it "nothing more than a sort of parody of the more dignified and graceful [*lakhon*]," adding,

> The performers in the *lik[ay]*, as now played, are for the most part clowns who sing and dance in a very indifferent manner, but as they generally contrive to be funny, in a sort of rough fashion, they are popular with a certain class of people who are not very discriminating in their taste.[74]

In fact, that "certain class of people" were in the majority, and constituted Cham's electorate and his audience. Despite King Vajiravudh's dismissive remarks, not only did *likay* survive, but it was strongly promoted by Phibun.

---

[71] "Nai Cham Tells Tribunal His Antics Publicity Acts," *Bangkok Post,* April 10, 1951, 1.

[72] *Sayam Nikon,* March 4, 1948, 1.

[73] See: Michael Smithies, "Likay: A Note on the Origin, Form, and Future of Siamese Folk Opera," *Journal of the Siam Society* 59, no. 1 (1971): 33–64; and Paradee Tungtang, "Shakespeare in Thailand" (PhD thesis, University of Warwick, 2011), 275–76.

[74] King Vajiravudh, "Notes on the Siamese Theatre," *Journal of the Siam Society* 55, no. 1 (1966): 3.

On the parliamentary stage, it was Cham who acted as the *dao rai*, the evil star, the subversive clown. Cham's insistence on treating the parliament as a theater was subversive on yet another level. As Craig Reynolds noted in his analysis of the sedition trial of Thim Sukkhayang,

> The court's concern for the corruption of "proper" speech by commoners intimates a more deep-seated concern that the vulgarization of high culture was but one weapon that might be arrayed against the ideology and institutions of the ruling elite.[75]

One of the many accusations against Cham was that he used language that an ordinary person would not. In fact, one might rather say his language was common. He created controversy by pointing at the face of a minister, while calling him *sengli,* and antagonized the parliamentary president through his interruptions and his word choices. His dress was likewise "vulgar" on occasion, whether through his use of peasant attire, or his stripping off most of his clothes to jump in the fountain. In this way he vulgarized the dignified façade of democracy that had been put in place.

None of this fully explains Cham's "madness," however. Actors are not really mad, they play roles. Khukrit Pramot once remarked, to Cham's delight, that if all MPs joined his Buddhist party, there would be no further arguing in parliament, rather they could come together and peacefully sing *nora* (southern slang for *manora*).[76] *Manora*, like *likay*, originated in the South. In *manora*, the role of the clown, who speaks in the southern dialect, and employs improvised, often satirical, topical verse, was even more prominent. It was also quite competitive, with stars competing to win the loyalty of audiences away from other troupes.[77] But whereas *likay* was intended for entertainment, *manora* was connected to the spirit world—as part of the *manora*, there is a call for ancestor spirits to take possession of the actors. As Ginsburg noted,

> In former times the *manora* master had a role in the community far beyond that of a mere entertainer. He was in fact the pre-eminent magician in the surrounding area, and was relied upon to perform rites involving the *khwan*, such as exorcisms, topknot ceremonies, ordinations, etc. ... The *manora* player and his family were feared in the past because of their occult powers ... great pains were taken to attempt to spoil the rival's performance by means of curses, and to protect one's own performance from the rival's curse...[78]

Cham's qualification in Buddhism, his use of the honorific *khru*, his frequent appeals to religion, and even his magic performances fit this profile.[79] And *manora*

---

[75] Craig J. Reynolds, "Sedition in Thai History: A Nineteenth-Century Poem and Its Critics," in *Thai constructions of knowledge,* ed. Manas Chitakasem and Andrew Turton (London: School of Oriental and African Studies, University of London, 1991), 27.

[76] *Sayam Nikon* May 6, 1948, 5.

[77] Henry Ginsburg, "The *Manora* Dance Drama: An Introduction," *Journal of the Siam Society* 60 (July 1972): 169–81. See also Alexander Horstmann, "*Manora*, Ancestral Beings, Possession, and Cosmic Rejuvenation in Southern Thailand," *Anthropos* 107 (2012): 103–14.

[78] Ginsburg, "The *Manora* Dance Drama," 177–78.

[79] Samnao provides multiple examples of Cham performing rituals both during election campaigns and at the parliament.

provides a clear explanation for Cham's "swallowing the sun" to enhance his power. To cite Ginsburg again,

> Even today every *nora* wears around his neck and waist a barrage of protective charms and amulets, in various forms, but mainly small images of the Buddha. And to protect or sanctify his own performance, just before appearing each player makes a prayer, which he combines with gestures in his own personal ritual. I saw one player grasp a handful of air from in front of the side curtain, then "swallow" it, and convey it to his navel. Then he brought his thumb upwards from the navel and into the roof of his mouth.[80]

To make the final connection to "madness" we need to keep in mind that Cham's time in parliament marked the rise of the science of psychiatry in Thailand.[81] Traditionally, it was thought that madness was the result of possession, and thus madness was treated by magicians and spirit mediums—just as the *manora* masters performed magic and exorcisms, and invited possession in their performances. For Cham, madness was connected to power, and his ability to master it, as a *nora* masters a possessing spirit, made him powerful.

Ultimately, the purpose of the 1932 uprising was progress, modernization, and the advance of reason and science. Under Phibun, the focus of these efforts sometimes included democratization and always included populism, thus perpetuating the survival of the old traditions from below.[82] By the time Sarit came to power in the late fifties, progress was seen in technocratic terms, proceeding from a strong, central, rational, and scientific authoritarian state. Psychiatry, which had already begun to push aside possession as an explanation for madness, in the Cold War context, was enlisted on the side of the authoritarian state, against its enemies. The enemies of the state, and belief in their ideologies, including communism, became abnormal, and their proponents mad. Increasingly, madness was seen not as possession by powerful spirits, but rather as aberrant behavior, including aberrant political behavior, and treated by doctors in hospitals. It is surely this transition that led to Cham's initial refusal to plead innocent by reason of insanity, for to make such a plea was to admit to having lost control of his power, and his message. For the authoritarian state, getting Cham to accept his madness would undermine the power of his message, for if he were irrational, then his message must also be irrational, and devoid of power and meaning. Of course, madness still was not criminal, it was an illness, so that madness continued to protect Cham from the authoritarian state through its own "science." While Cham would eventually bend to Sarit's use of "science," and in the process be released from prison and sent to a hospital, he did

---

[80] Ginsburg, "The *Manora* Dance Drama," 178.

[81] The best source on the history of psychiatry in Thailand is Walter Irvine, "The Thai-Yuan 'Madman' and the 'Modernizing, Developing Thai Nation' as Bounded Entities under Threat: A Study in the Replication of a Single Image" (PhD thesis, University of London, 1982).

[82] The return of populism and the rising influence of both technocratic and less technocratic forms of politics under Thaksin Shinawatra are certainly part of the reason for the return of magic to public politics, most clearly seen in the form of the blood curse cast by Red Shirt protestors on the Democrat Party headquarters. Despite Sarit and the rise of science, rationalism, and technocracy, black magic was still practiced privately. See Robert Horn, "In Thailand, A Little Black Magic is Politics as Usual," *Time*, March 20, 2010, http://content.time.com/time/world/article/0,8599,1973871,00.html, accessed November 5, 2014.

not break. To this day, he is widely and fondly remembered throughout the south, and the power and meaning, and even the (non)existence, of his madness, while clear to the people of Nakhon Sithammarat, remains unanswered, unresolved, and, ultimately, beyond the rationality of the authoritarian state.

CHAPTER SEVEN

BIG IS GOOD: THE BANHARN-JAEMSAI OBSERVATORY TOWER IN SUPHANBURI

Yoshinori Nishizaki

Many leaders in Asia have competed to build public buildings of superlative size. A good case in point is the Kuala Lumpur Tower (KL Tower, or Menara Kuala Lumpur) in Kuala Lumpur, Malaysia, which no visitor will fail to notice. At 421 meters in height (1,381 feet) and built on a hill, the tower soars above its surrounding buildings. As visitors ascend to its observation floor, they can see conspicuously displayed on the wall the KL Tower's standing vis-à-vis the world's other tall towers. At the time of my visit in 2005, the KL Tower ranked fourth after the CN Tower in Toronto, the Ostankino Tower in Moscow, and the Oriental Pearl Tower in Shanghai.

Most foreign tourists cannot help smiling cynically at this public display of *Malaysia Boleh*—an official slogan launched in the 1990s, meaning "Malaysia can do it!" While they are amazed at the height of the tower, many tourists tend to shrug it off as a silly, frivolous attempt at international competition. A tourist from California said to me, "The government should spend more money on helping the poor, instead of trying to emulate other countries." This comment is suggestive of a common Western mindset that adopts a utilitarian and rationalist perspective. Starkly put, a public good that does not bring economic benefits to the maximum number of individuals is no good. Such a viewpoint is not wrong. But as Milne and Mauzy aptly noted,[1] the tower is "designed not just to be serviceable or to meet economic needs, but to impress." It is what Malaysians can show off to the outside world as the symbol of their modernity.

An earlier and shorter version of this essay appeared with the title "The Gargantuan Project and Modernity in Provincial Thailand," *Asia Pacific Journal of Anthropology* 8, no. 3 (2007): 217–33. Craig Reynolds, whose many works, especially "The Plot of Thai History" (cited below), have influenced me, once visited the Banharn-Jaemsai Tower, and he has shared his views of it with me in our many conversations in Canberra and Singapore.

[1] R. S. Milne and Diane Mauzy, *Malaysian Politics under Mahathir* (London: Routledge, 1999), 67.

The individual behind the construction of the KL Tower, former Prime Minister Mohamad Mahathir (in power from 1981 to 2003), would agree. Starting in the late 1980s, he undertook several other grandiose projects, such as the Proton Saga (the first automobile to be made in the "Third World"), the Petronas Towers ("the world's tallest towers" at the time, until Taiwan's Taipei 101 was built in 2004), and the Penang Bridge (the third longest bridge in the world, "six times the length of the Marcos Bridge" in the Philippines).[2] In Mahathir's own words, as provided by Khoo Boon Teik, these projects aimed to show that Malaysia can "compete successfully against other rivals ... and to 'stand as tall as others.'" Mahathir wanted to create a society that is "psychologically subservient to none and respected by the peoples of other nations."[3] Widely condemned by economists as extravagant and ostentatious, his actions were motivated by his intense desire to boost Malaysia's national status. During my visit to Kuala Lumpur in 2005, I asked an ethnic Indian taxi driver what he thought of Mahathir. He answered: "Oh, I like him." The answer made me pause, given Mahathir's pro-Malay policies and authoritarian tendencies. Asked why he liked him, the driver pointed to the KL Tower and said: "He has made Malaysia famous. Thirty years ago, nobody knew where Malaysia was on the world map. Now everybody knows."

Mahathir is not the only leader who has a penchant for grandiose public projects. Leaders as diverse as Ferdinand Marcos and Suharto in the second half of the twentieth century[4] and Siamese kings and Chinese leaders at the turn of the last century,[5] have shown a similar predilection. This paper identifies such a leader in provincial Thailand as well. As political and economic power has devolved from the center to the countryside in many countries of Asia, several provinces or regions within those countries have come to assert their distinctive identities.[6] My case study illustrates such a trend in Thailand.

The province I spotlight is Suphanburi, located in the Chaophraya delta, about a hundred kilometers north of Bangkok. Like many other provinces, Suphanburi's economy has traditionally relied on agriculture. In 1974, for instance, agriculture accounted for 60.5 percent of Suphanburi's Gross Provincial Product (GPP). Among the then-seventy provinces in Thailand, only twelve relied more heavily on agriculture.[7] Although the relative importance of agriculture declined by 2002, it still

---

[2] *Asiaweek*, September 27, 1985, 58.

[3] Cited in Khoo Boon Teik, *Paradoxes of Mahathirism: An Intellectual Biography of Mahathir Mohamad* (Kuala Lumpur: Oxford University Press, 1995), 66, 183, 329.

[4] See: David Wurfel, *Filipino Politics: Development and Decay* (Ithaca: Cornell University Press, 1988), 272; and Jonathan Rigg, Anna Allott, Rachel Harrison, and Ulrich Kratz, "Understanding Languages of Modernization: A Southeast Asian View," *Modern Asian Studies* 33, no. 3 (1999): 587.

[5] See: Maurizio Peleggi, *Lords of Things: The Fashioning of the Siamese Monarchy's Modern Image* (Honolulu: University of Hawaii Press, 2002); and Qin Shao, *Culturing Modernity: The Nantong Model, 1890–1930* (Stanford: Stanford University Press, 2003).

[6] For examples on China, see: Hans Hendrischke and Feng Chongyi, eds., *The Political Economy of China's Provinces: Comparative and Competitive Advantage* (London: Routledge, 1999); and Tim Oakes, "China's Provincial Identities: Reviving Regionalism and Reinventing 'Chineseness,'" *Journal of Asian Studies* 59, no. 3 (2000): 667–92.

[7] National Economic and Social Development Board, *Phalitaphan Phak lae Changwat 2521* [Regional and Provincial Products 1978] (Bangkok: National Economic and Social Development Board, 1979).

remained the largest economic sector in Suphanburi, comprising 27.3 percent of GPP. As of 2004, this figure was the nineteenth highest among Thailand's seventy-five provinces, although it does not mean that Suphanburians are wretchedly poor.[8] While Suphanburi remains mainly an agrarian province, however, it stands out in one crucial respect: it has an array of grandiose public works and other projects that distinguish it from most other Thai provinces. Roads and schools top the list of those works. Suphanburi also boasts of having the world's largest dragon-shaped statue (*mangkon*)—eight meters wide, fifteen meters tall, and more than a hundred meters long. It has been built at the Town Shrine (*sarn chaopho lak muang*) in Muang District at a cost of 200 million baht. Another conspicuous project—the one I highlight in this chapter—is a soaring observation tower (123.25 meters tall) that stands in the heart of Suphanburi, a tower of unmatched height in provincial Thailand.

The construction of this tower, as well as many other public projects, is credited to one man: Banharn Silpa-archa, a member of parliament from Suphanburi (1976–2008) and also prime minister (1995–96). Throughout his political career, Banharn used a combination of his personal wealth and state funds to implement big public projects, including the tower. He was often accused of colluding with local contractors to skim off profits from such publicly funded projects. The civil servants who channeled those projects subsequently won promotions, allegedly thanks to Banharn's patronage. These lines of accusation were particularly common in the 1980s and 1990s, and Banharn's name became a de facto synonym for "money politics" (a euphemism for corruption) in Thailand. Yet most Suphanburians still lent strong support to him, as exemplified by his resounding victories at the polls.[9] Why? I argue that one (if not the sole) reason for Banharn's entrenched political authority is his role in enhancing Suphanburi's provincial prestige. I attempt to show how the observation tower—a seemingly wasteful and pretentious public project—has become a distinctive symbol (*sanyalak*) of Suphanburi's modernity, and how it has boosted Suphanburi's reputation. In particular, I highlight a ceremony held by Banharn in 1999 to celebrate and advertise the uniqueness of the tower, and to shape Suphanburians' positive provincial identity. In broad theoretical terms, I shed light on the social-psychological underpinning of Banharn's political authority at the local level.

My argument departs from the bulk of the literature (and media reports) on Thai politics that attribute the electoral success of rural-based politicians like Banharn to a range of unscrupulous means, such as violence, intimidation, electoral fraud (especially vote-buying), pork-barrel spending, patronage, and so forth.[10] These

---

[8] National Economic and Social Development Board, "Gross Regional and Provincial Products 2005," available at http://www.nesdb.go.th/Default.aspx?tabid=96, accessed January 14, 2015.

[9] Banharn won between 60 and 94 percent of the votes in all the elections he contested between 1976 and 2007.

[10] See, among others: Benedict Anderson, "Murder and Progress in Modern Siam," *New Left Review* 181 (1990): 33–48 (reprinted in Benedict R. O'G. Anderson, *Exploration and Irony in Studies of Siam over Forty Years* [Ithaca: Cornell Southeast Asia Program Publications, 2014], 101–15); Daniel Arghiros, *Democracy, Development, and Decentralization in Provincial Thailand* (Richmond, UK: Curzon, 2001); Ruth McVey, ed., *Money and Power in Provincial Thailand* (Honolulu: University of Hawaii Press, 2000), 1–122; Michael Nelson, *Central Authority and Local Administration in Thailand* (Bangkok: White Lotus, 1998); James Ockey, *Making Democracy: Leadership, Class, Gender, and Political Participation in Thailand* (Honolulu: University of Hawaii Press, 2004), 81–123; and Pasuk Phongpaichit and Sungsidh Piriyarangsan, *Corruption and Democracy in Thailand* (Chiang Mai: Silkworm, 1996), 57–107.

politicians allegedly attain and maintain political power by deceiving, buying off, or intimidating voters. Accordingly, the image of rural voters that emerges from such literature is wholly negative: submissive, venal, and timid. Readers are led to believe that rural voters are easy prey to the enormous coercive and financial resources that sleazy politicians, including mafia-type bosses or godfathers (*chaopho*), possess. Put another way, rural voters allegedly have little agency of their own to vote for the politicians they want to support. In fact, they may not even know who to vote for or how to distinguish "good" candidates from "bad" ones, because they are not educated or politically sophisticated enough. Such views supplied the military with a convenient justification for ousting Prime Minister Thaksin Shinawatra in a 2006 coup, despite his unprecedented electoral support from voters in rural Thailand.[11] These stereotyped views, barbarously simple and condescending as they may be, have long constituted the dominant discourse on rural Thai politics and society.

Based on my fieldwork in Suphanburi (and elsewhere in rural Thailand), I find such popular and scholarly discourse profoundly unsatisfying, incomplete, and stifling, if not wholly inaccurate. The scholars who have exposed the seamy problems of rural Thai politics and society have done enormous academic service; the value of their individual scholarship is beyond dispute. Nonetheless, the *sum* of their scholarship has produced the unintended effect of projecting the uncanny image of rural Thailand as a socially inferior and changeless "other"—a perennially problematic and incorrigible entity inhabited by a hopelessly docile and venal people. The scholars who have propounded the mainstream discourse on rural Thailand, no matter how well-intentioned they may be, are (unknowingly) complicit in reproducing and perpetuating this uniformly adverse "Orientalist" image. Yet, as Craig Reynolds reminds us by drawing on historiographer Hayden White, every phenomenon, individual, event, incident, accident, and so forth should have multiple "plots" without having any one ontologically absolute quality.[12] What kind of "plot" it has depends on how scholars invent or reconstruct it by imputing a certain structure of meanings to it. Each "emplotment" is based not on objective evidence, but rather on the subjective, selective, and creative interpretation of the available evidence—interpretations that reflect the scholars' respective worldviews or ideological positions. This relativist or deconstructivist approach has long been conspicuous by its absence in the studies of rural Thai politics. It is only in recent years that a small number of revisionist studies have appeared to subject the prevailing plot—the one that centers on debased politicians and their pliant, blighted voters—to critical scrutiny, and to offer alternative "plots."

More specifically, Anek Laothamatas—perhaps the trailblazer of revisionist scholarship—has drawn our attention to the two conflicting meanings of democracy that urban middle-class people and rural dwellers have come to embrace in the historical context of Thailand's uneven socioeconomic development. While

---

[11] Andrew Walker, "The Rural Constitution and the Everyday Politics of Elections in Northern Thailand," *Journal of Contemporary Asia* 38, no. 1 (2008): 84–85.

[12] Craig Reynolds, "The Plot of Thai History: Theory and Practice," in *Patterns and Illusions: Thai History and Thought*, ed. Gehan Wijeyewardene and E. C. Chapman (Canberra: Australian National University, 1992), 313–32. See also these volumes by Hayden White: *Metahistory: The Historical Imagination in Nineteenth-century Europe* (Baltimore: Johns Hopkins University Press, 1973); *Tropics of Discourse: Essays in Cultural Criticism* (Baltimore: Johns Hopkins University Press, 1978); and *The Content of the Form: Narrative Discourse and Historical Representation* (Baltimore: Johns Hopkins University Press, 1987).

economically well-off Bangkok residents (can afford to) define democracy as a set of high-sounding principles, such as freedom of speech and government transparency, rural voters, whose socioeconomic interests have long been neglected by the central state, regard democracy as a mechanism or process that brings them concrete material benefits. Accordingly, for rural voters, honest politicians who promote the abstract "national interests" of Thailand do not necessarily make good politicians. Instead, the rural voters' ideal politicians are "those who visit them often, address their immediate grievances effectively, and bring numerous public works to their communities."[13] Anek thus makes a simple yet important point that rural-based politicians do not (always) buy or kill their way into corridors of power; they get elected because they have the voters' support.[14]

Andrew Walker provides valuable empirical support to Anek's (unsubstantiated) point by highlighting the unwritten, time-honored "rural constitution"—a set of locally embedded moral values, norms, expectations, and aspirations—in Chiang Mai Province.[15] William Callahan also scrutinizes the allegedly rampant vote-buying in rural Thailand, suggesting that it is not so much an actual phenomenon as a biased discursive concept that is repeatedly invoked, exaggerated, demonized, and perpetuated by urban elites to maintain their self-righteous sense of moral superiority over the countryside.[16] More recently, Marc Askew has shown that the virtual hegemony of the Democrat Party in southern Thailand is based on the party's successful invention and manipulation of the voters' regional identity as "virtuous southerners" (although he accords due attention to the use of money and party machines in the region).[17] Drawing much inspiration from Reynolds's argument, I have sought elsewhere to contribute to this body of scholarship, too, by using the cases of Banharn and another rural-based politician, Ladawan Wongsriwong.[18]

I situate this paper as another small contribution to offering a more balanced and nuanced (or less pessimistic) picture of rural politics. Contrary to what the conventional plot has us believe, most Suphanburians viewed Banharn as their own

---

[13] Anek Laothamatas, "A Tale of Two Democracies: Conflicting Perceptions of Elections and Democracy in Thailand," in *The Politics of Elections in Southeast Asia*, ed. Robert Taylor (New York: Woodrow Wilson Center Press, 1996), 202.

[14] Ibid., 207.

[15] See: Walker, "The Rural Constitution and the Everyday Politics of Elections in Northern Thailand," 84–105; and Andrew Walker, *Thailand's Political Peasants: Power in the Modern Rural Economy* (Madison: University of Wisconsin Press, 2012).

[16] William Callahan, "The Discourse of Vote Buying and Political Reform in Thailand," *Pacific Affairs* 78, no. 1 (2005): 95–113. For similar, if brief, critiques, see: Thongchai Winichakul, "The Others Within: Travel and Ethno–Spatial Differentiation of Siamese Subjects 1885–1910," in *Civility and Savagery: Social Identity in Tai States*, ed. Andrew Turton (Richmond, UK: Curzon), 55–56; and Thongchai Winichakul, "Toppling Democracy," *Journal of Contemporary Asia* 38, no. 1 (2008): 24–26. For a historical account of the localist discourse on vote-buying in Chiang Mai, see: Katherine Bowie, "Vote Buying and Village Outrage in an Election in Northern Thailand: Recent Legal Reforms in Historical Context," *Journal of Asian Studies* 67, no. 2 (2008): 469–511.

[17] Marc Askew, *Performing Political Identity: The Democrat Party in Southern Thailand* (Chiang Mai: Silkworm, 2008).

[18] Yoshinori Nishizaki, *Political Authority and Provincial Identity in Thailand: The Making of Banharn-buri* (Ithaca: Cornell University Southeast Asia Program Publications, 2011); Yoshinori Nishizaki, "Prostitution and Female Leadership in Rural Thailand: The Story of Phayao Province," *Modern Asian Studies* 45, no. 6 (2011): 1535–97.

"legitimate" politician, and not as the prototype of unscrupulous, rural-based politicians who resort to guns, goons, and gold to attain power. Just like beauty, Banharn's legitimacy was in the eye of the beholder. People supported him because they wanted to, not because they were coerced, paid, or told to do so. In other words, they had their own agency or autonomous informed choice to act in accordance with their preferences. This argument does not deny or question Banharn's alleged corruption; my point is only that there is more to his resilient political authority in Suphanburi than we are often led to believe.

Unless otherwise noted, the information in this paper is based on my fieldwork conducted in 1999–2000, 2002, and 2004. This fieldwork involved (1) a direct observation of the aforementioned ceremony that Banharn held in 1999 to broadcast the symbolic value of the observation tower, and (2) open-ended interviews with civil servants, merchants, workers, students, and others in and outside Suphanburi. I also make extensive use of government documents and provincial newspapers to supplement my analysis.

A Brief Historical Background

In the post-Enlightenment global regime of visual and discursive representations, the products of superior technology—perceived metaphysically as things that are big, long, tall, bright, wide, clean, fast, beautiful, fragrant, orderly, organized, etc.—have been upheld, through a plethora of means (e.g., the media, colonial documents, world fairs), as marks of civilization, development, or modernity. Accordingly, the national and sub-national groups that possess such advanced technology have been able to despise, humiliate, and marginalize have-nots as inferior "others."[19] As the whole world has been mapped physically through the means of impersonal cartographic technology, another kind of geography—"the imaginary *social* geography," in which some territorial-based groups (e.g., nation-states and their component parts) enjoy (putatively) higher social status than others—has been symbolically and discursively constructed.[20] In this social geography that has survived into the post-colonial period, a deep social stigma is attached to people living in "backwardness," and these people are often driven to articulate their positive identity by acquiring visible signifiers of modernity or progress that supposedly superior social groups possess. Such signifiers, in other words, have collective non-material prestige value—value often overlooked by most political scientists or economists, who measure modernization in terms of socioeconomic material benefits alone (e.g., income distribution, employment, literacy rate, and access to education and public healthcare).

[19] See: Timothy Mitchell, *Colonising Egypt* (Berkeley: University of California Press, 1991); Michael Adas, *Machines as the Measure of Men: Science, Technology, and Ideologies of Western Dominance* (Ithaca: Cornell University Press, 1989); Arturo Escobar, *Encountering Development: The Making and Unmaking of the Third World* (Princeton: Princeton University Press, 1995); Anne Maxwell, *Colonial Photography and Exhibitions: Representations of the "Native" and the Making of European Identities* (London: Leicester University Press, 1999); Robert Rydell, *All the World's a Fair: Visions of Empire at America International Expositions, 1876–1916* (Chicago: University of Chicago Press, 1984); Thongchai Winichakul, "The Quest for 'Siwilai': A Geographical Discourse of Civilizational Thinking in the Late Nineteenth and Early Twentieth-century Siam," *Journal of Asian Studies* 59, no. 3 (2000): 528–49.

[20] Edward Said, *Orientalism* (New York: Vintage Books, 1979), 53–54, emphasis mine.

Framed in terms of social identity theory in psychology, people with an "inadequate" or "negative social identity"—that is, "a social identity that is not as positive as one with which the individual is satisfied"[21]—try to shed or overcome it by supporting "social competition" or "social action" that "would lead to desirable changes in the situation [in which their group is deemed as inferior and disadvantaged]." They do not resign themselves to the inferior social status foisted unilaterally upon them by dominant higher-status groups. They perceive the existing status hierarchy as unjust and illegitimate, and believe that another hierarchical system, one in which their group enjoys elevated social status, can and should be created through conscious human efforts.[22] From this perspective, a seemingly silly proclivity for public "bigness" can be seen as a desire on the part of "backward" people to escape that degrading label and to gain a sense of collective self-esteem.[23]

The case of Suphanburi lends empirical support to this argument. Suphanburi, in the words of a local historian, used to enjoy "more glory and splendor than any other town" in the Ayutthaya Kingdom.[24] But as Ayutthaya was defeated by Burma, and a new ruling dynasty, the Chakri Dynasty, was established in Bangkok in 1782, Suphanburi declined in relative importance. The new state pursued a skewed pattern of development that favored the new capital. By the middle of the twentieth century, Suphanburi had lapsed into a typical "backward" province in the *ban nok*, a pejorative designation for the socially inferior countryside vis-à-vis modern Bangkok.[25] Against this backdrop, Suphanburians tried to assert their provincial identity by playing up what few signs of distinction they could find. Several seemingly trivial newspaper reports are suggestive of such attempts. One report boasted of the newly constructed Buddha statue (twenty-six meters high) at Phai Rongwua Temple, in southern Suphanburi, as "the world's largest."[26] Another report gave high-profile coverage to a French archeologist who found that the present district of U-Thong was the "biggest" center of the Dvaravati civilization (which dates to the sixth century), and that it "possessed a larger trap for catching elephants than the ones found elsewhere ... The elephant traps in Ayutthaya, Nakhon Sawan, and Surin [Provinces] are just ordinary traps."[27] In reporting the discovery of a ten-meter-high waterfall in 1962, another report touted: "Our province has a beautiful waterfall just like other provinces, such as Nakhon Nayok, Prachuab Khirikhan, Chanthaburi, Kanchanaburi, and Chiang Mai," which "we can be proud of."[28]

Since his first election to parliament in 1976, Banharn (b. 1932), a native of Suphanburi, has built a series of mega public works that have appealed to such

---

[21] Donald Taylor and Fathali Moghaddam, *Theories of Intergroup Relations: International Social Psychological Perspectives* (New York: Praeger, 1994), 83.

[22] Ibid., p. 84; Henri Tajfel, "Social Categorization, Social Identity, and Social Comparison," in *Differentiation between Social Groups: Studies in the Social Psychology of Intergroup Relations*, ed. Henri Tajfel (New York: Academic Press, 1978), 64.

[23] For more details, see: Nishizaki, *Political Authority and Provincial Identity in Thailand*, 205–36.

[24] *Suphanburi Sarn*, December 25, 1987, 6.

[25] For details, see: Nishizaki, *Political Authority and Provincial Identity in Thailand*, 33–56.

[26] *Khon Suphan*, February 8, 1966, p. 1. For more details about this temple's uniqueness, see: Benedict Anderson, *The Fate of Rural Hell: Asceticism and Desire in Buddhist Thailand* (Chicago: University of Chicago Press, 2012).

[27] *Khon Suphan*, November 10, 1964, 16; and *Khon Suphan*, September 15, 1964, 1, 16.

[28] *Khon Suphan*, October 10, 1962, 1.

desires for provincial distinction. Perhaps the most visible and unique among them is the Banharn-Jaemsai Tower (hereafter B-J Tower), an observation tower named after Banharn and his wife.

Banharn-Jaemsai Tower, Suphanburi (author's photo)

BANHARN-JAEMSAI TOWER: SYMBOL OF SUPHANBURI

The origin of the B-J Tower dates to 1991, when Banharn set out to build Queen's Park (24,000 square meters) in the market area of Muang, the central district of Suphanburi. The provincial prison used to be in this area, but in the late 1980s the residents started expressing concern about having an increasingly cramped prison near their homes. In light of this, Banharn proposed that the prison be moved outside the market town and that a recreational park be built in its place and dedicated to Queen Sirikit, who was to celebrate her sixtieth birthday in 1992. Started in August 1991, the construction of the park was completed in October 1994.[29] The park's landmark is the B-J Tower, built over the next four years (1994-97). It is Thailand's second tallest observation tower, after the Baiyoke Sky Tower in Bangkok, most of which is actually occupied by a hotel. Other provinces in Thailand do not even have an observation tower.

---

[29] Muang Municipality of Suphanburi, *Rai-ngarn kitjakarn thesabarn muang Suphanburi 2534–2538* [Report on activities of Muang municipality of Suphanburi 1991–1995] (Suphanburi: Muang Municipality of Suphanburi, 1996), 91.

The signboard displayed at the park's entrance touts Banharn's motive in building the B-J Tower: to emulate the "many foreign countries" he "had visited before" and to "impress viewers ... both Thais and foreigners." One rumor has it that the tower was modeled after the 195-meter Telstra Tower in Canberra, Australia, which Banharn visited in 1994. It is not clear whether this is true, but the resemblance is, indeed, striking. What is clear is that the B-J Tower has been built to impress non-Suphanburians.

In terms of its absolute size, the B-J Tower may not appear worthy of special mention. Its significance becomes clearer, however, when it is placed in Suphanburi's physical context. As mentioned earlier, Suphanburi is a mainly rice-growing rural province in the flat Chaophraya delta. There are no high-rise buildings, not even in the provincial capital. The next tallest building around is the eleven-story building at Chaophraya Yommarat Hospital, the largest government hospital in Suphanburi,[30] which is still less than half the height of the tower. Thus, no building comes even close to matching the B-J Tower in size. It soars far above all other buildings in the market town area.

The construction cost was astonishing: 100 million baht (about US$4 million, in the exchange rate of the early 1990s). Banharn claims that 99 percent of the funds came from his own pocket, while popular donations made up the rest.[31] Some Suphanburians, however, assert that his personal "donations" actually came from his MP fund, an annual state fund of 20 million baht that each MP was allowed to tap to promote local development. The latter story is actually more plausible than the "99 percent" claim. By the early 1990s, Banharn had established four construction and chemical companies, but they all generated unimpressive and unstable profits since at least 1987, thus severely hampering Banharn's ability to build up, let alone donate, his wealth. Between 1987 and 1994, one of his companies actually operated in the red. The other three, while in the black, reaped profits totaling a modest 84.6 million baht during the same period.[32] These records cast doubt on Banharn's claim to generosity. The precise source of his "donation," however, does not seem to concern many of the Suphanburians to whom I talked. An elderly Sino-Thai merchant, who lives within a stone's throw from the B-J Tower, gave this typical comment: "It doesn't make any difference whether he used his own wealth or state funds. The important thing is that Banharn initiated the project, and thanks to that, our hometown has this tower."

Banharn has vigorously marketed the B-J Tower. At his behest, a drawing of the tower has come to be used as a provincial logo in travel brochures and other documents published in Suphanburi. Hats, T-shirts, mugs, and other goods with a similar drawing are sold at a souvenir shop inside the tower. In addition, he designated 1997 as the "Visit Suphanburi Year" to promote tourism.[33] He conducted a similar campaign in 2001–02, called "Amazing Suphanburi Year."[34] The B-J Tower

---

[30] Banharn constructed this building with state funds of 290.7 million baht over 1997–2001. See: Budget Bureau, *Ekasarn Ngop-pramarn 2544*, vol. 4, no. 9 (2000), 67.

[31] *Khon Suphan*, March 1, 1993, 1–2.

[32] Department of Business Development, Ministry of Commerce, Bangkok Company File No. 3893 (Saha Srichai Construction); No. 2164/2523 (Caustic Soda Thai); No. 330/2513 (BS International); and No. 7508/2533 (Siam Occidental Electrochemical).

[33] *Khon Suphan*, January 16, 1997, 1

[34] *Suphan Post*, April 1, 2001, 1, 8.

was the center of these promotional campaigns. The Tourism Authority of Thailand has extended active support to Banharn's campaigns by touting the tower on its website as the "must-see" item in Suphanburi. National newspapers have also assisted, if unintentionally, in promoting the tower nationwide by featuring its photo.[35]

The B-J Tower has consequently become an attraction for tourists from other provinces and even from abroad to visit this otherwise drab rural province. According to a receptionist at the tower, there is a daily average of about a hundred visitors.[36] Writing in 1988 to deplore Suphanburi's former backwardness, one local Thai newspaper carried a column titled (in translation): "50–60 Years Ago, Nobody Wanted to Come to Suphanburi."[37] Today, the fact that non-Suphanburians choose to visit the B-J Tower represents undeniably a temporal break with that past. Thanks to Banharn's vigorous promotion, media exposure, increasing ease of travels, and word of mouth, the B-J Tower has become well known among Thais in general, including even those who have never been to the province.

CEREMONIAL PRODUCTION OF PROVINCIAL IDENTITY

Banharn has used public ceremonies to further play up the distinctiveness of the B-J Tower and his personal role as its patron. The first such ceremony was held on December 5, 1994 (incidentally, King Bhumibol's birthday) to mark the laying of its foundation stone.[38] On September 18, 1999, he held another ceremony, which I observed and highlight in this chapter. This ceremony was meant to publicize the latest addition to Queen's Park, namely, its music fountain, "the first [electrically operated] fountain in Asia."[39] The ceremony served, in effect, to advertise the B-J Tower as well.

Numerous clients of Banharn were involved in the planning and staging of this ceremony. Planning and holding any ceremony, no matter how small, requires a collective effort; Banharn cannot plan, rehearse, and execute a ceremony all by himself. He has to rely on what Geertz calls "impresarios, directors ... the supporting cast, stage crew, and audience."[40] Here is the importance of his network of bureaucratic clients, which he has established by using his vast appointive and budgetary power in the central patrimonial state.[41] To the extent that his clients are

---

[35] See: *Thai Rat*, July 24, 1998, 6; *Bangkok Post*, July 7, 1996, 3; and *Bangkok Post*, August 11, 1996, 3.

[36] During my fieldwork in Suphanburi in 1999, I encountered tour groups from provinces as far as Surat Thani and Nakhon Sithammarat in southern Thailand.

[37] *Suphanburi Sarn*, December 25, 1987, 6.

[38] *Suphan*, March 2002, 7.

[39] *Suphan, Post*, October 1, 1999, 1. Banharn's son Worawuth (Suphanburi's MP, 2001–08), who had studied architecture in England, designed the fountain.

[40] Clifford Geertz, *Negara: The Theater State in Nineteenth-century Bali* (Princeton: Princeton University Press, 1980), 13.

[41] Since 1976, Banharn has held several key cabinet posts (deputy of industry, 1976; agriculture, 1980–81; communications, 1986–88; industry, 1988–90; interior, 1990, 1995–96; and finance, 1990–91); and was prime minister, 1995–96. He was also the leader of the Chart Thai Party (1994–2008). In Thailand's institutional context, marked by a fuzzy line between public and private, those positions have allowed him to wield enormous personal influence over

interested in maximizing their chances of obtaining promotions and state funds, they choose to make a public spectacle of their obsequious loyalty to him. Organizing a ceremony for the music fountain was but one manifestation of their desire to display such loyalty. The literature on provincial Thai politics has us believe that a clientele network represents an electoral machine for harvesting votes,[42] but that is not the case with Banharn's clients. Banharn's clients actually make up what Geertz might call a "system of ceremony production" on the stage of the "provincial theater."[43]

Two institutions—the Muang municipality government and the Provincial Office of Suphanburi—were in charge of the ceremony. They were led by the following three people who had close personal ties to Banharn:

Jaranai Injai-uea, mayor of Muang municipality (1985–2007). A former schoolteacher and daughter of a prominent Sino-Thai landowner, Sa-ngiam Charoensil, in Suphanburi, Jaranai became the mayor in 1985 by defeating her longstanding political rival, Manas Rung-rueng, with Banharn's help. Her mother, Kim Liang, was the elder sister of Winit Sribunma, Banharn's classmate and former director of Chaophraya Yommarat Hospital (1990–91). Banharn's brother-in-law, Bandit, was also director of this hospital (1989–90). Additionally, Jaranai's younger brother, Police Colonel Pridi Charoensil, used to be Banharn's vote canvasser. She also served as advisor to the Suphanburi Chamber of Commerce, of which Banharn is president.

Yodchai Sujit, Muang municipality councilor (1990–2007). Yodchai, also a Sino-Thai, is related by marriage to Banharn, as his mother, Hansa, is the half sister of Banharn's wife, Jaemsai. Hansa is the founder of Hansa Sujit Withaya School, officially opened by Banharn in August 1976.[44] Banharn channeled nearly 9.4 million baht from the Ministry of Education into the school in 1996–98.[45] Yodchai's elder brother, Somchai, is a prominent capitalist who serves as the provincial agent for Hino, Honda, Ford, and Shell Oil. Somchai, along with Hansa, sits on the board of directors of BS International, a chemical company founded by Banharn in 1970.[46] Both Yodchai and Somchai were members of the Suphanburi Chamber of Commerce.

Wiphat Khongmalai, former governor of Suphanburi (1998–2003). A native of Suphanburi and the son of a prominent local rice miller, Wiphat was governor of a small neighboring Singburi province from 1995 to 1998, when

---

bureaucratic promotions and funds allocation. For more details, see: Nishizaki, *Political Authority and Provincial Identity in Thailand*, 85–113.

[42] See, for example: James Ockey, "Business Leaders, Gangsters, and the Middle Class: Social Groups and Civilian Rule in Thailand" (PhD dissertation, Cornell University, 1992); and Pasuk Phongpaichit and Sungsidh Piriyarangsan, *Corruption and Democracy in Thailand* (Chiang Mai: Silkworm, 1996).

[43] Geertz, *Negara*.

[44] *Khon Suphan*, August 10, 1976, 1–3; and *Khon Suphan*, August 20, 1976, 2.

[45] See: Budget Bureau, *Ekasarn Ngop-pramarn 2539*, vol. 8, no. 5 (1995), 2–305; and Budget Bureau, *Ekasarn Ngop-pramarn 2540*, vol. 8, no. 6 (1996), 2–220.

[46] DBD/MC Bangkok Company File No. 330/2513 (BS International).

Banharn transferred him to Suphanburi. Wiphat was grateful to Banharn for the appointment that brought him back to his hometown. Wiphat, too, is related by marriage to Banharn. Wiphat's younger sister, Mukda, is married to Yodchai Sujit, son of Banharn's wife's half-sister, Hansa (see above). Additionally, Wiphat, like Jaranai and Yodchai, served as advisor to the Suphanburi Chamber of Commerce.

These three individuals and their subordinates, linked to Banharn through an interlocking web of personal ties, planned, executed, and attended the ceremony in his honor. First, they drew up a program for the ceremony (see the translation, below), which was then distributed to residents of the market town. At Jaranai's order, Muang municipality also erected public signboards outside Queen's Park and at key junctions in town, which announced the date of the ceremony to maximize popular attendance. As a result of this publicity, the ceremony attracted a crowd of about seven hundred ordinary residents.

PROGRAM[47]

Opening Ceremony for Music Fountain, Queen's Park

by

His Excellency Banharn Silpa-archa, Former Prime Minister

Saturday, September 18, 1999

18:00 — Committee members, officials, guests, and spectators get together at the venue of the ceremony
18:15 — Performance by brass band, Provincial Office of Non-technical Education
19:00 — Performance of Thai country pop music
19:30 — His Excellency Banharn Silpa-archa, former prime minister and guest of honor, arrives at the venue of ceremony
   — Brass band plays auspicious music
   — Muang municipality mayor gives a welcome speech
   — His Excellency Banharn Silpa-archa, guest of honor, gives a speech
   — His Excellency Banharn Silpa-archa opens the music fountain
   — Brass band plays auspicious music
19:40 — Performance 1 by College of Physical Education of Suphanburi
   — Performance 2 by Nathasin Dramatic Arts College
   — Performance 3 by Technical College of Suphanburi
   — Performance 4 by Nathasin Dramatic Arts College
   — Performance 5 by Sports School of Suphanburi
   — Performance 6 by Anuban School of Suphanburi
20:30 — End of ceremony

---

[47] This text has been translated by the author from a copy of the program obtained from a local merchant.

A signboard erected to broadcast the date of the opening ceremony (author's photo)

The spectators were joined by numerous civil servants, local media crew members, and policemen. Also present were traditional Thai dancers and brass bands mobilized by the ceremony organizers from five schools in Suphanburi. In 1995–98 alone, these schools, thanks to Banharn's stranglehold over the Ministry of Education,[48] had received funding in excess of 233 million baht.[49] School leaders gladly dispatched their students to the ceremony to say thanks to Banharn for his past patronage and in the expectation of receiving more in the future.

The master of ceremonies was Rarchan Thipanetr, a young schoolteacher who had achieved rapid promotions thanks to Banharn. Rarchan used to be an ordinary teacher at a small school in Suphanburi, but his fortunes picked up in 1988 when his father, Prasarn, also a schoolteacher and vote canvasser for Jongchai Thiangtham (MP from Suphanburi, 1983–2008), defected from the Social Action Party to the Chart Thai Party, along with Jongchai. Rarchan quickly climbed the bureaucratic ladder in subsequent years. At the time of the ceremony, he was an assistant to the schoolmaster of a prestigious upper secondary school, Sayaisom Withaya. An eloquent speaker, Rarchan was often invited to preside over Banharn's ceremonies, an invitation he eagerly accepted to reciprocate for the favors he had received.

Banharn made his appearance at the ceremony at 19:30, as scheduled. As a brass band played welcoming music, Rarchan, in his attention-grabbing tone of voice, shouted Banharn's name into the microphone: "There he is, the twenty-first prime minister of Thailand, Banharn Silpa-archa!" A horde of high-ranking civil servants, including the governor Wiphat, flocked to Banharn with a respectful *wai*, a Thai

---

[48] In 1997–2001, the Chart Thai Party members, including Banharn's younger brother (Chumpol) and daughter (Kanchana), monopolized cabinet posts in the ministry. Banharn also controlled the ministry as prime minister in 1995–96.

[49] See: Budget Bureau, *Ekasarn Ngop-pramarn 2539*, vol. 4, no. 8 (1995), 262–63, 432; and Budget Bureau, *Ekasarn Ngop-pramarn 2540*, vol. 4, no. 8 (1996), 454, 601, 611.

gesture of putting hands together to greet seniors. Banharn was then garlanded with flowers. As he stepped into the venue of the ceremony, the audience clapped their hands to welcome the return of *their* man, who was born and grew up in the same market town. (A shop house where Banharn lived as a child is located only about a hundred meters from Queen's Park.)

Once Banharn was seated in a large, embellished chair situated in the center of a special platform, Jaranai gave a speech to thank him for his numerous contributions to local development, including the B-J Tower. Banharn then stepped onto the stage to address the audience himself. Rarchan shouted his name out loud again, in the manner of an emcee announcing the champion's name at a major boxing match. Egged on by this truly dramatic announcement, the audience greeted Banharn with another big round of applause. During his brief speech, Banharn reiterated his motive behind building Queen's Park and its components: "I have traveled to many foreign countries. I noticed that people in those countries have a beautiful recreation park in their communities, where they can relax. I thought that our province, Suphanburi, should have one, too ... Therefore, I have built this music fountain and the observation tower for the happiness of Suphanburians."

Banharn talked in his usual monotone; he is certainly not an orator who can move the crowd with fiery words. What was striking, however, is the way the meaning of his speech was amplified and dramatized by the accompanying deft use of spectacle, sound, and words. As Banharn declared the music fountain open at the conclusion of his speech, a blast of colorful, thundering fireworks were shot into the sky, startling and impressing the audience. This was quickly followed by roaring firecrackers, the release of dry-ice vapor, the appearance of colorful balloons, the sound of trumpets, the beating of drums, and, finally, the release of dozens of birds. While the audience kept looking on, clapping their hands and taking photos in admiration and excitement, emcee Rarchan, in a show of his characteristically smooth and captivating eloquence, gushed passionate words into the microphone to whip up the spectators' provincialist pride:

> Look at the observation tower! Look at the music fountain! Can you believe that this is Thailand?! In the past, we Thais had to travel abroad to see things like these. Now we don't have to any longer. We can now see them in Thailand. But not in Bangkok. We can see them right here in our home, Suphanburi Province!

Thus, Rarchan effectively trumpeted the superlative quality of the B-J Tower and the music fountain. Suphanburi is not, he proclaimed, the socially obscure province that it was before. The effects of this message were sensationally magnified with the help of a dazzling array of aural and visual theatrical tools, all employed adroitly at the right time by Banharn's clients, who were strategically positioned throughout the venue.

As the aftereffects of Rarchan's words lingered on, the students assigned to provide entertainment performed traditional Thai dance and music. These performances were followed by a surprise concert by Surachai Sombatcharoen, a Suphanburi-born singer of Thai country music (*luk thung*), and a group of stunning— and scantily dressed—young female dancers.

Banharn surrounded by dancers (author's photo)

Surachai is the son of Suraphon Sombatcharoen, a nationally famous and legendary *luk thung* singer who, more than forty years after his death in 1968, is still referred to as "the king of *luk thung* singers."[50] Surachai's name was not on the ceremony program, so the audience was pleasantly surprised at his appearance on stage. Brimming with smiles and running out of breath, Surachai announced that he had just come back from Bangkok (where he lives now) at Banharn's invitation. "How could I say 'no' when the former prime minister asked me to give a concert in front of you all in my hometown?" exclaimed Surachai, drawing instant applause and screams from the people in the audience.[51] For these people, the concert was something of a reunion with Surachai, for he was also born in the market town and was personally familiar to most of them. His childhood Suphanburi home is located right next to Queen's Park. As he started singing upbeat *luk thung* songs, and the accompanying dancers wiggled their slender bodies and bottoms in a sensuous manner, a number of excited men in the audience started singing and dancing along, while the rest listened, laughed, whistled, heckled, and applauded. All those who had gathered at the foot of the beautifully illuminated B-J Tower—Banharn himself, civil servants, performers, and spectators—became one undifferentiated crowd. An energizing sense of togetherness, or, to quote Durkheim, "collective effervescence,"[52] was clearly in the air.

The entire well-orchestrated ceremony, the successful execution of which depended on the cooperation of Banharn's local clients, provided an occasion for

---

[50] Literally meaning "children of the field," *luk thung* songs, sung with a distinctively idyllic rhythm, are enormously popular among provincial Thais. Suphanburi is the birthplace of many nationally famous *luk thung* singers, including Suraphon.

[51] The concert was actually scheduled before Banharn's arrival, but Surachai did not arrive on time because he was caught in a Bangkok traffic jam. However, the ceremony organizers, contacting Surachai continually via mobile phone, were informed of his anticipated arrival time and rescheduled his concert accordingly.

[52] Emile Durkheim, *The Elementary Forms of the Religious Life*, trans. Karen Fields (New York: Free Press, 1995), 218–20

residents of the provincial town to visualize, affirm, celebrate, bask in, and embrace the dramatically glorified uniqueness of present-day Suphanburi in an ambience filled with pageantry, emotions, and populist fun. Thus, the ceremony proved an effective means of mobilizing, nurturing, and reinforcing provincial pride.

PROVINCIAL PRIDE

Having been successfully advertised through ceremonial and other means over the years, the B-J Tower has come to be regarded as the quintessential symbol of Suphanburi's "modernity." As such, it has become an important component of Suphanburians' provincial pride. The pride finds verbal expression in their numerous statements that play up the distinctiveness of the tower. For example, a printing office manager in the market town said: "They say the tower is the tallest tower in Asia, although I don't know if it's true. If it's true, that makes Suphan very special." A daughter from a farmer's family in the adjacent Song Phi Nong District made a similar remark: "We can see the observation tower from so far. Everyone can recognize that's where Suphan is. It has made Suphan famous. Ask people in other provinces, 'At the mention of Suphanburi, what comes to your mind?' They would say, 'The observation tower.'"

In praising the tower, many Suphanburians made comments that display or give away their sense of superiority. An elderly merchant said: "Suppose you blindfold me and take me outside Suphan. I open my eyes, but I wouldn't know where I am. Am I in Chainat, Singburi, or someplace else? How could I tell? They all look similar because there is nothing like the tower Suphan has." Another respondent, a middle-aged employee at the B-J Tower, observed: "Last week, I saw a group of tourists, about fifty senior civil servants, from Chaiyaphum Province [in the northeast], visiting the B-J Tower. I saw them running around and taking photos like small kids. They had never been to a place like this before, so they couldn't contain their happiness … I heard them saying, 'We want a tower like this in our province. Why can't we?' They were envious of Suphanburi." I do not know if this respondent was exaggerating the tourists' envy, but the point is that outsiders' (imagined) envy makes him happy and proud.[53]

During my fieldwork outside Suphanburi in 1999–2000, I heard many people express feelings of (sour) envy. To give but a few examples, a college student in the northern province of Phrae expressed unprompted admiration for the B-J Tower when he found out that I had lived in Suphanburi: "I've never been to Suphanburi, but I've seen a photo of the observation tower. It's unbelievable that there is such a thing in Thailand. In Phrae, the tallest building is a hospital, which is only five or six stories high." A Sino-Thai merchant in Lampang, another northern province, was more bitter: "Suphanburi is a small province. I had always thought little of it. But now it has become quite well known because it has that tall tower. Lampang is much bigger than Suphanburi, but what do we have to brag to others about?"

The B-J Tower, it must be noted, has a less admirable side to it as well. For one thing, Banharn used this project to benefit his personal clients. The company that constructed the B-J Tower was Ital-Thai, whose board of directors included Chaiyut Kanasoot, a descendent of the tenth governor of Suphanburi Yi Kanasoot (1911–23),

---

[53] On the importance of envy enjoyment, see: Jon Elster, *Alchemies of the Mind: Rationality and the Emotions* (New York: Cambridge University Press, 1999), 142–43.

who founded Kanasoot Secondary School.[54] This school, the oldest secondary school in Suphanburi, was the recipient of nearly 31.8-million-baht in state funds channeled by Banharn between 1990 and 1997.[55] Additionally, since 1997, the schoolmaster of Kanasoot has been Charnchai Thipanetr, the elder brother of Rarchan, who was the emcee for the opening ceremony discussed above. Likewise, Sahakit Bandit, the contractor for the music fountain, is run by Banharn's mother-in-law's family, Thepsutha.[56]

While Banharn's detractors would view these ties as additional evidence of his well-known nepotism, many Suphanburians actually have a different take on it. For example, some defend him by saying that everyone favors his family or friends, and that there is, therefore, little to condemn about his behavior. Others take a more pragmatic attitude, as exemplified by the comment of a street cleaner: "You cannot eliminate corruption in Thailand. Every MP is corrupt. Then we should not judge an MP on whether he is corrupt or not. We should judge him on what he has done for his people in return. I think Banharn is on the take, but he has done so much for Suphanburi. Look at all the things he has built." Foremost among those things is the B-J Tower. Thus, while some outsiders take a wholly intolerant view of corruption, some Suphanburians take a more permissive view.[57]

Equally noteworthy is the fact that not all Suphanburians have actually gone up the B-J Tower. As of 2002, the "public" Queen's Park charged an admission fee of 10 baht per person and another 30 baht (which was enough to buy a meal) to go up the tower. Many Suphanburians from low-income families, therefore, have no or limited access to the tower. Critics might interpret this fact to argue that the tower is a wasteful white elephant, but some 70 percent of my informants, including even those who had never gone up the tower, defended its presence by playing up its prestige value. A son of a rice farmer, who worked as a janitor near the tower, said: "If you are rich and are building a house, will you build a small house? No. You want to build as big a house as your money can buy. It's the same for the tower. Because Banharn built a big tower, Suphanburi has become famous for it. That's good." An elderly rice farmer similarly said: "He [Banharn] wanted to build a new symbol of Suphan. Then why should he have built anything small? It wouldn't have been worth the effort." A middle-aged garbage collector from a farming family is more

---

[54] Department of Business Development, Ministry of Commerce, Bangkok Company File No. 168/2501 (Ital-Thai). I thank Mike Montesano for first bringing to my attention Chaiyut's ties to the Ital-Thai company.

[55] See: Budget Bureau, *Ekasarn Ngop-pramarn 2533*, vol. 4, no. 5 (1989), 479; Budget Bureau, *Ekasarn Ngop-pramarn 2534*, vol. 4, no. 5 (1990), 490; Budget Bureau, *Ekasarn Ngop-pramarn 2535*, vol. 4, no. 5 (1991), 571; Budget Bureau, *Ekasarn Ngop-pramarn 2538*, vol. 4, no. 5 (1994), 859; Budget Bureau, *Ekasarn Ngop-pramarn 2539*, vol. 4, no. 8 (1995), 614, 640, 747; and Budget Bureau, *Ekasarn Ngop-pramarn 2540*, vol. 4, no. 8 (1996), 659, 685.

[56] Department of Business Development, Ministry of Commerce, Suphanburi Limited Partnership File No. 523 (Sahakit Bandit).

[57] Tolerance of corruption is not confined to Suphanburi. See Walker, "The Rural Constitution and the Everyday Politics of Elections in Northern Thailand," 95, for a similar example in Chiang Mai Province. For examples in the Philippines and Burma, respectively, see: Fernando Zialcita, "Perspectives on Legitimacy in Ilocos Norte," in *From Marcos to Aquino: Local Perspectives on Political Transition in the Philippines,* ed. Benedict Kerkvliet and Resil Mojares (Manila: Ateneo de Manila University Press, 1991), 266–85, 271; and Ardeth Thawnghmung, *Behind the Teak Curtain: Authoritarianism, Agricultural Policies, and Political Legitimacy in Rural Burma* (London: Kegan and Paul, 2003), 7.

reserved in her appraisal, but made a comment that reveals the importance of envy enjoyment. The B-J Tower, she said, "is actually a bit too extravagant, but when people in other provinces come to Suphan and say they want to have a similar tower in their provinces, I get happy and realize that Suphan is special."

These respondents admit that the B-J Tower has little socioeconomic value for them. All the same, they praise it as the most eye-catching thing about which Suphanburi can boast. It has taken on the semiotic character of a "prestige good" on display—a good that Suphanburians can flaunt to non-Suphanburians, a luxury that is to be admired and envied by non-Suphanburians. This collective non-material value compensates for its lack of economic value at the individual level. The tower, therefore, does not represent a waste of money. It is the prestige symbol of an otherwise undistinguished rural province. The tower has altered what might be called the "social geography" of Thailand,[58] in which Suphanburi previously lacked the fame, social recognition, and admiration that it enjoys now. The B-J Tower has consequently become an indispensable source of Suphanburians' positive social identity. In this light, we can make better sense of popular support for Banharn. To many Suphanburians, he is not the corrupted MP that scholars of Thai politics make him out to be; rather, he is a local hero who has improved the public image of their birthplace.

CONCLUSION

Let me conclude by drawing briefly two interrelated implications of this chapter. First, it shows, as Shao did for China,[59] that social identity is the product of visible public works. Suphanburi's putatively superior modernity is embodied, among other things, in the tangible form of the B-J Tower, around which the collective pride of Suphanburians from all walks of life is fostered and mobilized. Even a seemingly squandering and irrationally gargantuan project can be an essential ingredient of imagined provincial human community. The literature on collective identity formation overlooks or underestimates this element, privileging instead the role of education, social interaction, culture, museums, newspapers, maps, novels, and so on.[60] The case of Suphanburi suggests that a highly visible project of unmatched size can contribute to collective identity formation, too.

Second, this case calls into question the widespread materialist and utilitarian perspective in the post-Enlightenment era. If viewed from that standpoint, the B-J Tower would be merely a symbol of pretentious, hollow modernity. Suphanburians, however, are not the purely self-centered, utility-maximizing individuals that rational choice theory makes human beings out to be. Bread-and-butter issues of

---

[58] For an elaboration of this argument, see: Nishizaki, *Political Authority and Provincial Identity in Thailand.*

[59] Shao, *Culturing Modernity.*

[60] See: Benedict Anderson, *Imagined Communities: Reflections on the Origin and the Spread of Nationalism* (London: Verso, rev. ed., 1991); Tamara Hamlish, "Preserving the Palace: Museums and the Making of Nationalism(s) in Twentieth-century China," *Museum Anthropology* 19, no. 2 (1995): 20–30; Michael Hechter, *Internal Colonialism: The Celtic Fringe in British National Development, 1536–1966* (Berkeley: University of California Press, 1975); Charles Keyes, *Regionalism in Isan* (Ithaca: Cornell Southeast Asia Program Publications, 1966); and Thongchai Winichakul, *Siam Mapped: A History of the Geo-Body of Siam* (Honolulu: University of Hawaii Press, 1994).

daily economic survival certainly concern ordinary Suphanburians, but they are also keenly conscious of the image, status, or reputation of their province. As leading proponents of social identity theory remind us, human beings have a fundamental desire or need to "belong to groups that compare favorably with, and are distinct from, other groups." Belonging to such a group gives human beings "positive evaluations for themselves" or positive social identities, which they all desire or need.[61] This quest or penchant for collective pride is "the psychological 'motor' behind the individual's actions in the intergroup context."[62] To draw on David Laitin's phrase, this is "a point of concern" for all human beings.[63] In light of these points, we can better understand why Suphanburians covet and cherish anything that makes their province look "good." The B-J Tower serves the important social function of meeting this collective, non-material desire of Suphanburians. Based as it is on a dry simplification of human interests, the utilitarian paradigm that dominates many branches of social sciences is inadequate to capture the social value or meaning of the tower.

---

[61] Taylor and Moghaddam, *Theories of Intergroup Relations*, 83. See also: Henri Tajfel, "Individuals and Groups in Social Psychology," *British Journal of Social and Clinical Psychology* 18 (1979): 187–88; and Henri Tajfel, *Social Identity and Intergroup Relations* (New York: Cambridge University Press, 1982).

[62] Taylor and Moghaddam, *Theories of Intergroup Relations*, 79. For further elaborations of social identity theory and its relevance for Banharn's domination, see: Nishizaki, *Political Authority and Provincial Identity in Thailand*, 205–36.

[63] David Laitin, *Hegemony and Culture: Politics and Religious Change among the Yoruba* (Chicago: University of Chicago Press, 1986), 29.

CHAPTER EIGHT

MARKETING BUSINESS KNOWLEDGE AND CONSUMER CULTURE BEFORE THE BOOM: THE CASE OF *KHOO KHAENG* MAGAZINE

Villa Vilaithong

Khoo Khaeng (Competitor) magazine no longer exists. It ended publication in 1999—a victim of the 1997 financial crisis. *Khoo Khaeng* was founded before the economic boom of the mid-1980s, and over the next decade flourished along with the economy. As such, this magazine represents an excellent case study to trace the dynamic history of modern Thai business. As the Thai financial achieved domestic competitiveness, marketing (*kan talat*) also matured, and was able to drive the economy toward an increasingly affluent consumer culture. The magazine promoted the professionalization of corporate executives, marketers, salespeople, advertising and media people, marketing journalists, and academics by offering them a public space where they could exchange their knowledge, skills, and experiences. By producing specific kinds of marketing knowledge in the new context of economic globalization, these different types of professionals fostered in turn the emergence of segmented groups of consumers.

Khoo Khaeng developed a reputation for providing rich quantitative and qualitative marketing data. The information provided included market news, surveys, trends, interviews, reportage, and advertisements that acquired the status of business reference works, and influenced especially the business manuals that were popular during the years of the economic boom. In fact, manuals on how to achieve success were "a peculiarly global thing" that moved "back and forth effortlessly between East and West," as Craig Reynolds stated some time ago.[1] In the Thai context, such manuals acquired additional meanings about personal security and self-protection. They provided people with strategies (*yutthasat*) to manage their lives

---

[1] Craig Reynolds, "Tycoons and Warlords: Modern Thai Social Formations and Chinese Historical Romance," in *Sojourners and Settlers: Histories of Southeast Asia and the Chinese*, ed. Anthony Reid (Honolulu: University of Hawaii Press, 2001), 140.

and deal with "competitors in the business world or with rivals in the civil service."[2] Business was accordingly approached as warfare by other means, and publishers packaged and marketed business manuals that "purported to fuse ancient wisdom with new knowledge."[3]

This essay argues that *Khoo Khaeng* positioned itself as *khu mue kan talat*, or marketing manual, for businesspeople and students of marketing, offering content that was categorized under marketing's "4Ps": product, price, place, and promotion. Mirroring the development of the capitalist marketplace in Thailand and the onset of the economic boom, *Khoo Khaeng* affirmed the role of marketing research and consumer-oriented marketing. The magazine also provided news coverage about new global products and distribution channels (e.g., electronic appliances, fast-food chains, convenience stores, and consumer credit), which targeted segmented consumers.

A history of Thai marketing has yet to be written. Business history is still a new academic field in Thailand, and economic historians have so far not studied business magazines. As far as *Khoo Khaeng* is concerned, it is dealt with only in a master's thesis, which examines the contribution given to business education by the daily edition of *Khoo Khaeng*, and by the "Mini-MBA" courses it offered in the mid to late 1990s.[4] The present essay considers the period before the boom years by focusing on the *Khoo Khaeng* monthly magazine from its inception in 1980 until the end of the decade. These ten years of publication paved the way for the apex of success that was achieved with the launch of the weekly *Khoo Khaeng Raisapda* in 1992, and the daily *Khoo Khaeng Raiwan* in 1994. The following analysis draws conceptually from the literature on the history of business as well as of men's and women's magazines. In particular, Michael Augspurger's *An Economy of Abundant Beauty* examines the ways in which *Fortune* magazine forged during the 1930s identities for the new and evolving professional classes through "corporate liberalism." James S. Miller traces how *Fortune* sought to invent a "folk" history of American industrial capitalism, even though *Fortune* was tied to the institutions and operations of the new commercial society. Daniel A. Clark's *Creating the College Man* shows how popular magazines, such as *Munsey's* and *Cosmopolitan*, were key tools for the cultural reconstruction of college identities in the period 1890–1915. Finally, Jennifer Scanlon's influential study *Inarticulate Longings* investigates how mass-circulation magazines, and advertisements in them, contributed to strengthening capitalism and also women's self-realization.[5]

---

[2] Craig J. Reynolds, *Seditious Histories: Contesting Thai and Southeast Asian Pasts* (Seattle and London: University of Washington Press, 2006), 231.

[3] Craig J. Reynolds, "Sino-Thai Business Culture: Strategies, Management, and Warfare," *Asia-Pacific Magazine*, nos. 6–7 (1997): 37. See also: Reynolds, "Tycoons and Warlords," 115–47.

[4] Songwit Kulsukdinun, "Bot bat nangsuephim *Khoo Khaeng* raiwan nai kan hai kan sueksa dan thurakit kap khwam phueng pho jai kong naksueksa '*Khoo Khaeng* mini MBA" (The role of business education of *Khoo Khaeng* daily newspapers and gratification of *Khoo Khaeng* Mini-MBA students) (MA thesis, Chulalongkorn University, 1998).

[5] See: Michael Augspurger, *An Economy of Abundant Beauty: Fortune Magazine and Depression America* (Ithaca: Cornell University Press, 2004); James S. Miller, "White-Collar Excavations: *Fortune* Magazine and the Invention of the Industrial Folk," *American Periodicals: A Journal of History, Criticism, and Bibliography* 13 (2003): 84–104; Daniel A. Clark, *Creating the College Man: American Mass Magazines and Middle-Class Manhood, 1890–1915* (Madison and London: University of Wisconsin Press, 2010); and Jennifer Scanlon, *Inarticulate Longings: The Ladies' Home Journal, Gender, and the Promises of Consumer Culture* (New York: Routledge, 1995).

THE BIRTH OF *KHOO KHAENG*

Two accounts of the origins of *Khoo Khaeng* magazine can be proposed. The first one locates its origins in a political context, the other one in the economic conditions of the time. The political situation in the first half of the 1970s significantly influenced the publishing industry, and prompted interest in business magazines in the decade's latter half. The more liberal atmosphere that followed the overthrow of the military dictatorship in October 1973 promoted the publication of a wide range of newspapers. But after the coup of October 5, 1976, the government closed down a number of newspapers and imposed rigid censorship on the reporting of political news. Some in the media industry objected to the censorship and argued that freedom of expression should be allowed, and that newspapers should not be associated with individuals or political parties, and ought to be free from conflict between capital owners and employees.[6]

Ruam Prachachat, a newspaper focusing on politics, charted a new direction by launching the business magazine *Khemthit Thurakit Raisupda* (Business Compass Weekly) in February 1977, during the reactionary Thanin Kraivichien government. This magazine's title was later changed to *Prachachat Thurakit* (Business Nation). By reporting economic and business news from both the government and private sectors,[7] this twelve-page, five-baht magazine became a model for subsequent business magazines published in the early stages of industrialization in the 1980s.[8]

The development of the Thai economy also affected the birth of *Khoo Khaeng*. The influx of foreign investment, improvement in productivity, expansion of the manufacturing sector, and changes in the industrial structure in the 1960s led to economic growth in the following decades.[9] Thailand's gross domestic product (GDP) increased constantly from 164.3 billion baht in 1972 to 755.8 billion baht in 1981, and 1,210 billion baht in 1987.[10] Akira states that domestic capitalist groups in the three major sectors of the Thai economy (import-substitution industries, finance, and agribusiness) played a dominant role in the 1960s and 1970s.[11] This period saw the emergence of a mass-production economy, which generated in turn the need for mass markets. Endo Gen notes further that "from the early 1980s until the mid-1990s, especially in the latter half of this fifteen-year period, Thailand's consumer market expanded considerably."[12] Producers became aware of the necessity of understanding consumer demand before raising productivity. Accordingly, a

---

[6] Malee Boonsiripan, *Seriphap nangsuephim thai* (The freedom of the Thai press) (Bangkok: Thammasat University Press, 2005), 97–104.

[7] *Siam phimphakan: Prawatsat kan phim nai phrathet thai* (Siam Printing: The history of printing in Thailand) (Bangkok: Matichon, 2006), 456–58. The magazine's contents were divided into the following sections: news summary, foreign affairs, economy, banking-finance, opinions, articles, tourism industry, sports-entertainment, and business society.

[8] Malee, *Seriphap nangsuephim thai*, 103.

[9] See: James C. Ingram, *Economic Change in Thailand, 1850–1970* (Stanford: Stanford University Press, 1971); Suehiro Akira, *Capital Accumulation in Thailand, 1855–1985* (Chiang Mai: Silkworm Books, 1989); and Pasuk Phongpaichit and Chris Baker, *Thailand: Economy and Politics* (New York: Oxford University Press, 1995).

[10] Department of Commercial Economics, *Sathiti kankha pracham phi 2530* (Statistics on Trade of 1987) (Bangkok: Chumchon Sahakorn Kan Kaset Haeng Prathet Thai, 1988), 291.

[11] Suehiro, *Capital Accumulation in Thailand*, 218.

[12] Endo Gen, *Diversifying Retail and Distribution in Thailand* (Chiang Mai: Silkworm Books, 2013), 35.

gradual shift occurred from mass marketing to consumer marketing. Advertising served as a marketing device to increase consumption.

The Thai economy was not much affected by the 1973 oil crisis and the Thai advertising industry grew rapidly in the 1970s and the 1980s in response to the abundance of products manufactured both locally and internationally. More international advertising agencies also entered the Thai market—Lintas Bangkok (1970), Thai Hakukodo (1973), Ogilvy & Mather (1973), Leo Burnett (1974), and Dentsu (1974)—to serve, at least initially, clients from the firms' mother countries. In the 1980s, a number of local agencies were also set up.[13] Production companies theorized that increasing their advertising budgets would sustain their businesses. Accordingly, advertising expenditure increased from 1,557 million baht in 1979 to 5,349 million baht in 1985, and was 10,414 million baht in 1989.[14]

Market expansion also led to growth in the media industry. Several "consumer magazines" started publication in 1980 at the same time as *Khoo Khaeng: Phuean wai run* (Teenager's Friend), *Donti thirak* (Dear Music), *Sapot khlap* (Sport Club), and *Rot* (Cars).[15] Historian Hong Lysa has drawn attention to the role that a segmented magazine such as *Sinlapa watthanatham* (Art and Culture), launched in 1979, played in defining the social meaning of art and culture during the 1980s and 1990s.[16] *Sinlapa watthanatham* and *Khoo Khaeng* played a similar role in educating the Thai middle class in the age of economic and cultural globalization by, respectively, popularizing historical knowledge that validated "Thainess" (*khwampenthai*) and providing readers with marketing knowledge to be used as a weapon with which to fight in the increasingly competitive business world.

Khoo Khaeng was founded by professionals from the marketing and advertising industry who had witnessed the rise of corporate capitalism. Thanks to their experience and contacts, they were able to access marketing information and business news. Realizing the significance of marketing information, they started by setting up a data center company, Media Focus, which collected, summarized, and sold business and advertising data about products and services from every media channel.[17] Exploiting its own data bank, Media Focus launched *Khoo Khaeng* in July 1980 as a monthly magazine with a clear objective: to offer marketing news, data, and information to manufacturers, entrepreneurs, and advertising practitioners.

---

[13] Advertising Association of Thailand, "Samsipsi pi thurakit khosana lae samakhom khosana thurakit heng prathetthai" (Thirty-four years of the advertising business and the advertising association of Thailand), in *Annual Report & Membership Directory 2000* (Bangkok: M. C. D. Publishing, 2000), 30.

[14] Advertising Association of Thailand, "Advertising Trends: Advertising Expenditure," in *Annual Report & Membership Directory, the 25th Anniversary* (Bangkok: Advertising Association of Thailand, 1991), 100.

[15] Rawiwan Prakopphon used the term "consumer magazines" to characterize the publishing industry's products in the 1980s. See: Rawiwan Prakopphon, *Nitthayasan thai* (Thai magazines) (Bangkok: Research Promotion Project, Chulalongkorn University, 1987), 329. Rawiwan classified "consumer magazines" into eight categories: (1) women's (2) men's [car, sports, stereo, video, and computer], (3) children, (4) family [home, interior, travel, and health and hygiene], (5) politics, (6) economy and business, (7) art and culture, and (8) entertainment.

[16] Hong Lysa, "Twenty Years of *Sinlapa Watthanatham*: Cultural Politics in Thailand in the 1980s and 1990s," *Journal of Southeast Asian Studies* 31, no. 1 (2000): 26–47.

[17] Media Focus was established on September 13, 1977, with a registered capital of 100,000 baht. See "Talat kho mun khuek khak kluen muea nangsuephim long ma len duai" (The information market is more lively with the newspapers), *Phujatkan* (December 1985), 65.

Thawat Palungtepin, *Khoo Khaeng*'s founding director, recalled that before the magazine came into being, marketing information was not divulged. Business firms did not want to disseminate their information to the public. After *Khoo Khaeng*'s launch, however, many firms were keen to provide it with information directly because doing so would help their business.[18]

In line with its mission, *Khoo Khaeng*'s first, seven-page issue covered a seminar on "Consumers and Advertising."[19] The column "Business Focus" featured a story about Sunanthan Tulayadhan, the first female managing director of the Thailand office of the international advertising agency Ogilvy & Mather.[20] The number of pages steadily increased to thirty with the first five issues, and by the end of 1988 *Khoo Khaeng* had reached 300 pages.[21] In 1989, Media Focus expanded its business by dividing the company into the departments of marketing, distribution and membership, and human resources, catered by new staff in the positions of marketing executives and reporters.[22] Within this arrangement, business journalists gained prominence.

MARKETING PROFESSIONAL NETWORK

Media Focus firmly believed that information was the real source of marketing power. Thus, *Khoo Khaeng* built professional networks to acquire and share new marketing knowledge, bridging a gap between marketing academics and marketers. It organized seminars where respected practitioners were invited to be speakers. On October 4, 1983, marketers from industry, finance, advertising, and media companies were invited to trace the history of the Thai market over the past twenty years, and to discuss possible trends for the next decade. The seminar proceeding explained that knowledge could be gained from historical studies.[23] In 1986, the newly christened *chomyut midia* (media warriors), the managing directors of advertising and media agencies, gathered at a seminar to recall and discuss their professional experiences.[24] That same year, *Khoo Khaeng* collaborated with educational and academic institutions in the organization of seminars—for example, "The Management of Modern Marketing"[25] and "Ways to Be the Professional Marketer"[26]—which were convened with the marketing department of Chulalongkorn University. The seminars suggested the authoritativeness of the marketing knowledge produced by university professors, and such collaborations could be used to strengthen the magazine's image as a strong advocate of public education.

---

[18] Interview, Thawat Palungtepin, Bangkok, 2009.

[19] *Khoo Khaeng* 1, no. 1 (July 1980), 1.

[20] Ibid., 2.

[21] *Khoo Khaeng* 6, no. 72 (September 1986) and *Khoo Khaeng* 9, no. 99 (December 1988).

[22] *Khoo Khaeng*, 9, no. 101 (February 1989).

[23] "Phoet lok kan talat" (Opining the marketing world), *Khoo Khaeng* 4, no. 37 (October 1983): 148–70.

[24] "Poet prasopkan chomyut midia" (Revealing media warriors' experiences), *Khoo Khaeng* 6, no. 69 (June 1986): 59–68.

[25] "Sammana *Khoo Khaeng*," (*Khoo Khaeng* seminar), *Khoo Khaeng*, 6, no. 64 (January 1986): 47.

[26] "Sammana *Khoo Khaeng* naew, tang su kan pen nak kan talat mue achip" (The *Khoo Khaeng* seminar, ways to become professional marketers), *Khoo Khaeng* 6, no. 66 (March 1986): 97–102.

The people at *Khoo Khaeng* realized that advertising was an attractive subject for university students. In 1986 the magazine initiated an advertising-campaign competition among students who studied marketing, advertising, and communications. The first year's contest, with the theme *"niyom thai"* (Favoring Thai), attracted forty-eight teams comprising 450 students from major universities in Bangkok and Chiang Mai. This campaign promoted the "Made in Thailand" government policy, launched in 1985, which sought to encourage the consumption of national products. The campaign's judging committees consisted of well-known marketing and advertising practitioners, university lecturers, and the magazine's owner and editors. Surat Osathanukro, the then-minister of commerce, presided over this very successful event, and the campaign was featured in *Khoo Khaeng*'s September 1986 issue. The following year the competition was again well received: sixty-nine teams and a total of 540 students participated to develop ad campaigns to promote the theme "banana." In the third year, *Khoo Khaeng* formed an alliance with the Creative Association and The Magic Eyes Project to organize the contest around the theme *"chan rak chaophraya"* (I Love the Chao Phraya River).[27] To grow its reputation at the global level, *Khoo Khaeng* also co-sponsored the Fifteenth International Asian Advertising Conference, held in July 1986, at the Hyatt Central Plaza Hotel.[28] Without support from its professional network, *Khoo Khaeng*'s participation in this international conference would have been impossible.

COMPETITIVE MARKETS

Khoo Khaeng clearly differentiated itself from other business magazines to satisfy its target audiences. Thai business magazines published in the first half of the 1980s can be divided into three groups: those focusing on finance and banking, including *Thurakit kan ngoen* (Finance Business), *Kan ngoen kan thanakan* (Finance & Banking), and *Dokbia* (Interest); those targeting business executives, such as *Phuchatkan* (Manager) and *Phunam* (Leader); and, finally, those concentrating on more specific aspects of business, such as *Thurakit Thidin* (Property Business) and *Thurakit ahan sat* (Animal Food Business).[29] *Khoo Khaeng*'s title—Competitor—was indicative of the competitive, aggressive nature of the 1980s markets, which were compared to battlefields by reference to the genre of Chinese martial stories such as *Romance of the Three Kingdoms*, whose Thai translation as *Sam Kok* became a top selling book.[30] In fact, there were several wars and many opposing warriors, and each side needed to win its war (*suek*) in order to become *chao yutthachak* (the market's king). On its first anniversary, *Khoo Khaeng* told its readers that the magazine would try harder to improve its content and design, [31] and noted that marketing and advertising

---

[27] "The 3rd Year Advertising Campaign Competition," *Khoo Khaeng* 9, no. 100 (January 1989): 175–80.

[28] "Khui kap than phu an" (Talking to the readers), *Khoo Khaeng* 6, 70 (July 1986): 5. Besides offering coffee breaks, a special international edition of *Khoo Khaeng*, *The Competitor*, was distributed to the thousand participants.

[29] *Thurakit kan ngoen* 1, no. 1 (1982); *Kan ngoen kan thanakan*1, no. 1 (1982); *Dokbia* 1, no. 1 (1982); *Phuchatkan* 1, no. 1 (August 1983); *Phunam* 1, no. 1 (January 1983); *Thurakit thidin* 1, no. 1 (May 1983); and *Thurakit ahan sat* 1, no. 1 (October–December 1984).

[30] Reynolds, "Tycoons and Warlords."

[31] "Thueng phu an duai khwam nupthue" (To readers with respect), *Khoo Khaeng* 2, no. 13 (September 1981): 5.

strategies were "the name of the game" in the commercial world. Warfare terminology was employed in the titles of many of its cover stories. For example, *"Hang sappasinkha poet suek"* (Department stores start wars, October 1980), *"Suek phongsakfok raboet"* (The detergent war begins, April 1982), *"Cogat raboet suek flu-o-lai"* (Colgate starts the fluoride war, July 1983), and *"Suek ching dam chao yutthachak sunkankha"* (The final round for the king of department stores, March 1984). Even though the academic cultivation of marketing knowledge in Thailand had American origins, the language of *Khoo Khaeng* combined Western, Chinese, and local business and marketing vocabularies.

Khoo Khaeng normally published news and stories from provincial, national, and international sources about products and services, such as: retail stores, real estate, consumer products, and consumer credit; and about the sports, entertainment, and advertising industries. Pictures of industrialists, manufacturers, and marketing and advertising professionals were usually displayed alongside product news. The columns on provincial and regional markets reported on production, wholesaling, and retailing in each province in the style of illustrated journalist reportage.[32] On reading these articles, one could argue that *Khoo Khaeng* acted as a sort of "marketing anthropologist" that provided its readers geographic, ethnic, and historical backgrounds on the provinces. By contrast, the columns "Talking across the World"[33] and "International" dealt with mostly American, Japanese, and, later on, Korean products and markets. By the mid-1980s, *Khoo Khaeng* had added one more P—public relations—to the four Ps of marketing;[34] and a sixth P—packaging—was introduced in 1989.[35] The magazine also traced the history of products and advertising seriously by recording the recollections of practitioners in the field and reproducing old advertisements.[36]

One of the most competitive markets about which *Khoo Khaeng* provided detailed accounts was retailing. The magazine's stories contained a wealth of product details, statistical data of market size and sales volumes, interviews with executives, and more. In 1983, *Khoo Khaeng* announced the golden age of *yutthachak khaplik* (retail), the consequence of the rapid transformation brought about by international marketing and business trends.[37] Next, decrying businesspeople's neglect of retail marketing, the magazine explained how shopping venues must be categorized for

[32] The column on provincial markets ("Talat tang changwat") first appeared in *Khoo Khaeng* in its first year of publication.

[33] "Khui kham lok doi Wisit Sueksakan" (Talking across the world by Wisit Sueksakan), *Khoo Khaeng* 2, no. 16 (December 1981). This column started appearing in the second year of publication.

[34] "Chomyut phi a rai khatha ko kan kae tong mi kuen" (The PR guru casts his spell: The importance of savvy PR in business), *Khoo Khaeng* 6, no. 71 (August 1986): 70

[35] "Phaekketching p tua thi ha gaem ruk thi ham kraphrip ta" (Packaging, the fifth P: The offensive strategy that must be noted), *Khoo Khaeng* 9, no. 108 (September 1989): 77–78, 81–82, 85–86, 89–90.

[36] These columns were entitled "Malai rotjana" and "Kho-sa-na" (*khosana* means advertising). An example is the special article "Suek ya si fan nai adit" (The toothpaste war in the past), which provided a brief history of toothpaste products from before the Second World War through the early 1980s. Examples of toothpaste advertisements were shown in the article.

[37] "Yutthachak kha plik" (The retailing battlefield), *Khoo Khaeng* 4, no. 38 (November 1983): 160–70.

retailing,[38] and also familiarized readers with new retail destinations such as the shopping centers that proliferated in Bangkok's suburban areas in the mid and late 1980s.[39]

RESEARCHING THE MARKET AND THE CONSUMER

Marketing, as an academic discipline, was new to Thailand in the late 1960s, when the courses taught at vocational schools, colleges, and universities covered such topics as marketing itself, marketing management, and marketing research. The government and educational institutions, and the advertising, research, and media industries played a vital role in spreading the new approach of consumer-oriented marketing in the 1970s. Ministry of Industry officials, and lecturers from the faculties of commerce and accountancy at Thammasat and Chulalongkorn universities, began publishing marketing textbooks based on marketing knowledge from the United States, and employed a social-science approach to understanding consumer behavior. Consumer behavior could not be explained purely through the lens of economics, because it also fell within the analytic purview of the behavioral sciences—an idea that had been recognized in American business since the 1950s. According to Cohen's *A Consumers' Republic*, American leaders in business and government developed after the Second World War a political economy and a political culture that fostered a mass-consumption economy.[40] Cohen shows how marketers and advertisers shifted business strategies from mass to segmented markets, and argues that by developing "market segmentation" by age, income, and lifestyle, the new markets "promised greater, steadier profits through expanding the pool of potential consumers."[41]

A similar shift to a consumer-oriented market also took place in the Thai market during the 1980s, when new marketing approaches from the United States made an impact among academics and professionals. Thongchai Santiwong's popular textbook, *Phuethikam Phuboripok* (Consumer behavior), first published in 1972, stated that "consumer behavior" was the newest trend among business administration

---

[38] Retailing entrepreneurs categorized their products into three groups—trading areas (e.g., Wang Burapha, Phahurat, Ban Mo, Penang market), department stores, and trade centers. Department stores were significant outlets for distributing goods to consumers in Bangkok. This "retailing war" also extended to the big provinces.

[39] "Suek ching dam jao yutthajak sunkankha" (The final round of the war to be the retailing warrior), *Khoo Khaeng* 4, no. 43 (April 1984): 135–40, 143–45. The first shopping centers in Thailand, including Amarin, Pantip, Mabunkhrong, City Plaza, River City, Peninsular Plaza, City Landmark, and Mahathun Plaza, opened in Bangkok in the early 1980s. In the second half of the 1980s, a number of department stores were constructed in the suburban areas of Bangkok and the northeastern and southern provinces. In 1988, the department store business was worth about 15 billion baht generated from three hundred department stores in Thailand (fifty in Bangkok). See: "Suek ching dam chao yutthachak sunkankha" (The final round of the war to be the retailing king), *Khoo Khaeng* 4, no. 43 (April 1984): 136; the cover stories of *Khoo Khaeng* 6, no. 66 (March 1986) and 8, no. 87 (December 1987); and "Yutthachak kan kha plik ... saep saep ... kan kan ... tae man di" (The battle of retail: a fierce but thrilling competition, *Khoo Khaeng* 9, no. 99 (December 1988): 101.

[40] Lizabeth Cohen, *A Consumers' Republic: The Politics of Mass Consumption in Postwar America* (New York: Alfred A. Knopf, 2003).

[41] Ibid., 298.

subjects.[42] Thongchai affirms that the behavioral sciences benefited from other social science disciplines, such as sociology, anthropology, and especially psychology,[43] that helped explain how each person's perception, attitudes, emotions, and opinion affected their purchase actions.[44] The book devoted a whole chapter to social classes.[45] The anthropology chapter concentrated on the meaning of culture and cultural standards.[46] The reference section listed a number of acclaimed American books on marketing and behavior published in the 1960s and early 1970s, along with articles from business and social sciences journals such as the *Journal of Marketing*, *Psychological Review*, and *American Sociological Review*.[47] The introduction of a social-science approach to teaching marketing in Thailand is even clearer when considering graduate studies. Master's theses on consumer behavior were first submitted at Chulalongkorn University's business school in the early 1970s; their number gradually increased in the 1980s.[48] Selected theses' topics are revealing of the chief product categories then prevalent in the market. Students also made use of consumer research questionnaires to collect data. Marketing was thus elevated to the status of an academic discipline.

In the commercial world, too, marketing, media, and advertising research steadily gained more attention after the 1970s. Manufacturers, traders, and advertising agencies set up research departments in their companies. The well-known research company Demar was established in 1970 as a research department of Diethelm (Thailand), and over the next two years became an independent entity (and in 1975 it was bought by the Survey Research Group). Media Focus, as already mentioned, was founded in 1977 with the aim of collecting data that show where companies were spending their advertising dollars (e.g., television, print), and how much they were spending. Research and Data Researches (RDR), founded in 1979 by ItalThai and its affiliated companies, became Demar's main competitor. By the mid-1980s, research business, especially media research, had become more vigorous. Demar and RDR increasingly used computer technology and video monitoring of consumer behavior.[49] According to *Khoo Khaeng*, three types of market research services were prevalent in the mid-1980s.[50] These were research departments within

---

[42] Thongchai Santiwong, *Phuetthikam phu boriphok* (Consumer behavior), second edition (Bangkok: Thai Watthana Phanit Press, 1974), "Introduction to the first edition."

[43] Ibid., 20–27.

[44] Ibid., 25–26.

[45] Ibid., 26–27.

[46] Ibid., 27–28.

[47] See, for example: George Katona, *The Powerful Consumer* (New York: McGraw-Hill, 1960); James F. Engel, David T. Kollat, and Roger D. Blackwell, *Consumer Behavior* (New York: Holt, Rinehart and Winston, Inc., 1968); Blair Kolasa, *Introduction to Behavioral Sciences for Business* (New York: Wiley, 1969); Rom Markin, *The Psychology of Consumer Behavior* (Englewood Cliffs: Prentice-Hall, 1968); and Thomas Robertson, *Consumer Behavior* (Glenview: Scott, Foresman and Company, 1970). See also Thongchai, *Phuetthikam phu boriphok*, 275–76.

[48] These theses are kept at the library of the Faculty of Commerce and Accountancy and the Office of Academic Resources, Chulalongkorn University.

[49] "Talat kho mun khuek khak kluen muea nangsuephim long ma len duai" (The information market is more lively with the newspapers), *Phuchatkan* (December 1985): 60–66.

[50] "Song lok wichai" (Looking at the research world), *Khoo Khaeng* 5, no. 50 (November 1984): 158–74. This article stated that marketing research was not a new service. Unilever is one of the oldest companies that valued marketing research.

Thai and Thailand-based multinational companies, independent research companies, and consulting services by academics. *Khoo Khaeng* pioneered the science of consumer research that serves as the foundation upon which much work has been built since.

In an article published in *Khoo Khaeng*'s fourth anniversary issue, Krairit Bunyakiat, a renowned marketer, claimed that the consumer, the market, and the marketer were the three major components of marketing. The market belonged to the consumer, or "buyer's market," in his words.[51] Krairit suggested that the following key trends in consumer behavior should be taken into account. First, consumers had acquired a distinctive lifestyle as a result of the diminishing size of the typical household unit, and the increase in and diversification of outlets for consumption.[52] Second, consumers had become more individualistic, each favoring multiple brands.[53] Third, Krairit highlighted the increasing value of time: with all family members being busy, they increasingly desired products to help them save time (e.g., bigger refrigerators, gas ovens, and disposable goods).[54]

In 1985, the magazine put together a team to conduct market research and collect more market data. All research findings were kept in Media Focus's data bank.[55] In the same year, Walada Chulawatthanakun, director of research and advertising in the media department of Ogilvy and Mather (Thailand), contributed a special article on how marketers should use research.[56] *Khoo Khaeng* also investigated its readers' expectations for improvements in the magazine in cooperation with Chai-narong and Associates, a marketing research company.[57] In 1986, *Khoo Khaeng* emphasized the concept of consumer segmentation by claiming that people of all ages and social backgrounds were potential consumers. The consumer behavior of urbanites (*khon mueang*) and villagers (*khon chonnabot*) had become more homogeneous due to the influence of mass media (especially radio), and the diffusion of urban lifestyles to the

[51] Krairit Bunyakiat, "Prakotkan kan talat nai rop si phi 1981–1984" (The marketing phenomenon in the past four years, 1981–1984), *Khoo Khaeng* 4, no. 48 (September 1984).

[52] Ibid., 116–118, 122. Krairit noted that increasing numbers of consumers shopped at shopping centers, food centers, and chain stores. In terms of eating habits, psychological factors (health, luxury, social awareness, and convenience) increasingly affected consumers' food choices. For example, the growing fast-food sector added convenience and saved time for some people while other consumers became more sensitive to issues of food hygiene and safety. In terms of their media habits, consumers reported being interested in reading economic and financial news, watching television, and listening to music from cassette tapes. Consumers had more choices of magazine selection. In a white-collar family, a husband and wife might choose a magazine that offered specific, topical content. Bankers read *Kan ngoen kan thanakan* (Finance & Banking), marketers read *Khoo Khaeng*, entrepreneurs and academics chose *Klang samong* (Brain Bank), and executives opted for *Satai* (Style).

[53] Krairit, "Prakotkan kan talat nai rop si phi 1981–1984," 122. Krairit used the example of a typical household in which three daughters might use nine brands of shampoo, eleven brands of soaps, and six brands of toothpaste.

[54] Ibid., 122–23, 125. The appearance and acceptance of packaged food and new packaging forms—canned food, plastic bags, the UHT (Ultra High Temperature) system—were also indicative of consumers' desire to save time.

[55] "*Khoo Khaeng* tueng phu an thi khaorop" (Khoo Khaeng to respected readers), *Khoo Khaeng* 6, no. 61 (October 1985), 9.

[56] Wanlada Chulawatthanakun, "Nak kan talat khuan chai kan wichai yang rai" (How marketers should use research findings), *Khoo Khaeng* 4, no. 43 (March 1985): 158–64.

[57] "*Khoo Khaeng* tueng phu an thi khaorop," 9.

countryside by returning villagers who had earlier moved to Bangkok to work.[58] Still, *Khoo Khaeng* accorded priority to urban consumers, who were categorized by age, sex, income, and lifestyle. Another article published in 1986 (whose opening lines stated "in today's consumer-oriented society ... the lifestyles and desires of consumers are at the core of our country's marketing strategies") presented research findings from some three hundred middle-class couples with at least one child.[59] Details of spending habits usually kept in the family were thus made public by this new method of marketing research.

SEGMENTING THE CONSUMER

Khoo Khaeng promoted marketing segmentation by positioning old and new commodity brands vis-à-vis distinct groups of consumers as defined by gender, class, occupation, age, lifestyle, and geography. Thailand's most valuable consumers were categorized as urbanized, middle-class, globally connected, and short on time. *Khoo Khaeng* endorsed in particular the idea that consumption reflects female agency as women construct through it their own selves and social position. Although all female consumers were categorized by class and profession, most marketing was aimed at middle-class housewives, who were targeted with consumer products, such as instant food (e.g., instant noodles, fast food, seven-minute rice) and electric appliances such as microwave ovens. The microwave oven entered middle-class Thai households in the late 1980s, when Japanese and Korean manufacturers introduced low-priced models (8,000-20,000 baht). According to *Khoo Khaeng*, "the middle-class housewife can use the microwave oven and not get dirty from being in the kitchen."[60] A 1989 advertisement for the Goldstar microwave featured the images of two women dressed in work attire. One woman, looking very tired, was cooking at a gas stove, and below it the caption read "yesterday." The other woman, who stood next to a microwave oven, was smiling and looking relaxed, with a caption that read "today ... beautiful ... comfortable ... the style of a genius housewife."[61]

The development of the microwave-oven market was aided by a novel mode of food preparation and consumption that accorded with the new urban lifestyle. The "TV dinner"—a prepackaged frozen meal—entered the Thai market in the 1980s, but did not grow fast at first because it faced direct and indirect competition from market food, delivered food, and ready-to-eat meals, whose prices were lower. In 1988, Rim Khlong restaurant, a pioneer in developing prepackaged frozen meals, realized the market opportunity of this concept from its success in the United States and the fact that Thai society was moving in the same direction. Rim Khlong's innovative TV dinner menus featured local curry dishes (priced from 15 to 50 baht), and the affordable price and familiar tastes hastened consumers' acceptance of the new products.[62] In 1989, Q.P. (a brand of the Sahapat group) entered Thailand's

---

[58] *Khoo Khaeng*, "Chap chipphachon consummoe...waek krop phueatthikam mai," (Checking consumer pulse ... breaking new behavior), *Khoo Khaeng* 6, no. 68 (May 1986): 61–67.

[59] "Chiwit khwam pen yu lae laisatai khon chan khlang nai krungthep" (The life and lifestyle of the middle class in Bangkok), *Khoo Khaeng* 7, no. 73 (October 1986): 119–20.

[60] "Tao-op mikhowep khayai tua su than lang" (The microwave oven [market] expands to the lower class), *Khoo Khaeng* 6, no. 69 (June 1989): 41.

[61] See *Khoo Khaeng* (June 1989), 90.

[62] Their good taste and quality was guaranteed by Shell Chuan Chim, a food award conferred by the most prominent food critic of that period, M. R. Thanatsri Sawatdiwat.

convenience-food market by introducing instant Japanese food (soup, curry, stir-fried dishes) and targeting students living on their own as well as housewives.[63]

In addition to housewives, children and teenagers became more prominent and powerful consumers. In 1985, Chainarong Intaramisup, CEO of CSN & Associates and a contributor to *Khoo Khaeng*'s column "Song wichai" (Looking at the research), cited survey results to predict that, in 1990, those below age twenty in Thailand would outnumber those aged twenty to thirty-nine.[64] Kindergartens, music schools, ballet and computer classes and clubs, health care services, and sport centers were booming as a result of the increasing number of children in the general population and the changing urban lifestyle that enabled families to afford such services and opportunities.[65] In 1983, there were only about 385 private kindergartens catering to almost 85,800 pupils in Bangkok.[66] By 1985, the number of kindergartens had increased to six hundred.[67] In 1984, the kindergarten market was worth approximately 300 million baht.

The youth market likewise grew into a lucrative target for manufacturers, marketers, and advertisers. In Thailand, marketing practices reaching out to young people did not seem to be different from those observed in the West. Writing about the United States, Lizabeth Cohen states that "teenagers became defined as a unique consumer experience: buying certain kinds of things—records, clothes, makeup, movies, and fast food—in certain kinds of places—shopping centers, drive-in theaters, and car-hop restaurants."[68] Thai teenagers were approached through similar product categories and at similar venues.

Khoo Khaeng reported on the fast growth of the fashion industry, which targeted urbanites, middle-class consumers, and youths. Boutique shops like Domon, Tempopo, Kurobo, Charles Michels, Magic Pin, Punch, and La Foret opened in shopping centers in Siam Center (not far from Chulalongkorn University) and the Ratchadamri area in Bangkok. Owners decorated their shops stylishly, changed window displays every two weeks, and played trendy music to attract teenagers. Merchants also advertised in the teenagers' fashion magazines, sponsored the wardrobes of television dramas, and organized fashion shows in the shopping centers where their shops were located.[69] In the 1980s, both Thai and international fashion brands competed with each other to gain the largest share of the youth fashion market. The fashion war became even more intense when shopping centers were built in every major corner of Bangkok and the large provinces.

---

[63] "Thi wi din noe kan toep to bon sen thang khlong khon run mai" (TV dinner: The growth on the path of the new generation), *Khoo Khaeng* 9, no. 101 (February 1989): 28–29.

[64] Chainarong Intarameesup, "Song Wichai" (Looking at the research), *Khoo Khaeng* 5, no. 60 (September 1985): 49.

[65] "Naew nom talat khun nu sotsai" (The future for children's market is bright.), *Khoo Khaeng* 5, no. 55 (June 1985): 135–48.

[66] "Phoei talat rong rian anuban 300 lan" (Revealing the 300 million baht kindergarten market), *Khoo Khaeng* 4, no. 45 (May 1984): 147.

[67] "Naew nom talat khun nu sotsai," 28.

[68] Cohen, *A Consumers' Republic*, 319.

[69] Looking back in history, a market for teenagers' fashion began emerging in Thailand with the establishment of the American military bases in the mid-1960s, when "dressing like an American is the best." See "Yutthachak buthik thueng yuk thi 'thong pen mue pro'" (The time for the boutique world "must be professional"), *Khoo Khaeng* 7, no. 76 (January 1987): 24.

As reported in *Khoo Khaeng*, marketers came up with a new approach to marketing both music and branded products. In the early 1980s, Yum Yum instant noodles extended its target market to teenagers by promoting its minced pork flavor to young people and selecting a male band, Grand Ex, to be in Yum Yum commercials.[70] Brands like Coca-cola and Pepsi successfully used their international marketing strategies to introduce Thai teens to a global teen culture. Coke gave two million baht to sponsor Carabao, the most famous "songs-for-life" band in the mid to late 1980s, whose album *Made in Thailand* (1984) achieved the extraordinary sales volume of more than one million cassettes.[71] With its campaign "New Generation," Pepsi built consumer awareness of youthful lifestyles and gender equality. In 1989, Pepsi chose Pornthip Nakhirunkanok as its spokesperson due to her huge popularity for being crowned Miss Universe for 1988–89 (only the second Thai woman to ever hold that title). She was young, beautiful, well-educated, and recognized internationally.[72]

The arrival of a convenience store like 7-Eleven is another example of how *Khoo Khaeng* promoted lifestyle consumption to urban consumers.[73] In 1984, Nimit Watthanawarin, a US-based columnist who wrote on international marketing, introduced this new type of store to Thai consumers: "7-Eleven is a small convenience store which is brave enough to stand beside big supermarts, such as Safeway, Saveon, Ralphs, Mayfairs, Thrifty, and Vons. Instead of selling at cheaper [prices] than supermarts, [7-Eleven] sells products which are 10 to 40 percent more expensive." Niwat also analyzed the store's customers and their purchasing habits, and even explained how to buy a franchise.[74] Nevertheless, it was not until 1988, as reported by *Khoo Khaeng*, that the C. P. Group, Thailand's then-largest agribusiness group, signed a contract with 7-Eleven to open franchises in the country. The first 7-Eleven store was located at C. P. Tower, in Bangkok's Silom district.[75]

The credit card was another global product that served as a status symbol to identify middle- to upper-class conspicuous consumers. The market for credit cards in Thailand was influenced by international trends.[76] *Khoo Khaeng* started reporting

---

[70] "Bami thueng chut 'phlik chom' ma ma ching ok 'miao-jo' thalom talat song pan lan" (The noodles "turning point"... Ma Ma launched "Myojo" to bombard the two billion baht market), *Khoo Khaeng* 5, no. 50 (November 1984): 182.

[71] Thiwa Sarajutha, "Sip pi met in Thailand" [The tenth anniversary of Made in Thailand album], *Si san* 7, no. 6 (2537), http://www.9dern.com/rsa/view.php?id=116, accessed October 29, 2013.

[72] Villa Vilaithong, "Americanization and Thai Magazine Advertising, 1987–1996" (master's thesis, University of Auckland, 2001), p. 36.

[73] In *Khoo Khaeng*'s articles, this chain store's name was given as "711."

[74] "'711' Rang khlong cham thi bang art khai khlong paeng ka suppoemaket" (7-Eleven: A convenience store that dares to to sell [its products] for more than do supermarts), *Khoo Khaeng* 4, no. 43 (April 1984): 48–53.

[75] "Yutthachak kan kha plik ... saep saep ... kan kan ... tae man di," 95, 97–98. Harboring doubts as to the commercial viability of convenience stores in Thailand, the C. P. group, before signing the franchise contract, tested the market by opening "Food Vill" at the Samakorn housing estate in Bangkok (approximately two thousand households), which was selected because of the concentration there of target consumer groups.

[76] The massive proliferation of credit cards began in the United States in the 1960s. See Jan Logemann, "Different Paths to Mass Consumption: Consumer Credit in the United States and West Germany during the 1950s and '60s," *Journal of Social History* 41, no. 3 (Spring 2008): 525–59.

on credit cards in the early 1980s; a 1982 column, "Yai miaw jai talat" (Grandma Miew goes shopping), explained how credit cards were replacing money.[77] As is typical for many new products that enter the Thai market, a Thai term was not immediately coined for "credit card," and so the transliteration *khredit kat* became current. Kasikorn Bank (Thai Farmer Bank) and Srinakorn Bank (Bangkok Metropolitan Bank) were the pioneers in offering such a service.[78] An advertisement for the Kasikorn Thai credit card published in *Khoo Khaeng* featured Bancha Lamsam, the bank's president and CEO, stating: "These cards are necessary in some circumstances."[79] By 1984, Thai commercial banks were collaborating with international credit-card companies, for example, Bangkok Bank with American Express and Thai Commercial Bank with VISA.

In the first half of the 1980s, the majority of credit-card users in Thailand were tourists; few Thais used them. Credit cards were only accepted in Bangkok, at first-class hotels, big restaurants, department stores, jewellery shops, and travel. There were rather strict criteria to be eligible for a credit card, and those automatically limited the number of Thai clients. A 1983 consumers' opinion poll determined that there were only 56,000 cardholders in the kingdom. Its survey of 240 cardholders in the Bangkok metropolitan area found out that approximately 78 percent were men and 22 percent were women.[80] These were high-, middle-, and low-level executives who worked in government organizations, state enterprises, financial institutions, and private companies. American Express was the most popular card, and M. R. Kukrit Pramoj, former prime minister of Thailand, was the spokesperson for American Express's first advertising campaign in Thailand in 1984.

By the late 1980s, business entrepreneurs and marketers moved vigorously to target "high-class" consumers, that is, those with much disposable cash. The category "luxury marketing" was created, which aimed to reach those consumers who had substantial capital at their disposal. The article "Opening the Door to the High-Class Product" elaborated that being prepared to cater to this group was important because Thai society had become an "affluent society."[81] The consumer lifestyles and purchasing behavior of this new generation of affluent urbanites were markedly different from those of their parents, for they used "future money" (i.e., credit cards) instead of money from their saving accounts. This new generation of wealthy consumers also earned more than the previous generation since many worked for private enterprises, and some inherited lands and benefitted from land and property development. The article estimated that "millionaire consumers, accounting for 2 percent of the whole population," were already models of consumption for this newly wealthy class.[82] Products and services targeting them

---

[77] "Bat thaen ngoen" (The card that replaces money), *Khoo Khaeng* 3, no. 19 (March 1982): 20, 23.

[78] *Khoo Khaeng* 4, no. 48 (September 1984), 61.

[79] Kasikorn Thai credit-card advertisement, *Khoo Khaeng* 5, no. 55 (April 1985), 109.

[80] Achara Kriengkraisakul, "Kan sueksa khwam khit khong phuboriphok nai khet krungthepmahanakhon thi mi tho bat khredit thi ok doi sathaban kan ngoen" (A study of consumer opinions in Bangkok metropolitan area regarding credit cards issued by financial institutions) (master's thesis, Chulalongkorn University, 1986), 43–44.

[81] "Poet pratu su talat hi-khlas" (Opening the door to high-class market), *Khoo Khaeng* 8, no. 93 (June 1988): 37.

[82] Ibid., 40.

included condominiums by the sea, expensive restaurants, golf and exclusive clubs' memberships, and expensive, high-fashion clothing from international brands. Between 1986 and 1988, when the economy started booming, various gold-color products (credit cards, toilets, even swimming suits) were created to symbolize the wealth, luxury, and privilege flaunted by the new rich.[83]

"Luxury marketing" also applied to the real-estate market. As the demand for middle- and low-income houses became more competitive, concentrating on the premium market was more lucrative for investors. Real-estate companies initiated high-end projects that catered to consumer demand. For instance, the unique Ban Rieu Mai project of forty-nine housing units on Bangkok's Wiphawat Rangsit Road was developed solely for executives and entrepreneurs who passed the project owner's selection criteria. The unit prices ranged from 3 to 10 million baht, and the development company sent project brochures directly to prospective clients.[84] Magazine advertisements for such exclusive housing developments encouraged those who could afford it to live in elegant houses that were located in safe, and environmental friendly, housing estates in suburban areas not far from Bangkok's central business areas.

ADVERTISING TO THE CORPORATE MAN

Khoo Khaeng depended mainly on advertising revenue rather than subscription fees for its income. Advertising rates were clearly announced in the magazine's first issue.[85] Indeed, since *Khoo Khaeng*'s circulation figures are not available, an indication of its leading position in the periodicals market is the continuous increase in the number of its ad pages during the 1980s, which shows advertisers' confidence in the magazine's ability to reach out to target consumers. For *Khoo Khaeng*'s two hundred page, sixth-anniversary issue, in September 1986, advertisements were indexed in a table of contents.[86] By the end of 1988, the total pages of an issue had increased to approximately three hundred.[87] Increasing revenue from advertisements allowed *Khoo Khaeng* to launch "Khoo Khaeng Extra," a special report on particular business sectors (the first issue was on housing).[88] These advertisements targeted corporate types by presenting a range of stylish images of desirable consumer goods, from expensive watches to Thai and international ready-to-wear clothing (especially in the magazine's early years).[89] They advised this target group how to dress for success, and how to flaunt a distinctive style and lifestyle by wearing particular attire for

---

[83] Ibid.

[84] "'Watthanawekin' ruk khuep khao talat thi yu a sai" ("Watthanawekin" penetrates housing market), *Khoo Khaeng* 9, no. 94 (July 1988): 36, 39.

[85] A full page, four-color advertisement cost 8,000 baht; a full page, black-and-white ad, 5,500 baht; and a half page, black-and-white ad, 3,000 baht. The number of advertisements published in *Khoo Khaeng* increased steadily during the 1980s.

[86] *Khoo Khaeng* 6, no. 72 (September 1986): 6.

[87] *Khoo Khaeng* 9, no. 99 (December 1988).

[88] "Khui kap than phu an" (Talking to the readers), *Khoo Khaeng* 6, no. 71 (August 1986): 5.

[89] See more details about the men's ready-to-wear market and examples of advertisements in "Talat suea pha samret rup phuchai ... thueng yuk bran nok hom kranam" (Men's ready-to-wear market reaches the point when international brands are active), *Khoo Khaeng* 9, no. 101 (February 1989): pp. 61–64, 70–72.

particular occasions. The new menswear, reflecting notions of refinement, self-discipline, and Westernization, transformed middle-class corporate men's appearance both at work and at play. While projecting ideals of masculine success and authority, fashion advertisements tended to depict women in marginal roles.

As more commercial buildings were developed, a new concept of business center was introduced in the 1980s. For instance, the Chamnan Phenchat project comprised a computer room, storage room, parking area, exhibition hall, meeting and seminar room, restaurant, product show room, sport club, and swimming pool. Other similar projects (e.g., the 42-floor Sin Sathon Tower and the 35-floor R. S Tower) were located along central arteries, such Silom, Sukhumvit, Asoke-Din Daeng, Ratchadaphisek, and Rama 9 Road.[90] Printed advertisements depicted corporate offices as being equipped with ergonomically designed furniture as well as communication equipment produced by American, European, and Japanese manufacturers. On the whole, advertisements targeting male corporate consumers portrayed a fantasy lifestyle in which drinking imported whisky, dining at international restaurants, and living in seaside condominiums were highly desirable forms of conspicuous consumption. Conspicuous consumers were expected to pay for their expenses not with cash, but by credit card; and the more they used premium credit cards, the more economic and social status was attached to them.

CONCLUSION

The caption for the image from *Khoo Khaeng*'s 1989 New Year card reads: "The golden rule for 1989: Consumers are powerful, so everybody has to please them."[91] On the jacket sleeves covering the multiple arms that are shown bestowing a crown and a sceptre on the central figure are inscribed the words: "retailing," "computer," "bank," "car," and "dress." *Khoo Khaeng* championed a new social ethic centered on material abundance and conspicuous consumption at the same time that it inaugurated business journalism in Thailand, serving as a model for later publishing initiatives. The political and economic situation during the second half of the 1970s paved the way for the birth of *Khoo Khaeng*. Journalists and news entrepreneurs launched business periodicals in response to the political uncertainty of the period, when news reporting was under strict government control. In 1980, when *Khoo Khaeng* started publication, the government led by General Prem Tinsulanonda issued the Prime Ministerial Order that put an end to communist insurgency. During the 1980s, Thailand witnessed the decline of socialist ideology and the last phase of the Cold War in global politics, while "guided democracy," or "Premocracy," was developed in accordance with the expansion of industrialist capitalism.[92]

---

[90] "Consep mai offit biwding" (New concept: Office building), *Khoo Khaeng* 9, no. 102 (March 1989): 23–24.

[91] *Khoo Khaeng* 9, no. 100 (January 1989): 9.

[92] See: Thikan Srinara, "Khwam kit thang kan mueang khong 'panyachon fai khan' phai lang kan tok tam khong krasae khwam kit sangkhomniyom nai prathetthai" (Political thoughts of "the opposition intellectuals" after the decline of the socialist ideology in Thailand, 1981–1950) (PhD dissertation, Chulalongkorn University, 2012); Uchen Cheangsen, "Prawatthisat kan mueang phak prachachon: khwamkhit lae pratibatkan khong nak kitchakam tangkan mueang nai pratchuban" (A history of people's politics: The ideas and practices of political activists (MA thesis, Thammasat University, 2012).

Industrial and economic development required new business approaches. The study of marketing was initiated to provide entrepreneurs and business owners with information about markets, products, consumer buying habits, purchasing power, competitor data, and the like. Marketing and advertising professionals were well aware of the competitive value of marketing knowledge. A small group formed a data bank, and eventually they also created *Khoo Khaeng* magazine, to fill this void in creating, analyzing, storing, and accessing marketing information and knowledge. *Khoo Khaeng* steadily built a strong connection with manufacturers, marketers, media people, advertisers, academics, and students, which made possible the professionalization of marketing. The magazine followed in the footsteps of business schools and research companies by promoting market research, and inviting research specialists to contribute regular articles and conduct several types of research. Although the magazine focused initially on traditional product-oriented marketing, it also promoted new consumer-oriented marketing. The marketing of product and service categories revealed the classification of consumers by gender, age, occupation, income, class, and lifestyle. Advertisements in the magazine strengthened modern concepts of business practices, routines, and manners. The ads articulated an ideal vision of corporate businessmen. As a marketing manual, *Khoo Khaeng* provided a forum for negotiation involving the meanings and identities of market, products, consumers, and advertisements in the context of a major transformation of Thai business culture.

CHAPTER NINE

"GOVERNANCE" IN THAILAND

Kasian Tejapira

What I propose to do in this chapter is to look at the introduction and trajectory of the concept and practice of "governance" in Thailand from the perspective of cultural politics, focusing on the politics of translating and transforming governance into the Thai language and culture, as well as its practical activation.[1] The underlying idea is that the movement of discourse—the cross-language, cross-cultural adoption of special idioms and an unfamiliar lexicon—is a complex process (involving translation, transformation, reinterpretation, and selection), wrought with politics. So is its activation and manipulation in local culture and politics. This essay will relate the soft power of cultural political practice in the Thai context with the hard political economic reality of a dominant neoliberal global policy regime, demonstrating how the Thais managed to mess up "good governance" in the process.[2]

THE NEOLIBERAL SHOCK DOCTRINE

The occasion of the coming of "governance" to Thailand is directly related to what Naomi Klein, a leading North American intellectual of the global justice movement, called the "shock doctrine" in her acclaimed book of the same title.[3] According to Klein, a general collective shock, be it induced by an economic crisis, a military coup and subsequent brutal repression, real or imagined terrorist threats, or

---

[1] This essay was first presented as a paper at the Tokyo University Institute of Social Science, Shaken International Symposium on "Governance of Contemporary Japan," December 1, 2010 (http://jww.iss.u-tokyo.ac.jp/publishments/issrs/issrs/pdf/issrs_47.pdf, accessed December 2, 2014), and was published in a revised version in the Institute of Social Science Research Series, no. 47 (2011).

[2] My research into the politics of translation and discourse in Thailand was inspired by the pioneering, insightful, and sophisticated work of Craig J. Reynolds on the political semiotics of the term *sakdina* (feudalism) as used by Jit Poumisak, a celebrated Thai radical intellectual of the post-WWII period. See Craig J. Reynolds, *Thai Radical Discourse: The Real Face of Thai Feudalism Today* (Ithaca: Cornell Southeast Asia Program Publications, 1987).

[3] Naomi Klein, *The Shock Doctrine: The Rise of Disaster Capitalism* (London: Penguin Books, 2007).

even a natural disaster, is crucially instrumental in stunning the populace, stifling people's resistance, and imposing generally unpopular neoliberal economic policy packages that typically involve a massive transfer of resources from the public sector to the corporate sector of the economy, and from the bottom to the top of the economic hierarchy. Moreover, this astute practical observation, which actually drove the drastic redirection of economic policy under the Pinochet regime in Chile (1973–90), had been developed into a conscious strategy by the most influential advocate of the neoliberal economic doctrine, as well as the highest-profile personal adviser to General Pinochet, namely the University of Chicago's Professor Milton Friedman, a Nobel laureate in economics.[4] As Friedman stated in the preface to the new edition of his celebrated book *Capitalism and Freedom,*

> Only a crisis—actual or perceived—produces real change. When that crisis occurs, the actions that are taken depend on the ideas that are lying around. That, I believe, is our basic function: to develop alternatives to existing policies, to keep them alive and available until the politically impossible becomes politically inevitable.[5]

Two years later, he further expanded upon the so-called shock doctrine by specifying the limited time frame available for imposing policies:

> A new administration has some six to nine months [following a crisis] in which to achieve major changes; if it does not seize the opportunity to act decisively during that period, it will not have another such opportunity.[6]

In Thailand, a shock-inducing economic crisis struck in 1997,[7] and then spread to the wider East Asian region, in the form of currency free-fall, financial collapse, severe economic contraction and depression, widespread bankruptcy and unemployment, rising poverty, and fire sales of assets to foreign financial investors. Thai GDP contracted by a massive 10.8 percent in 1998.[8] One hundred, or over a quarter of all firms, were delisted from the Stock Exchange of Thailand, half of them because of bankruptcy or collapse. About a quarter of the top business groups in pre-crisis Thailand (seven of the top thirty, and over fifty of the top 220) either vanished

---

[4] Ibid., 80–83. For Milton Friedman's background and his relation to the so-called Chicago School of Economics, see Eric Schliesser, "Friedman, Positive Economics, and the Chicago Boys," and Robert Van Horn and Philip Mirowski, "Neoliberalism and Chicago," both in *The Elgar Companion to the Chicago School of Economics,* ed. Ross B. Emmett (Northampton, MA: Edward Elgar, 2010).

[5] Milton Friedman, *Capitalism and Freedom,* rev. ed. (Chicago: University of Chicago Press, 1982), ix.

[6] Milton Friedman and Rose Friedman, *The Tyranny of the Status Quo* (San Diego: Houghton Mifflin Harcourt, 1984), 3.

[7] The general account in this section is derived from Kasian Tejapira, "Post-crisis Economic Impasse and Political Recovery in Thailand: The Resurgence of Economic Nationalism," *Critical Asian Studies* 34, no. 3 (September 2002): 323–56.

[8] Bank of Thailand, *Key Economic Indicators* (Bangkok: Bank of Thailand, February 28, 2002), 5.

altogether or drastically shrank.[9] Nearly two-thirds of big Thai capitalists went bankrupt, thousands of companies folded, and two thirds of the pre-crisis private commercial banks went under and changed hands. One million Thai workers lost their jobs and three million more fell below the poverty line.

It was precisely amid such an economic crisis, and resultant psychic shock in the region, that an alternative to the pre-crisis, dirigiste and developmentalist (if crony-capitalist) economic policy was imposed in most of East and Southeast Asia in the form of Wall Street-pushed (and US-government-supported) IMF loan conditionality.[10] This neoliberal policy-reform package essentially comprised further economic liberalization, business deregulation, privatization of state enterprises and higher education, cuts to social spending and government subsidies, and, last but not least, governance reform, or "good governance."[11]

The following first-hand account illustrates the IMF's high-handed, imperial attitude toward the crisis-ridden emerging market countries. According to the then-Thai deputy prime minister, Veerapong Ramangkura, an academic-turned-leading-economic-minister, who was the Thai government's point man in its difficult negotiations with the IMF over the loan rescue package, the then-IMF first deputy managing director, Stanley Fischer, invited him and the Bank of Thailand governor to a working breakfast at the luxurious Oriental Hotel in Bangkok. Veerapong suggested to Fischer that, when the deal being worked out by the Thai government and IMF negotiating teams was finally ready, he and Fischer should review it together in the same manner that professors review a student's dissertation. However, Fischer curtly brushed aside the amicable suggestion on the grounds that he had no time, since he had to look after so many countries around the world. Instead he advised Veerapong to trust Hubert Neiss's (IMF's then-director for Asia and Pacific) economic policy prescriptions, since Neiss had dealt with various countries in similar dire economic situations. Veerapong argued that each country had its own particular economic structure and culture, so how could a single formula be universally applied? Fischer simply replied: "Don't worry. The single formula can be applied all over," leaving Veerapong saddened and dismayed.[12]

The Thai Cultural and Political Buffer—A Shock Absorber

The way in which Thai political society in general, and Thai public intellectuals in particular, coped with such an overwhelming shock-inducing and externally

---

[9] According to the findings of Professor Akira Suehiro, cited in Chang Noi (Chris Baker), "10 Years after the 1997 Crisis," *The Nation* [Thailand], June 12, 2007, www.nationmultimedia.com /option/print.php?newsid=30036611.php, accessed December 2, 2014.

[10] For an analytical account of the pre-crisis dirigiste and developmental states in East Asia and their neoliberalization in the aftermath of the crisis, see: Meredith Woo-Cumings, ed., *The Developmental State* (Ithaca and London: Cornell University Press, 1999); and Meredith Jung-En Woo, ed., *Neoliberalism and Institutional Reform in East Asia: A Comparative Study* (New York: Palgrave Macmillan and UNRISD, 2007).

[11] See, in this connection: Jolle Demmers, Alex E. Fernandez Jilberto, and Barbara Hogenboom, eds., *Good Governance in the Era of Global Neoliberalism: Conflict and Depolitisation in Latin America, Eastern Europe, Asia, and Africa* (London and New York: Routledge, 2004); and Barbara Orlandini, "Consuming 'Good Governance' in Thailand: Re-contextualising Development Paradigms" (PhD dissertation, University of Florence, 2001).

[12] See Veerapong Ramangkura, "Khon doen trok" column, *Prachachat Thurakij*, July 12, 2004: 2.

imposed policy diktat owed much to what Prince Wan Waithayakon Worawan[13] called *phutthiphrom haeng phasa*, "the creative intelligence of the Thai language."[14] As he stated in a public lecture on the Siamese language in 1932, the year of the constitutionalist coup against the absolute monarchy by the People's Party,

> It is the Thai language that will guarantee the security of the Thai nation. This is because if we favor the use of Thai transliterations of Western words about ideas, we may walk too fast. That is, we may imitate other people's ideas directly instead of pre-modifying them in accord with our ideas. But if we use Thai words and hence must coin new ones, we will have to walk deliberately.[15]

In effect, Prince Wan's coinage guideline amounts to a cautious and conservative reception of Western modernity, based on a considered political manipulation of language and translation. By controlling the spelling and pronunciation of words, Wan contends, one controls their meanings; by controlling their meanings, one controls people's thinking; and by controlling people's thinking, one controls the people. Although registering the opposite political intent, Prince Wan's dictum finds unexpected resonance in Prasenjit Duara's concept of "the body cultural."[16]

Situated at the margins of a national language, translation guards the linguistic border and integrity of a nation-state's body cultural. Where language is standardized and coinages need to be sanctioned by central authorities (as in modern Thailand), the translation of key foreign political and ideological words becomes a highly politicized and fiercely contested boundary. At the point of translation, the language "border patrol" tries to screen newly translated lexical immigrants so as to discriminate against the radical ones and declare them *lexica non grata*. Failing at that, the central authorities proceed to retranslate (in some cases even pre-translate) such radical terms so as to turn them into either quarantined and alien permanent nonresidents, or emasculated and tamed, harnessed and domesticated, incorporated and de-radicalized, naturalized neuters. At the same time, the unauthorized radical translators seek incessantly to smuggle in and procreate their illegitimate lexical brainchild.[17]

---

[13] Prince Wan Waithayakon Worawan, or *Kromamun* Naradhip Bongsprabandh (1891–1976), was the Oxford and École Libre des Sciences Politiques-educated doyen of official lexical coiners, as well as first chairperson of the Royal Institute and a top Thai diplomat.

[14] HRH Kromamun Naradhip Bongsprabandh, *Witthayawannakam* [Scholarly writings] (Bangkok: Phraephitthaya, 1971), 243–322 (esp. 270, 315). For a profile of Prince Wan, see "Prince Wan Waithayakon (Thailand) Elected President of the Eleventh Session of the General Assembly," General Assembly of the United Nations, www.un.org/en/ga/president/bios/bio11.shtml, accessed December 2, 2014.

[15] Prince Naradhip Bongsprabandh, *"Pathakatha ruang siam phak"* [Lecture on the Siamese language], in *Chumnum praniphon khong satsatrajan pholtri phrajaoworawongthoe kromamun naradhip bongsprabandh* [Selected writings of Professor Major General Prince Naradhip Bongsprabandh], ed. Songwit Kaeosri (Bangkok: Bangkok Bank, 1979), 416.

[16] Prasenjit Duara, *Rescuing History from the Nation: Questioning Narratives of Modern China* (Chicago: University of Chicago Press, 1995).

[17] My interpretation of Duara's concept is derived from Craig J. Reynolds, "Identity, Authenticity, and Reputation in the Postcolonial History of Mainland Southeast Asia," keynote speech given at the International Conference on Post Colonial Society and Culture in Southeast Asia, Yangon, Myanmar, December 16–18, 1998. I am also inspired by Thongchai

Take, for example, the translation and transformation into Thai of the Western term "democracy," also discussed in this volume by Patrick Jory.[18] The standard Thai equivalent of "democracy" is *prachathipatai* and the current system of government is normally referred to as "a democratic regime of government with the king as head of the state."[19] In fact, the term *prachathipatai*, which was coined by King Vajiravudh as early as 1912, originally meant "republic" (i.e., a non-monarchical government).[20] The shift in meaning from "republic" to "democracy" followed on from a compromise between the People's Party and the throne in the aftermath of the coup of June 1932, when a constitutional monarchy was decided upon in place of a republic.[21] The ultimate result of this process is the characterization of the present Thai political system as *rabob prachathipatai an mi phramahakasat song pen pramuk,* or, if one sticks to the original meaning of *prachathipatai,* "a republic with the king as head of the state," an oxymoron made possible by the successful taming, or metathesis, of a foreign-derived radical signifier.

In the case of the forceful coming to Thailand of IMF-style good governance, its latter-day lexical buffer, or shock absorber, was coined by Chaiwat Satha-anand, of the Faculty of Political Science, Thammasat University, following in the footsteps of Prince Wan. A Thai Muslim of Indian descent, and a foremost scholar of peace studies and non-violent conflict resolution, Chaiwat strategically translated "good governance" as *thammarat,* literally meaning a righteous state or a state guided by *thamma* (Pali, *dhamma*; Sanskrit, *dharma,* i.e., moral righteousness, truth, law). His idea was to make it possible to interpret *thammarat,* or Thai-style good governance, as the norm to control, regulate, and discipline the Thai state, providing implicitly a legitimate justification for civil disobedience against it.[22]

Chaiwat's cultural political initiative was picked up and developed into a public campaign by Thirayuth Boonmi, a lecturer at Thammasat University. A former student leader and guerrilla fighter-turned-academic-cum-suave-political-publicist, Thirayuth redefined *thammarat* in a broad, consensus-seeking manner, as a tripartite self-reform of the state, business, and civil society, to achieve efficient and just public administration. Thirayuth then deployed his clout as public intellectual, and his political and business connections, to build it up into a widely publicized national agenda and high-profile reform campaign.[23] From then on, *thammarat* was

---

Winichakul, *Siam Mapped: A History of the Geo-Body of a Nation* (Honolulu: University of Hawaii Press, 1994), especially the section "The Border of Thainess," pp. 169–70.

[18] Patrick Jory, "Republicanism in Thai History," chapter five in this volume.

[19] See Section 2 of the official English version of the current constitution by the Constitution Drafting Commission, Constituent Assembly, in *Constitution of the Kingdom of Thailand, B.E. 2550,* trans. Pinai Nanakorn (Bangkok: Bureau of Printing Services, Secretariat of the House of Representatives, 2007), 4.

[20] King Vajiruvudh, *Chotmaihet raiwan khong phrabatsomdet phramongkutklao jaoyuhua r.s. 131* [Diary of King Vajiravudh, 1912 CE] (Bangkok: Duang Kamol, 1981), 7.

[21] For a standard account of the 1932 revolution, see Thawat Mokarapong, *History of the Thai Revolution: A Study in Political Behaviour* (Bangkok: Chalermnit, 1972).

[22] See the statement entitled *"Khosanoe waduai thammarat fa wikrit setthakij-kanmueang"* [A proposal on good governance in the face of political economic crisis], which Chaiwat as chairperson was authorized to draft on behalf of the meeting of the Faculty of Political Science, Thammasat University, and which was published in *Matichon,* August 10, 1997: 2.

[23] See Thirayuth Boonmi, *Thammarat haeng chat: Yutthasat koo haiyana prathet thai* [National good governance: Strategy for salvaging Thailand] (Bangkok: Sai Than Publishing House, 1998).

appropriated, and variously interpreted, by leading representatives of various strategic groups in the Thai political society, based on their respective political proclivities and socio-economic interests, as summarily illustrated by the following figures.[24]

Figure 1: The Five Versions of *Thammarat*

IMF-mandated terms
↓
"Good Governance"
↓
Thammarat

(*Thamma + Rat* → Moral Righteousness, Truth, Justice, Law and Rules, and State)

State-civilizing *Thammarat*	National-concensus *Thammarat*	Authoritarian *Thammarat*	Liberal *Thammarat*	Communitarian *Thammarat*
The use of *Thamma* to control, regulate, and discipline the state, thus providing a legitimate ground for civil disobedience	A tripartite self-reform of state–society–business, not just the state, for efficient and just public administration	The state imposes *Thamma* on the people in a top-down manner	Orientation to management, efficiency, and results + depoliticization	Weaving social fabric together → generating social energy → pushing for national *Thammarat* → building an ideal *Santi Prachatham* society
Promoted by Chaiwat Satha-anand et al. (academic community)	Promoted by Thirayuth Boonmi (pluralist political activist and strategist)	Promoted by Gen. Bunsak Kam-haengritthirong (military, National Security Council)	Promoted by Anand Panyarachun (former prime minister, business leader,)	Promoted by Dr. Prawase Wesi (royalist medical doctor, civic leader, and NGO sage)

THE AFTER-EFFECTS OF *THAMMARAT*

Given the tradition of Thai coinage of cultural–political buffers and shock absorbers, have the Thais been able to resist the shock-induced, and IMF-imposed, neoliberal alternative? Seventeen years on, the record is mixed. The populist and royal-nationalist force of organized labor and farmers, old business elite, middle-class entrepreneurs, NGO activists, and intellectuals mounted a determined resistance to prescribed neoliberal policy reform. But their success has been partial, uneven, and sectorial.

Due to an IMF-loan-conditioned series of new regulations, the Thai economy has become structurally more open. The penetration of foreign capital is deeper and more widespread than before the crisis. The inflow of foreign investment in the post-crisis decade (1997–2006) was three times higher than in the previous ten years

---

[24] These figures are adapted from Kasian Tejapira, "*Thammarat*—Good Governance in Glocalizing Thailand," in *Words in Motion: Toward A Global Lexicon*, ed. Carol Gluck and Anna Lowen Haupt Tsing (Durham and London: Duke University Press, 2009), 320–21.

Figure 2: The Three Meanings of *Thammarat*

Issues	Authoritarian version	Liberal Version	Communitarian Version
Power	State-centralized power over a monolithic, harmonious nation	Has limitations; checks and balances of power; allows for conflict	Decentralization of power
Market	Compliance to market forces	Takes as its premise the triumph of free-market capitalism	Takes as its premise the failure and injustice of capitalism; seeks space for a "sufficiency economy"
Democracy	Thai-style	Considers *thammarat* and democracy as two separate issues, the former being about administrative process, the latter having to do with power relations; a country can have *thammarat* without democracy, e.g., Singapore	*Thammarat* and democracy can not be separated; hence, all forms of dictatorship—whether monarchical, military, or communist—are emphatically not *thammarat*.

(1987–96) when measured in US dollars, and five times higher when measured in bahts. At the height of the boom, 112 of the world's top 500 multi-national corporations (MNCs) had an operation in Thailand. That figure is now over 250, or more than double.[25] Certain key lucrative state enterprises were privatized, such as petroleum and natural gas,[26] telecommunications,[27] and electronic media.[28] But privatization of other state enterprises met stiff resistance by vested interests and was repeatedly delayed, partly compromised (at leading national universities),[29] or even reversed in one important case (electricity generation).[30]

---

[25] Chang Noi, "10 Years after the 1997 Crisis."

[26] The Petroleum Authority of Thailand (PTT, established in 1978) was privatized under Corporatization Act B.E. 2542 (1999 CE) and became the PTT Public Company Limited in 2001. See "Background," PTT, http://www.pttplc.com/EN/About/pages/Background.aspx, accessed December 2, 2014.

[27] The Communications Authority of Thailand (CAT, established in 1977 on the basis of the preexisting Post and Telegraph Department) was privatized under Corporatization Act B.E. 2542 (1999), and became the CAT Telecom Public Company Limited in 2003. See "Corporate Info," www.cattelecom.com/site/en/company_detail.php?cat=375, accessed December 2, 2014.

[28] The Mass Communication Organization of Thailand (MCOT, established in 1977 on the basis of the Thai Television Company Limited, which had been founded in 1955) was privatized under Corporatization Act B.E. 2542 (A.D. 1999) and became the MCOT Public Company Limited in 2004. See "Thurakij khong borisat" [Company's business], MCOT, http://mcot-th.listedcompany.com/business.html, accessed February 19, 2013.

[29] See: "Korani rang phraratchabanyat mahawitthayalai nai kamkab khong rat" [The case of the autonomous university bills], *Siam jodmaihet: Bantheuk khaosan lae hetkan,* pi thi 31 pho.so. 2549 [CD] [Siam archives: Record of news and events, vol. 31 B.E. 2549] (Bangkok: Siamban Company Limited, 2006), 1660, 1661; "Rang phraratchabanyat mahawitthayalai nai kamkab khong rat" [Autonomous university bill] *Siam jodmaihet: Bantheuk khaosan lae hetkan,* pi thi 32 pho.so. 2550 [CD] [Siam archives: Record of news and events, Vol. 32 B.E. 2550] (Bangkok: Siamban Company Limited, 2007), 1046; "Rang phraratchabanyat chulalongkorn-

For example, a nine-year delay (1997–2006) in privatizing higher education was due to persistent opposition not only from university students but especially from the faculty, researchers, and administrative staff members who wanted to hold on to their status as government officials with job security and lifetime welfare benefits. To overcome that resistance, the government offered university employees—faculty, researchers, and staff—a choice between retaining the status of being a permanent government official and that of becoming a contracted state employee (albeit with better pay) when the university was transformed from a state institution to an autonomous (independent) one. Having made the offer, it was then possible to push ahead with the mandated privatization. (Newly hired university personnel are all employed on a contractual basis.[31])

More significantly, the Electricity Generating Authority of Thailand (EGAT, established in 1969 on the basis of three preexisting state-owned regional electricity generating plants) was privatized under Corporatization Act B.E. 2542 (1999) and became the EGAT Public Company Limited in 2005, amid fierce and continuing protests by the EGAT trade union and consumer groups. In the lawsuit against the privatization of EGAT filed by the Foundation for Consumers and its allies, the administrative court ruled in 2006 that the privatization was not done in accordance with the law, and hence was null and void. Consequently, EGAT's status has since reverted to a state enterprise.

In the aftermath of the overthrow of the elected Thaksin Shinawatra government, which had been pursuing a crony capitalist-oriented globalizing/neoliberalizing policy,[32] by a palace-blessed military coup in September 2006, a substantial number of consumer-group and labor-union activists, as well as royalist-nationalist public intellectuals, were appointed by the ARC to the National Legislative Assembly.[33] These appointees submitted a bill to the National Legislative Assembly to abrogate the act that privatized EGAT, so as to put an end to the "nation-selling" privatization of state enterprises,[34] while the ARC-installed government of Prime Minister General

---

mahawitthayalai" [Chulalongkorn university bill], *Siam jodmaihet* 2550 [CD], 1663, 1666, 1669; and "Kanprachum saphanitibanyat haeng chat" [National legislative assembly's session], *Siam jodmaihet* 2550 [CD], 1722.

[30] See "Kham phiphaksa sal pokkhrong soongsud khadi mailek dam thi f. 14/2548 wanthi 15 phreussajikayon pho.so. 2548" [The ruling of the Supreme Administrative Court, Case No. F 14/2548, 15 November B.E. 2548], http://www.senate.go.th/lawdatacenter/includes/FCKeditor/upload/Image/b/ad7.pdf, accessed January 19, 2015.

[31] See, for example, the case of Thammasat University, which has yet to change its status in "Thangdoen khong mahawitthayalai Thammasat soo kanpen mahawitthayalai nai kamkab khong rat (nab tae pho.so. 2541 theung pajjuban)" [The path of Thammasat University toward autonomous status (from 1998 to the present)], Thammasat University, http://legal.tu.ac.th/ (link to /tu_51/tu_control/pdf/), accessed January 26, 2015; and "Rang phraratchabanyat mahawitthayalai thammasat pho.so ..." [Thammasat University Bill], Thammasat University, http://legal.tu.ac.th (link to /tu_51/tu_control/pdf/), accessed January 26, 2015.

[32] See Kasian Tejapira, "Toppling Thaksin," *New Left Review* 39 (May/June 2006): 5–37.

[33] Kasian Tejapira, "Ratthaprahan 19 kanyayon pho.so. 2549 kab kanmueang thai" [The 19 September 2006 coup and Thai politics], *Ratthasatsan* 29, no. 3 (September–December 2008), esp. pp. 58–60.

[34] Senator Sophon Suphapong and others, "Ekkasan prakob kanphijarana rang phraratchabanyat yokleok phraratchabanyat thun ratthawisahakij pho.so 2542 pho.so ... " [Supplements to the Abrogation of the Corporatization Act B.E. 2542 Bill B.E ...], *Wutthisapha*, http://library2.parliament.go.th/giventake/content_nla/2550_48.pdf, accessed January 19, 2015.

Surayud Chulanont (a former commander-in-chief of the army, supreme commander of the armed forces, and privy councilor) submitted another bill to replace the Corporatization Act in an effort to rectify and regulate the existing flawed and corruptible privatization process.[35] Their separate and uncoordinated moves eventually doomed the anti-neoliberal legislative thrust; the attempt at a legislative repeal/reform of the Corporatization Act was divided and weakened, whereas the pro-privatization and financial market force was alarmed and jolted into inflexible opposition. The first bill was rejected by the National Legislative Assembly; the second bill passed its second reading but was left to expire; the Corporatization Act is still in force, though politically unusable in face of widespread public suspicion and opposition.[36] Apparently, privatization is stalled for the time being.[37] (In 2014 the coup-installed military government of Prime Minister General Prayuth Chan-ocha invited foreign public and private corporations from China, Japan, and South Korea to take part in the state's high-speed rail-system and water-management megaprojects. As for existing major state enterprises, none has been slated for privatization, although one that chronically lost money was dissolved.)

Cuts in social spending have been largely offset by major populist programs introduced by the deposed Thaksin government in what may be called *compensatory,* as against *disciplinary,* neoliberalism, such as affordable health care and housing, village funds, and SME (Small and Medium Enterprise) credits.[38] As for good governance itself, it has been normalized, i.e., retranslated as *thammaphibal* (the fostering and maintenance of *thamma*), and as *kanborihan kitchakan banmueang thi di* (good administration of public affairs).[39] It has also been bureaucratized by virtue of

---

[35] "Poed rang pho.ro.bo. praeroop ratthawisahakij" [Unveiling the State Enterprise Corporatization Bill], *FTA Watch*, http://www.ftawatch.org/node/11655, accessed September 27, 2013.

[36] This information and observation is kindly provided by Pokpong Junvith, a lecturer at the Faculty of Economics, Thammasat University, who was directly involved in drafting the improved but aborted new corporatization bill through Chalongphob Sussangkarn, a former president of the Thailand Development Research Institute-turned-minister of finance under the Surayud Chulanont Government (Pokpong Junvith, personal e-mail correspondence, February 19, 2011).

[37] This recent *rapprochement* between the former left and the former right in Thai politics under a nationalist banner against the globalizing other is taken to task by Thongchai Winichakul in "6 tula nai khwamsongjam khong faikhwa 2519–2549: ak chaichana soo khwamngiab (tae yang chana yoo di)" [The October 6th incident in the memory of the right B.E. 2519–2549: From victory to silence, albeit still victorious], in Chaiwat Satha-anand, ed., *Khwamrunraeng son/ha sangkhom thai* [Hidden/seeking violence in Thai society] (Bangkok: Matichon Press, 2010), 482–86. For an earlier theoretical discussion, of the anti-globalization political shift, albeit with the opposite political import, see Pierre Bourdieu, "Neo-liberalism, the Utopia (Becoming a Reality) of Unlimited Exploitation," in his *Acts of Resistance: Against the Tyranny of the Market*, Richard Nice, trans. (New York: The New Press, 1998).

[38] See Kasian, "Toppling Thaksin," 27–28; Pasuk Phongpaichit and Chris Baker, "Thaksin's Populism," *Journal of Contemporary Asia*, 38, no. 1 (2008): 62–83. The two versions of neo-liberalism are derived from Perry Anderson, "Editorial: Jottings on the Conjuncture," *New Left Review*, 48 (November/December 2007): 24.

[39] The two new translated Thai equivalents of good governance appear interchangeably in the text of the current constitution, which was drafted by the military junta-appointed constituent assembly and approved in a nationwide referendum in 2007. Aee "Ratthathammanoon haeng ratcha-anajakthai" [The constitution of the kingdom of Thailand], *Royal Thai Government Gazette* 124, Section 47 ko. (August 24, 2007), sections 74, 78, and 84; pp. 20, 22, 25.

the cabinet-issued Royal Decree on Criteria and Procedures for Good Governance, B.E. 2546 (2003),[40] which established the Office of the Public Sector Development Commission and its affiliated Institute for Good Governance Promotion to develop and promote good governance ideas and practice in the state bureaucracy. As a result, good governance is safely and securely lodged in officialdom and become part of bureaucratic and academic jargon.[41]

More significantly, good governance has also been politicized by populist and royalist-nationalist forces and then used as a rallying cry in their anti-corruption campaign in general, and in the anti-Thaksin movement in particular. Evidence for this is that good governance figures prominently in the military junta-promoted current Constitution of 2007 (Sections 74, 78, and 84), whose aim is "to prevent future Thaksins gaining power," as described by former Royal Thai Air Force Squadron Leader Prasong Soonsiri, a veteran state intelligence official, self-proclaimed key conspirator of the 2006 coup, and chairperson of the Constitution Drafting Commission.[42] The relevant sections of this anti-Thaksin constitution reads in part as follows:

> Section 74. A government official, official or employee of a government agency, a state agency, a state enterprise or other state official shall have a duty to act in compliance with the law in order to protect public interests, and provide convenience and services to the public in accordance with *the good governance principle* ...;

> Section 78. The state shall pursue directive principles of state policies in relation to the administration of the state affairs, as follows: ... (4) to develop the working system in the public sector with particular emphasis on the development of the quality, conscience, and ethics of state officials in tandem with the improvement of patterns and methods of work in order to achieve efficiency of the administration of the state affairs, and to promote the application of *the good governance principle* amongst state agencies ...; [and]

> Section 84. The state shall pursue directive principles of state policies in relation to economy, as follows: ... (2) to promote the application of righteousness,

---

[40] See a tentative official translation at http://thailaws.com/law/t_laws/tlaw17512.pdf, accessed January 26, 2015.

[41] There exists, for instance, a much-promoted research and training institute called Soon Borikan Wichakan Thammaphibal (the Center for Good Governance Academic Services), affiliated with a doctoral program at the Chandrakasem Rajabhat University in Bangkok. See its official website at http://tinyurl.com/csri-or-th-index, accessed February 4, 2015. As for a typical scholarly publication on the topic of Thai good governance, see Amporn Thamronglak, ed., *Kanborihanpokkhrong satharana (Public Governance) kanborihan ratthakij nai satawas thi 21* [Public Governance: Public Administration in the 21st Century] (Bangkok: Textbook and Publication Program, Faculty of Political Science, Thammasat University, 2010).

[42] Cited in Nattaya Chetchotiros, *"Charter Defended: Prasong Says Aim Was to Prevent Future Thaksins Gaining Power,"* Bangkok Post, August 18, 2007: 3. As to Prasong's alleged role in the 2006 coup, see his interview in Rodney Tasker, "Grumbles, Revelations of a Thai Coup Maker," *Asia Times* Online, www.atimes.com/atimes/Southeast_Asia/HL22Ae01.html, accessed December 2, 2014.

ethics, and *good governance* in tandem with the operation of business ... (emphasis added).[43]

The trajectory of discourse and practice of good governance in Thailand has thus followed the dynamics and vagaries of intense political conflict in Thailand in recent years. In short, good governance has become part of the resurgent anti-democratic discourse in Thailand. This can be seen in a series of public statements made by key actors in the monarchical network and their populist NGO allies in recent years. First, there is Sumet Tantivejkul, a French-educated close aide to King Bhumibol Adulyadej, secretary-general of the Chaipattana Foundation under royal patronage since its establishment in 1988,[44] and president of Thammasat University Council from 2005 to 2011.[45] On March 16, 2004, Sumet gave a public lecture, entitled "The State and Private Sectors' Common Front against Corruption," which he claimed was inspired by King Bhumibol's uncharacteristic verbal curse on corruption to an audience of provincial governors on October 8, 2003. Sumet propounded what was in effect a typical conservative Thai reception of Western discourse, that is to say, there was nothing new under the (Thai) sun. He claimed that Thai-style good governance—*thammaphibal* or *thammarat*—actually predated Western good governance for decades, as evidenced by King Bhumibol's accession speech in 1950: "I shall reign by Dhamma, for the benefit and happiness of all the Thai people."[46] Thus it fell upon all loyal Thais to help rid the country of corruption and uphold *thamma*, as called upon by the king. To carry out this royally ordained mission, Sumet also chaired a pioneering, well-connected, and high-profile anti-corruption NGO, called *Moonnithi prathetthai sai sa-ad*, or "Foundation for a Clean and Transparent Thailand" (FaCT), which had been set up on the advice of key leaders of the monarchical network in 2001.[47]

Next came Borwornsak Uwanno, a leading royalist scholar of public law, secretary of the cabinet under Prime Minister Thaksin Shinawatra, and secretary-

---

[43] *Constitution of the Kingdom of Thailand*, B.E. 2550 (2007), pp. 30, 32–33, 37.

[44] The Chaipattana (literally, "winning development") Foundation is a royal NGO that finances royally initiated development projects nationwide from private donations to avoid restrictive government rules and regulations. See "Background," Chaipattana Foundation, http://www.chaipat.or.th/, accessed January 26, 2015.

[45] See: Chanida Chitbundid, *Khrongkan an neuang ma jak praratchadamri: Kansathapana praratcha-amnajnam nai phrabatsomdej phrajao yoo hua* [The royally iInitiated projects: The making of royal hegemony] (Bangkok: The Foundation for the Promotion of Social Science and Humanities Textbooks Project, 2007), 329–56, 404–20. This book was developed from Chanida's path-breaking master's thesis.

[46] Cited from Borwornsak Uwanno, "Ten Principles of a Righteous King," *Bangkok Post*, June 12, 2006: 8. The spellings of *"thamma"* and *"dhamma"* are interchangeable here. A slightly different translation is given as: "We shall rule with righteousness for the benefit and happiness of the people of Siam." See: Nicholas Grossman, editor-in-chief, *Chronicle of Thailand: Headline News since 1946* (Bangkok and Singapore: *Bangkok Post* and Editions Didier Millet, 2009), 48.

[47] "Kong baeb buranakan, dr. sumet yam rabsang nailuang song thon maidai chaeng khontujjarit" [Integrated cheating, Dr. Sumet Stresses the king couldn't help cursing corrupted people], *Thaipost*, March 17, 2004. FaCT maintains a website with VDO clips and publications about its objectives and activities at www.fact.or.th/fact/, accessed April 17, 2014. For FaCT's background, see "Thi ma khong moonnithi" [The foundation's background], http://www.fact.or.th/fact/index.php/2008-11-28-04-14-17/2012-02-09-07-33-21.html, accessed April 17, 2014.

general of King Prajadhipok's Institute (a research and training think tank affiliated with the Thai Parliament).[48] After his timely and politically expedient resignation from the waning Thaksin government on June 10, 2006[49] (about three months before the military coup), and subsequent ordination as a Buddhist monk, Borwornsak published a series of articles in both Thai and English in the local press on the subject of the Thai monarchy and politics. In these articles, Borwornsak argued that King Bhumibol's diligent and consistent practice of *dasarajadhamma* (Buddhism's ten righteous principles for monarchs) accorded with good governance, making His Majesty the King a *dhammaraja* (righteous king), and adding a warm, compassionate, and uniquely Thai paternalistic quality to royal governance under his reign.[50]

After the coup and the installment of General Surayud Chulanont as prime minister (October 2006–January 2008), the Surayud government came under attack by ousted and self-exiled former Prime Minister Thaksin for lack of credibility, especially among foreign investors. Prime Minister Surayud retorted that had the elected Thaksin government practiced *thammaphibal,* there would not have been any problem.[51]

Among the populist NGO allies of the monarchical network, Rosana Tositrakul, a long-time Buddhist consumer-rights and public-health activist who turned into a high-profile anti-corruption and anti-Prime Minister Thaksin crusader, and who was elected senator for Bangkok (2006 and 2008), commands a formidable reputation for having put the first-ever corrupted cabinet minister behind bars, and reversed the

---

[48] See Borwornsak's profile and interviews on his personal background and work in the Thaksin government in "Borwornsak Uwanno," *Thailand Political Base,* http://politicalbase.in.th/index.php/, accessed February 27, 2011. Borwornsak Uwanno, "Botsamphas sastrajan do.ro. borwornsak uwanno lekhathikan khanaratthamontri meua wansuk thi 23 phreussaphakhom 2546" [Interview with professor Dr. Borwornsak Uwanno, secretary of the sabinet on Friday, May 23, B.E. 2546], by Nantawat Boramanand, *Public Law Net,* www.pub-law.net/publaw/view.aspx?id=172, accessed February 27, 2013; "Botsamphas sastrajan kittikhun do.ro. borwornsak uwanno wanangkhan thi 24 tulakhom 2549" [Interview with professor emeritus Dr. Borwornsak Uwanno on Tuesday, October 24, B.E. 2549], by Nantawat Boramanand, *Public Law Net,* www.pub-law.net/publaw/view.aspx?id=999, accessed February 27, 2011.

[49] "Lekhathikan khana ratthamontri la ok jak tamnaeng" [Secretary of the cabinet resigns], *Siam chotmaihet: Bantheuk khaosan lae hetkan, pi thi 31 pho.so. 2549* (CD) [Siam archives: Record of news and events, vol. 31 B.E. 2549 (CD)] (Bangkok: Siamban Company Ltd, 2006), 778.

[50] About Borwornsak Uwanno, see: "Ten Principles of a Righteous King," *Bangkok Post,* June 12, 2006: 8; "Thailand's Dhammaraja," *Bangkok Post,* June 13, 2006: 10; "King and the Constitution," *Bangkok Post,* June 14, 2006: 12–13; "A Proof beyond Any Shadow of Doubt," *Bangkok Post,* June 15, 2006: 12; and "The King's Paternalistic Governance," *Bangkok Post,* June 16, 2006: 10. See also: "Dynamics of Thai Politics," a paper presented at the seminar "The United States-Thailand Relationship and Southeast Asia," organized by the Royal Thai Embassy, Holiday Inn, Arlington, Virginia, May 9–10, 2007, http://www.kpi.ac.th/kpith/index.php?option=com_content&task=view&id=119&Itemid=214, accessed January 26, 2015.

[51] "Rai thammaphibal jeung don lai, surayud suan maew" [Surayud retorts that Thaksin was driven from power for lack of good governance], *Matichon,* January 25, 2007: 1. See, in addition, Thaksin's address to the Japan National Press Club during his visit to Tokyo (April 3, 2007), in Prime Minister General Surayud Chulanont, "Japan and Thailand: Celebrating a New Era of Intensified and Sustainable Partnership," Royal Thai Government House Media Center, http://www.thaigov.go.th/news/item/55823.html, accessed February 4, 2015.

privatization of EGAT.[52] As chairperson of the Senate Committee on Studying and Inspecting Corruption and Strengthening Good Governance (*Khanakammathikan seuksa truajsob reuang kanthujjarit lae soemsang thammaphibal*),[53] Senator Rosana has been censuring the military-backed government of Prime Minister Abhisit Vejjajiva (in office from December 2008 to August 2011) for failing to adhere to *thammaphibal* in several major instances.[54]

Last but not least, we have the yellow-shirted mass movement, ironically called People's Alliance for Democracy, or PAD, which, since its inception in early 2006, has helped the ARC oust elected Prime Minister Thaksin, then occupied Government House and Bangkok international airports (Don Mueang and Suvarnabhumi) to oust the successive pro-Thaksin governments of elected prime ministers Samak Sundaravej and Somchai Wongsawat, in 2008. PAD has consistently, and self-righteously, campaigned on the royal-nationalist platform of New Politics, i.e., defense of the monarchy, moralistic and clean politics, economic prosperity, and good governance, which old electoral politics could not deliver—or so PAD claims.[55]

All in all, good governance, as the IMF and World Bank's global preferred discursive enforcing agent of neoliberal political economic order, has paradoxically been turned on its head, or glocalized, by Thai royalist-nationalist intellectuals into *thammarat* or *thammaphibal*. The result is a national discursive saboteur that is bent on wreaking havoc and creating chaos in the vain attempt to impose a conservative, even reactionary, undemocratic, and unconstitutional Thai moral order on its compatriots.[56]

POSTSCRIPT (2014)

In November 2013, Suthep Thaugsuban—former secretary-general of the opposition Democrat Party, and deputy prime minister responsible for the bloody suppression of the Red Shirt demonstrators in 2010—launched an insurgent mass

---

[52] *"Rosana tositrakul,"* Wikipedia, accessed 27 February 2011, th.wikipedia.org/wiki/rosana_tositrakul; and *"Rakkiat sukthana,"* Wikipedia, accessed February 27, 2011, th.wikipedia.org/wiki/rakkiat_sukthana.

[53] See the committee's official website: http://www.senate.go.th/w3c/senate/comm.php?comm_id=74, accessed January 26, 2015.

[54] "Rosana fak 3 khamtham thuang thammaphibal nayok" [Rosana calls on the prime minister to respond to three questions about good governance], *Khao Thairath* Online, created September 23, 2010, http://www.thairath.co.th/content/113470, accessed January 26, 2015; "Chamlae rak wikrit sangkhomthai, 'ao leuad hua ma lang tin' tong mai koed kheun" [Dissecting the roots of Thai society's crisis, "off with their heads" must not happen], www.prachachat.net, created March 30, 2010, www.prachachat.net/news_detail.php?newsid=1269951068, accessed December 3, 2014. For a contrarian view of Senator Rosana's forceful role, see "Ruangkrai yuen po.po.cho.-ko.ko.to. thod ko.mo.tho. sob thujjarit chai amnaj maichob" [(Senator) Ruangkrai petitions the national anti-corruption commission and the election commission to dismiss the senate committee on inspecting corruption for abuse of power], *Khao Thairath* Online, created September 27, 2010, http://www.thairath.co.th/content/114438, accessed January 26, 2015.

[55] Kasian, *"Toppling Thaksin,"* 5–10; and Kasian Tejapira, *Songkhram rawang si: kon theung jud thi mai aj huanklab* [Warring colors: Before the point of no return] (Bangkok: Openbooks, 2010).

[56] In this connection, see: Kasian Tejapira, "Rabob prachathipatai an mi phramahakasat pen pramuk khong sondhi limthongkul" [The democratic regime of government with the king as head of the state *à la* Sondhi Limthongkul], *Songkhram rawang si*: 120–35.

protest movement, centered mostly in the Democrat Party's strongholds in Bangkok and the South.[57] The movement, allegedly able to mobilize at its height over a million street protesters, has been trying since to oust the Yingluck government and eradicate the Thaksin regime through "reform before election." During the past six months of its continuing protest, the so-called People's Committee for Absolute Democracy with the King as Head of State, or PDRC-led movement, with Suthep as its secretary-general, has forcefully occupied various key government offices and central business quarters in Bangkok, partly obstructed a general election, intermittently engaged in armed clashes with police and political opponents, and managed to paralyze to a large extent the normal functioning of the government, bureaucracy, electoral politics, and economy, resulting in more than a score of conflict-related deaths and over seven hundred casualties.

The rank-and-file of this self-styled "people's revolution" movement consists of those from the relatively affluent and well-educated Bangkok upper and middle classes, along with lower-middle-class villagers from the South. These disparate groups are led, financed, and supported by a network of conservative royalist-nationalist Democrat politicians, big business tycoons, NGO activists, state enterprise labor unionists, university professors, students and school administrators, medical and public health personnel, journalists, TV personalities, movie stars, popular singers, conservative lawyers and judges, and some leading members of the Privy Council and the royal family. Regardless of its new and different moniker, the PDRC substantially shares many prominent cadres as well as the basic strategy and tactics with the now-defunct PAD. Most significant are the occupation of key government offices and business quarters by a combination of unarmed militants and armed guards; the use of various constitutional checks-and-balances mechanisms, such as the constitutional and the administrative courts, the National Anti-Corruption Commission, and the Electoral Commission, to delegitimize the authority of the elected government and remove it from office; the staging of anti-government mass demonstrations to provide a populist excuse for street anarchy; and presumed state failures that could be a pretext for and invitation to military intervention and coup.

The idea is actually a familiar, Friedman-like one: make the politically impossible become politically inevitable, reasonable, and even respectable, through an engineered crisis. Targets that may be considered "politically impossible" include the subversion of political equality and universal suffrage, the abolition of constitutional rule, the nullification of a general election, the installation of an unelected government and legislative "people's council" through a judicial coup, and the replacement of "government by the people" with a "government for the people" led by an enlightened despotic minority. The public intellectual rationalization and justification of this reversal of democracy had again been led, with much fanfare reminiscent of good governance, by—alas—Thirayuth Boonmi. In total disregard of the brutal suppression but steadfast presence of the resentful and vengeful, pro-government and pro-democracy, rural-based majority Red Shirt movement, together with the impending aggravation of violent conflict, he acclaimed the PDRC seditious tactics as a "whistle of people's revolution" unprecedented in Thai history, in which

---

[57] He was able to do this by taking advantage of the fatal political mistake of the government led by Yingluck Shinawatra (in office 2011–14; the youngest sister of deposed prime minister Thaksin Shinawatra, a fugitive in exile for corruption charges since 2008) in rushing through the House of Representatives a hugely criticized across-the-board amnesty bill that would have allowed Thaksin to return home a free and pardoned man.

the "Great Multitude of the People" *(muan maha prachachon)* would exercise their right to revolt against a corrupt and abusive government, so as to usher in a corruption-free, self-regulatory democracy.[58]

Unfortunately, though actually unsurprising, it led instead to the military coup of the National Council for Peace and Order (NCPO), led by General Prayuth Chan-ocha, the commander-in-chief of the army, on May 22, 2014, and a subsequent military-bureaucratic authoritarian regime bent on arbitrary and heavy-handed governance of the populace without any effective checks and balances in the political system. Under martial law and the absolute power of General Prayuth, the constitution was scrapped, democracy cut short, and human rights and the rule of law indefinitely suspended. Those ideals, along with "good governance," became merely empty slogans for the justification of dictatorship.

---

[58] Thirayuth Boonmi, "Kan patiwat nokweed mong sheumyong kab panha anakhot kanmueang thai" [The whistle revolution in relation to the future of Thai politics], *Fa Dieo Kan* 11,3 (October–December 2014): 71–76. This same issue of *Fa Dieo Kan* also contains my criticism of Thirayuth's thesis, "Jak sangkhom khemkhaeng soo sangkhom anaraya: Toe thirayuth boonmi phoo uppatham thang khawmkhid khong suthep na ko.po.po.so" [From civil to uncivil society: Against Thirayuth Boonmi the ideational patron of Mr. Suthep@PDRC]: 56–70.

APPENDIX

PUBLICATIONS BY CRAIG J. REYNOLDS (UPDATED TO FEBRUARY 2015)

MONOGRAPHS

1973　*The Buddhist Monkhood in Nineteenth-Century Thailand*. Doctoral dissertation, University of Michigan. University Microfilms International.

1979　*Prawattisat sangkhom khu arai* [What is social history?]. Bangkok, Thai Khadi Research Institute, Thammasat University. Thai and English (Thai version reprinted in 1984 and 2007; see below).

1987　*Thai Radical Discourse: The Real Face of Thai Feudalism Today*. Ithaca: Cornell University Southeast Asia Program Publications. Reprinted 1994. Published in Thai as *Khwam khit waek naew khong thai*, trans. Anchali Susayan (Bangkok, 1991).

2006　*Seditious Histories: Contesting Thai and Southeast Asian Pasts*. Seattle: University of Washington Press.

2007　*Chaosua khunsuk sakdtina panyachon lae khonsaman* [Tycoons, warlords, feudalists, intellectuals, and common people]. Bangkok: Textbook Foundation Project for the Humanities and Social Sciences, Thammasat University. Trans. and ed. Varuni Otsatharom. Reprinted 2013.

EDITED VOLUMES

1979　*Autobiography: The Life of Prince-Patriarch Vajiranana of Siam, 1860–1921* (ed., trans., introduction). Athens, OH: Ohio University Press.

1991a　Jennifer W. Cushman, *Family and State: The Formation of a Sino-Thai Tin-Mining Dynasty, 1797–1932* (ed.). Singapore: Oxford University Press.

1991b　*National Identity and its Defenders: Thailand, 1939–1989* (ed.). Clayton, Victoria: Monash University, Centre of Southeast Asian Studies. Reprinted 1993, Chiang Mai: Silkworm Books.

2002　*National Identity and its Defenders: Thailand Today* (ed.), rev. ed. Chiang Mai, Silkworm Books.

2008　O. W. Wolters, *Early Southeast Asia: Selected Essays* (ed., introduction). Ithaca: Cornell University Southeast Asia Program Publications.

ARTICLES AND CHAPTERS IN BOOKS

1973   "The Case of K. S. R. Kulap: A Challenge to Royal Historical Writing in Nineteenth-Century Thailand," *Journal of the Siam Society* 61, 2: 63–90. Thai translation published by the Siam Society, 1995.

1976   "Buddhist Cosmography in Thai History, with Special Reference to Nineteenth-Century Culture Change," *Journal of Asian Studies* 35, 2: 203–20.

1979a   "Monastery Lands and Labor Endowments in Thailand: Some Effects of Social and Economic Change, 1868–1910," *Journal of the Economic and Social History of the Orient* 22, 2: 190–227.

1979b   "A Nineteenth-Century Buddhist Defense of Polygamy and Some Remarks on the Social History of Women in Thailand," in *Proceedings, Seventh Conference, International Association of Historians of Asia,* 927–70. Bangkok, Chulalongkorn University Press.

1979c   "Religious Historical Writing and the Legitimation of the First Bangkok Reign," in *Perceptions of the Past in Southeast Asia,* ed. David G. Marr and A. J. S. Reid (Singapore: Heinemann Educational Books), 90–107.

1983a   (with Hong Lysa) "Marxism in Thai Historical Studies," *Journal of Asian Studies* 43, 1: 77–104.

1983b   "Bibliography: Radical Literature in Thailand," *Cormosea Bulletin* 11, 2: 18–23.

1983c   (with Akin Rabibhadana and Wanwipha Burutratanaphan) *Raingan wichai ruang khaniyom* ... [Research report on values, customs, and attitudes concerning the relationship between people and the state ...]. Academic Seminar on the Development of Human Rights in Thailand. Bangkok, Thammasat University, Thai Khadi Research Institute.

1985   "Feudalism as a Trope or Discourse for the Asian Past with Special Reference to Thailand," in *Feudalism: Comparative Studies,* ed. Edmund Leach, S. N. Mukherjee, and John Ward (Sydney: Sydney Association for Studies in Society and Culture), 136–54.

1986   "The Author-Function and Thai History," *Asian Studies Association of Australia Review* 10, 1: 22–28.

1989   (with A. J. Day) "The Concept of Peasant Revolt in Southeast Asia" in *Revolution as History,* ed. S. N. Mukherjee and J. O. Ward (Sydney: Sydney Association for Studies in Society and Culture), 105–12.

1991b   "Introduction: National Identity and its Defenders," in *National Identity and its Defenders,* 1–40. See 1991b and 2002 rev. ed. in edited volumes.

1991c   "Sedition in Thai History: A Nineteenth-Century Poem and its Critics," in *Thai Constructions of Knowledge,* ed. Manas Chitakasem and Andrew Turton (London: School of Oriental and African Studies), 15–36.

1992a   "Poststructuralism and History," 106–113, and "Asian History," 170-177, in *History at Sydney, 1891–1991: Centenary Reflections,* ed. Barbara Caine et al. (Sydney, University of Sydney, Department of History).

1992b   "Authenticating Southeast Asian History in the Absence of Colonialism: Burma," *Asian Studies Review* 15, 3: 141–51.

1992c   "The Plot of Thai History: Theory and Practice," in *Patterns and Illusions: Thai History and Thought in Memory of Richard B. Davis,* ed. Gehan Wijeyewardene and E. C. Chapman (Canberra: Richard Davis Fund and the Department of Anthropology, Research School of Pacific Studies, Australian National University), 313–32. Thai translation by Ratchaniphon Janthara-ari et al. in *Thai khadi suksa ruam botkhwam thang wichakan phua sadaeng muthitajit* [Thai studies: Collected academic essays in honour of Dr. Neon Snidvongse], ed. Sunthari Atsawai et al. (Bangkok: privately published).

1992d   "Poststructuralism in a Department of History," *Australian Historical Association Bulletin,* 72 (December): 26–33.

1993   "Chao sua lae khun suk watthanatham lae kanmuang khong sangkhom thai lae sam kok [Tycoons and warlords: Culture and politics in Thai society and *Sam Kok,*" *Warasan thammasat* 19, 2: 7-37.

1994   "Predicaments of Modern Thai History," *Southeast Asia Research* 2, 1: 64–90.

1995   "A New Look at Old Southeast Asia," *Journal of Asian Studies* 54, 2: 419–46.

1996a   "Tycoons and Warlords: Modern Thai Social Formations and Chinese Historical Romance," in *Sojourners and Settlers: Histories of Southeast Asia and the Chinese,* ed. Anthony Reid (St. Leonards, NSW: Allen & Unwin), 115–47. Repr. Honolulu: University of Hawai'i Press, 2001.

1996b   "Thailand," in *Communities of Thought,* ed. Anthony Milner and Mary Quilty (Melbourne: Oxford University Press), 110–25.

1997a   (with Thaveeporn Vasavakul) "Elections in Thailand 1996: What is Missing?" *Current Affairs Bulletin* 73, 6: 4–9.

1997b   "Sino-Thai Business Culture: Strategies, Management, and Warfare," *Asia-Pacific Magazine* 6–7: 33–38.

1998a   "Globalisation and Cultural Nationalism in Modern Thailand," in *Southeast Asian Identities: Culture and the Politics of Representation in Indonesia, Malaysia, Singapore, and Thailand,* ed. Joel S. Kahn (Singapore: Institute of Southeast Asian Studies), 115–45.

1998b   "Public Intellectuals—A View from Southeast Asia: Located Knowledges," *Items* (of the Social Science Research Council) 52,4 (December): 79–81.

1998c   "Self-cultivation and Self-determination in Postcolonial Southeast Asia," in *Southeast Asian Studies: Reorientations*, the Frank H. Golay Memorial Lectures 2 and 3 (Ithaca: Cornell University Southeast Asia Program Publications), 7–35.

1998d   "The Study of Indochina and Burapha University," *Warasan manutsayasat lae sangkhomsat mahawitthayalai burapa. Chabap phiset indochinsuksa* [Special Issue: Indochinese Studies]: 15–28. In Thai and English.

1998e   "Thai Revolution," in *The Encyclopedia of Political Revolutions*, ed. Jack A. Goldstone (Washington, DC: Congressional Quarterly), 479–80.

1999a   "Internationalizing Social Science: A New Architecture," *Dialogue* (Newsletter of the Academy of the Social Sciences in Australia) 18, 1: 23–26.

1999b   "On the Gendering of Nationalist and Postnationalist Selves in Twentieth-century Thailand," in *Genders and Sexualities in Modern Thailand*, ed. Peter A. Jackson and Nerida M. Cook (Chiang Mai: Silkworm Books), 261–74.

2000a   "The Ethics of Academic Engagement with Burma" in *Burma Myanmar: Strong Regime, Weak State?* ed. Morten B. Pedersen et al. (Adelaide: Crawford House Publishing), 123–37.

2000b   "Icons of Identity as Sites of Protest: Burma and Thailand Compared," Academica Sinica PROSEA Research Paper no. 30 (Taipei).

2000c   (with Tony Day) "Cosmologies, Truth Regimes, and the State in Southeast Asia," *Modern Asian Studies* 34, 1: 1–55.

2001a   "Globalisers vs. Communitarians: Public Intellectuals Debate Thailand's Futures," *Singapore Journal of Tropical Geography* 22, 3: 252–69.

2001b   "The Economic History of the Thai Village and Communitarianism," *Journal of the Economic and Social History of the Orient* 44, 3: 400–402. Reprinted [in Thai] in *With Pride*, ed. Sirilak Sampatchalit and Siriphorn Yotkamolsat (Bangkok: Sangsan Press, 2002), 553–58.

2002   "Thai Identity in the Age of Globalisation," in *National Identity Thailand and its Defenders: Thailand Today*, rev. ed., ed. C. J. Reynolds (Chiang Mai: Silkworm Books), 308–38.

2003   "Tai-land and its Others," *South East Asia Research* 11, 1: 113–20.

2004a   "Kansang phet phawa khong tuaton baep chatniyom lae langchatniyom nai prathetthai chuang kritsatawat thi 20," in *Phet phawa kan thathai rang kankhonha tuaton* [The power of gender: Contesting bodies, searching for selves], ed. Suchada Thawisit

(Chiang Mai: Centre for Women's Studies, Faculty of Social Science, Chiang Mai University), 255–85. [Trans. of 1999b.]

2004b   "Thailand's Democratic Traditions," in *The Development of Thai Democracy since 1973: Proceedings of the Thai Update 2003*, ed. Cavan Hogue (Canberra: National Thai Studies Centre, Australian National University), 25–42.

2004c   "Tailandia en la era de la globalización," in *El sudeste asiático. Una visión contemporánea*, ed. Juan Ignacio Piovani and Sebastián Bagnoli (Buenos Aires: Editorial de la universidad nacional de tres de febrero), 123–46.

2005a   "Power" in *Critical Terms for the Study of Buddhism*, ed. Donald Lopez Jr. (Chicago: University of Chicago Press), 211–28.

2005b   "Nation and State in Histories of Nation-Building, with Special Reference to Thailand," in *Nation-Building: Five Southeast Asian Histories*, ed. Wang Gungwu (Singapore: Institute of Southeast Asian Studies), 25–38.

2008a   "Thailand," *The Oxford Encyclopedia of the Modern World*, vol. 7, 244–49.

2008b   "The Professional Lives of O. W. Wolters," in *Early Southeast Asia,* ed. C. J. Reynolds, 1–38, (see 2008, Edited Volumes, above).

2008c   "A Very Short History of Anthropology in Thailand with Special Reference to the North," in *Crossing the Boundary of Thai Social Science Knowledge: A Festschrift to Anan Ganjanapan*. Special Issue of *Warasan sangkhomsat* 20, 2: 17–53.

2008d   "The Origins of Community in the Thai Discourse of Global Governance," in *Tai Lands and Thailand: Community and State in Southeast Asia*, ed. Andrew Walker (Singapore: NUS Press), 24–40.

2009a   *"Chumchon/*Community in Thailand," in *Words in Motion: Toward a Global Lexicon*, ed. Carol Gluck and Anna Lowenhaupt Tsing (Durham, NC, and London: Duke University Press), 286–305.

2010   "Thai Institutions of Slavery: Their Economic and Cultural Setting," in *Tracks and Traces: Thailand and the Work of Andrew Turton*, ed. Nicholas Tapp and Philip Hirsch (Amsterdam: Amsterdam University Press), 103–14. Trans. Soimat Rungmani in *Senthang lae rongroi muangthai kap ngan khong aendru thoetan* (Chiang Mai: Silkworm Books, 2014), 145–64.

2011a   "Rural Male Leadership, Religion, and the Environment in Thailand's Mid-south, 1930s–1960s," *Journal of Southeast Asian Studies* 42, 1: 39–57.

2011b   (with Nicholas Farrelly and Andrew Walker) "Practical and Auspicious: Thai Handbook Knowledge for Agriculture and the Environment," *Asian Studies Review* 35: 235–51.

2012a   "The Social Bases of Autocratic Rule in Thailand," in *Bangkok May 2010: Perspectives on a Divided Thailand*, ed. Michael J. Montesano, Pavin Chachavalpongpun, and Aekapol Chongvilaivan (Singapore: Institute of Southeast Asian Studies), 267–73.

2012b   (and Team) "Time's Arrow and the Burden of the Past: A Primer on the Thai Un-State," *Sensate: A Journal for Experiments in Critical Media Practice*, http://sensatejournal.com/2012/05/craig-reynolds-et-al-times-arrow/>, accessed March 22, 2015.

2012c   "Policing and the Power of Thai Amulets," *Australian-Thailand Association Newsletter* 38, 4 (October–December): 4–5.

2013a   "Chatthip Nartsupha, His Critics, and More Criticism," in *Essays on Thailand's Economy and Society for Professor Chatthip Nartsupha at 72*, ed. Pasuk Phongpaichit and Chris Baker (Bangkok: Sangsan), 1–22.

2013b   *Kanpatirup lae maechik nai satsanaphut baep thai* [Reform and Magic in Thai Buddhism] in *Prawattisat satsana watthanatham lae kansuksa ruam botkhwam thaisuksa phua raluk thung satrachan ichi-i yoneo* [History, Religion, Culture and Education: Collected Essays in Memory of Professor Ishii Yoneo] ed. Chatthip Nartsupha and Chalong Soontravanich (Bangkok: Sangsan Press), 263-279. Trans. Chatthip Nartsupha.

2014   "Homosociality in Modern Thai Political Culture," *Journal of Southeast Asian Studies* 45,2: 258–77.

n.d.   "Applied Sciences for Hedging Risk and Anticipating Outcomes in Police Work," *Thammasat Journal of History* (forthcoming).

n.d.   "Buddhism in Southeast Asia," in *The Buddhist World*, ed. John Powers (Routledge, forthcoming).

n.d.   "Magic and Buddhism," in *The Buddhist World*, ed. John Powers (Routledge, forthcoming).

OTHER PUBLICATIONS

1970   (with Robert B. Jones and Ruchira C. Mendiones, eds.) *Thai Cultural Reader* (Ithaca: Cornell Southeast Asia Program Publications), Book I, revised edition.

1988   Preface in Adrian Snodgrass, *The Symbolism of the Stupa* (Ithaca: Cornell Southeast Asia Program Publications), i.

1991   Foreword in Jennifer Cushman, *Family and State: The Formation of a Sino-Thai Tin-Mining Dynasty 1797–1932* (Singapore: Oxford University Press), vii-xvi.

2001   "Obituary: O. W. Wolters (8 June 1915–5 December 2000)," *Journal of the Siam Society* 89, 1–2: xvi–xix.

2002   Foreword in Maurizio Peleggi, *The Politics of Ruins and the Business of Nostalgia* (Bangkok: White Lotus), ix-x.

2010   "Behind the Thai Crisis," *Inside Story* (April 29), at http://inside.org.au/behind-the-thai-crisis/, accessed February 23, 2015.

2013   Foreword in Saichol Sattyanurak, *Phya Anuman Rajadhon: A Commoner Philosopher, Creator of the Myth of Thainess* (Chiang Mai: Chiang Mai University Press) [in Thai].

2014a   Foreword in *Good Coup Gone Bad,* ed. Pavin Chachavalpongpun (Singapore: Institute of Southeast Asian Studies), ix-xi.

2014b   Foreword in Sulak Sivaraksa, *Puey Ungpakorn: An Honest Siamese in a Class of His Own* (Bangkok: Foundation for Children Publishing House), v-vi.

BOOK REVIEWS

1974   Wachirayan warorot, Prince-patriarch, *Collected Works of Prince-patriarch Wachirayan warorot* [in Thai]. *Journal of the Siam Society* 62, 2 : 365–68.

1975   George Coedès and Charles Archaimbault, *Les trois mondes*. *Journal of the Siam Society* 63, 1: 283–85.

1977a   Charnvit Kasetsiri, *The Rise of Ayudhya, A History of Siam in the Fourteenth and Fifteenth Centuries*. *Asian Studies Association of Australia Review* 1, 2: 103–5.

1977b   Kitsiri Malalgoda, *Buddhism in Sinhalese Society, 1750–1900: A Study of Religious Revival and Change*. *Asian Studies Association of Australia Review* 1, 2: 129–31.

1979   David G. Marr, ed. *Reflections from Captivitiy: Phan Boi Chau's "Prison Notes," Ho Chi Minh's "Prison Diary."* *Asian Studies Association of Australia Review* 3, 1: 83–84.

1980   Mattani Rutnin, *Modern Thai Literature: The Process of Modernization and the Transformation of Values*. *Journal of Southeast Asian Studies* 11, 2: 406–8.

1982   Walter F. Vella, *Chaiyo! King Vajiravudh and the Development of Thai Nationalism*. *Journal of Southeast Asian Studies* 13, 1: 192–93.

1984   David K. Wyatt and Alexander B. Woodside, eds., *Moral Order and the Question of Change: Essays on Southeast Asian Thought*. *Journal of Asian Studies* 43, 2: 374–75.

1985   Somboon Suksamran, *Buddhism and Politics in Thailand*. *Asian Studies Association of Australia Review* 8, 3: 99–100.

1988a   Yoneo Ishii, *Sangha, State, and Society: Thai Buddhism in History. Journal of Southeast Asian Studies* 19, 1: 162–63.

1988b   [review essay] Charles F. Keyes, *Thailand: Buddhist Kingdom as Modern Nation-State;* and Somsakdi Xuto, ed., *Government and Politics of Thailand. Journal of Asian Studies* 47, 4: 940–42.

1990   Anthony Reid, *Southeast Asia in the Age of Commerce, 1450–1680,* vol. 1, *The Lands below the Winds. Review of Indonesian and Malaysian Affairs* 24: 177–80.

1991   Kennon Breazeale and Snit Smukarn, *A Culture in Search of Survival: The Phuan of Thailand and Laos. Review of Indonesian and Malaysian Affairs* 25, 2: 104–6.

1998   John Girling, *Interpreting Development: Capitalism, Democracy, and the Middle Class in Thailand. Review of Indonesian and Malaysian Affairs* 32, 1: 220–22.

2001   Kasian Tejapira, *Commodifying Marxism: The Formation of Modern Thai Radical Culture, 1927–1958. Journal of the Siam Society* 89, 1–2: 137–39.

2004   Victor Lieberman, *Strange Parallels: Southeast Asia in Global Context, c. 800–1830,* vol. 1, *Integration on the Mainland. American Historical Review* 109, 5: 1535; http://asiapacific.anu.edu.au/newmandala/2009/05/31/review-of-lieberman/, accessed February 23, 2015.

2006   Han ten Brummelhuis, *King of the Waters: Homan van der Heide and the Origin of Modern Irrigation in Siam. New Zealand Journal of Asian Studies* 8, 2: 209–12; http://asiapacific.anu.edu.au/newmandala/2009/05/27/review-of-brummelhuis/, accessed February 23, 2015.

2007   Tamara Loos, *Subject Siam: Family, Law, and Colonial Modernity in Thailand. Asian Studies Review* 31, 3: 381–83; http://asiapacific.anu.edu.au/newmandala/2009/ 06/04/review-of-loos/, accessed February 23, 2015.

2009a   Anne Hansen, *How to Behave: Buddhism and Modernity in Colonial Cambodia, 1860–1930. Asian Studies Review* 33, 1: 129–31; http://asiapacific.anu.edu.au/ newmandala/2010/01/14/review-of-hansen/, accessed February 23, 2015.

2010a   Chang Noi, *Jungle Book: Thailand's Politics, Moral Panic, and Plunder, 1996–2008, Journal of the Siam Society* 98: 254–56; http://asiapacific.anu.edu.au/ newmandala/2010/04/23/review-of-chang-noi/, accessed February 23, 2015.

2010b   *Daily World Today* [lok wan ni], comp. *Punching above My Weight: Nattawut Saikua Tells his Story* [*chok kham run* nattawut saikua lao ruang]; http://asiapacific. anu.edu.au/newmandala/2010/10/27/review-of-nattawut-saikua-biography/, accessed February 23, 2015.

2010c   Justin Thomas McDaniel, *Gathering Leaves and Lifting Words: Histories of Buddhist Monastic Education in Laos and Thailand*; http://asiapacific.anu.edu.au/newmandala/2010/02/07/review-of-mcdaniel/, accessed February 23, 2015.

2010d   Kong Bannathikan Matichon [Matichon Editorial Team]. *Withi tamruat kla 'ja phian'* [Sgt. 'Phian: The Path of a Brave Policeman], http://asiapacific.anu.edu.au/newmandala/2010/08/20/review-of-sgt-phian/, accessed February 23, 2015.

2010e   Peerasak Chaidaisuk, *Chat sua wai lai* [A Tiger Doesn't Change Its Stripes]; http://asiapacific.anu.edu.au/newmandala/2010/03/12/review-of-peerasak/, accessed February 23, 2015.

2011a   Richard A. Ruth, *In Buddha's Company: Thai Soldiers in the Vietnam War*; http://asiapacific.anu.edu.au/newmandala/2011/06/09/review-of-ruth/, accessed February 23, 2015.

2011b   Yoshinori Nishizaki, *Political Authority and Provincial Identity in Thailand: The Making of Banharn-buri*; http://www.academia.edu/2419710/Review_of_Yoshi_Nishizaki_Political_Authority_and_Provincial_Identity_in_Thailand, accessed February 23, 2015.

2012   Wissanu Krea-ngam, *This World's a Stage* [Lok ni khue lakhon]; http://asiapacific.anu.edu.au/newmandala/2012/04/18/review-of-this-worlds-a-stage/, accessed February 23, 2015.

2013a   Claudio Sopranzetti, *Red Journeys: Inside the Thai Red-Shirt Movement;* http://www.prachatai.com/english/node/3528, accessed February 23, 2015.

2013b   Tyrell Haberkorn, *Revolution Interrupted: Farmers, Students, Law, and Violence in Northern Thailand*; http://www.prachatai.com/english/node/3513, accessed February 23, 2015.

CONTRIBUTORS

EDITOR

Maurizio Peleggi is associate professor of history at the National University of Singapore and editor of the *Journal of Southeast Asia Studies*. He is the author of *Thailand: The Worldly Kingdom* (2007), *Lords of Things: The Fashioning of the Siamese Monarchy's Modern Image* (2002), and *The Politics of Ruins and the Business of Nostalgia* (2002), as well as several journal articles and book chapters. His new book, to appear in 2016, is entitled *Monastery, Monument, Museum: Sites and Artifacts of Thai Cultural Memory*.

CONTRIBUTORS

Chris Baker formerly taught Asian history at Cambridge University. His most recent publications, co-written with Pasuk Phongpaichit, include *Thailand: Economy and Politics* (second ed., 2002), *A History of Thailand* (second ed., 2009), and *The Tale of Khun Chang Khun Phaen* (2012), winner of the 2013 Becker Translation Prize from the Association of Asian Studies.

Patrick Jory, senior lecturer in Southeast Asian history at the University of Queensland, Brisbane, was formerly the coordinator of the Regional Studies Program at Walailak University in southern Thailand. He has authored numerous journal articles and is the editor or co-editor of *Ghosts of the Past in Southern Thailand: Essays onm the History and Historiography of Patani* (2013) and, with Michael Montesano, *Thai South and Malay North: Ethnic Interactions on a Plural Peninsula* (2008).

Kasian Tejapira, professor of political science at Thammasat University, Bangkok, is the author of *Commodifying Marxism: The Formation of Modern Thai Radical Culture, 1927–1958* (2001) and has published many journal articles and book chapters. He is also a regular columnist in the Thai press.

Tamara Loos is associate professor of Southeast Asian history at Cornell University. Her first book, *Subject Siam: Family, Law, and Colonial Modernity in Thailand* (2006), focused on gender, justice, modernity, and national identity in Thai history. Her forthcoming second book, *Bones Around My Neck: Silence and Secrets under Siamese Absolutism*, is about Prince Prisdang Jumsai (1852–1935).

Yoshinori Nishizaki is assistant professor of political science at the National University of Singapore. He is the author of *Political Authority and Provincial Identity in Thailand: The Making of Banharn-Buri* (2011) and several journal articles.

James Ockey is an associate professor (reader) in political science at the University of Canterbury in Christchurch, New Zealand. His research interests cover many aspects of Thai politics, including democratization, local politics, civil–military relations, electoral politics, and political conflict.

Pasuk Phongpaichit is emeritus professor of economics at Chulalongkorn University, Bangkok. His most recent publications, co-authored with Chris Baker, include *Thailand: Economy and Politics* (second ed., 2002), *A History of Thailand* (second ed., 2009), and *The Tale of Khun Chang Khun Phaen* (2012), an annotated translation of the Thai folk epic that won the 2013 Becker Translation Prize from the Asdsociation of Asian Studies.

Thongchai Winichakul, professor of history at the University of Wisconsin-Madison, was president of the Association for Asian Studies in 2013–14. His book *Siam Mapped: A History of the Geo-body of a Nation* (1994) was awarded the Harry J Benda Prize in 1995, and the grand prize from the Asian Affairs Research Council (Japan) in 2004, following the publication of its Japanese translation. He is currently working on a book on the memories of the 1976 massacre.

Villa Vilaithong teaches history at Chulalongkorn University. Her research interests include Thai cultural and business history, the advertising and fashion industries, and consumer culture. She is the author of *"Thantakan" khong Jit Phumisak lae nak thot kan mueang* (Prison time: Jit Phumisak and other political detainees, 2013), and is currently working on a history of beauty institutions in Thailand.

9 780877 277668